Microsoft Azure Administrator Exam Prep (AZ-104)

Make Your Career with Microsoft Azure Platform
Using Azure Administered Exam Prep

Lalit Rawat

www.bpbonline.com

FIRST EDITION 2021

Copyright © BPB Publications, India

ISBN: 978-93-89898-767

Distributors:

BPB PUBLICATIONS
20, Ansari Road, Darya Ganj
New Delhi-110002
Ph: 23254990/23254991

DECCAN AGENCIES
4-3-329, Bank Street,
Hyderabad-500195
Ph: 24756967/24756400

MICRO MEDIA
Shop No. 5, Mahendra Chambers,
150 DN Rd. Next to Capital Cinema,
V.T. (C.S.T.) Station, MUMBAI-400 001
Ph: 22078296/22078297

BPB BOOK CENTRE
376 Old Lajpat Rai Market,
Delhi-110006
Ph: 23861747

To View Complete
BPB Publications Catalogue
Scan the QR Code:

Published by Manish Jain for BPB Publications, 20 Ansari Road, Darya Ganj, New Delhi-110002 and Printed by him at Repro India Ltd, Mumbai

www.bpbonline.com

iii

Dedicated to

Narendra Kumar Rawat and Narmada Rawat

To my Parents: Thank you for your unconditional support in any and every situation. Thanks for your blessings and support.

Radhika and Mayra Rawat
My daughters who have made my life easy!

About the Author

Lalit is a Cloud Architect, Azure MVP, MCT, and author of the 'Azure Interview Q and A' book. He likes to share his knowledge through his blog (**https://azure4you. com/**) and share his technical skills in a wider community like AzureTalk, Local Meetup Group, and so on. He has written several articles on Microsoft Azure and changed many lives from his articles and his hands-on training programs and workshops.

He is "Speaker" and delivered the session on a big platform, including MS Global Bootcamp, Local user group, Expert Live India, and other events.

Moreover, and to his credit, he has delivered 500+ training sessions to professionals worldwide in Microsoft Azure technologies and other technologies, including SCOM and Windows Server. He has also provided instructor-led online training and hands-on workshops.

His technical prowess and capability of exploring new frontiers of technology and imparting them to his aspiring team members is his trademark. His execution is priceless and bringing forth his approach will help you realize your dreams, goals, and aspirations into reality.

About the Reviewers

❖ **Gaurav Aroraa** is a serial entrepreneur and start-up mentor. He has done an MPhil in computer science. He is a Microsoft MVP award recipient. He is a lifetime member of the Computer Society of India (CSI) and an advisory member and senior mentor at IndiaMentor. He is certified as a Scrum trainer and coach, ITIL-F certified, and PRINCE-F and PRINCE-P certified. He is an open source developer and contributor to the community.

❖ **Pulakesh Mahanta** is a technology addict and always feels happy when he learns new things, explores new technology, or shares personal IT experience. His career started as a desktop engineer way back in 2007 and he worked as a System Administrator for more than 6 years. For the last 5 years, he has been working on public cloud. He is Microsoft Azure and AWS Certified Architect having extensive experience in data center design, implementation, consolidation, and migration. He believes in automation and integration of the new cloud digital platform He is highly skilled in the new digital platform which also demands EUC (End User Experience) such as AWS Workspace and AppStream, Citrix VDI, Azure WVD (Windows Virtual Desktop), Self-Bot, and so on.

❖ **Arun Pachehra** is a certified Azure Architect and has more than 11 years of industry experience. He is currently working with one of the best cloud service providers in the world which deals with all kinds of public and private clouds. He has been working with public cloud technologies for more than 5 years. His focus areas include cloud consulting, architecture, designing, and migration. He comes from a Windows background; hence, Azure is always welcoming. However, he is always exploring and learning new things. He has also completed the AWS certification, and nowadays, he is exploring the modernization of application with Docker, Kubernetes, and DevOps. He is well versed in IAC via Terraform. He believes in knowledge sharing and also hosts technical blogs and YouTube channels.

Acknowledgement

There are a few people I would like to thank for the continued and ongoing support they have given me during the writing of this book. First and foremost, I would like to thank my wife, Punita Rawat, and two daughters, Radhika and Mayra, for putting up with me while I was spending many weekends and evenings on writing. I could have never completed this book without their support.

This book wouldn't have happened if I hadn't got the support from my family, followers, friends, and so on. My gratitude goes to the AzureTalk core team, especially Niraj Kumar, for providing valuable insights into some of the new features and providing mentorship and guidance.

I would like to thank Gaurav Aroraa for his wonderful support, guidance and helping me while writing the Azure Administrator book.

Thank you, Deepak Rajendran Sir, for providing your guidance to do something new and contribute more and more.

Finally, I would like to thank Gaurav and BPB Publications for giving me this opportunity to write my first book for them.

Preface

Microsoft Azure is a platform where you can start your journey of cloud learning. In this book Azure Administration (AZ-104), we have explained about the day-to-day tasks which you can take up and learn about Azure administration. We have explained Azure core concepts in this chapter and add the lab-based scenario, which will help you clear the core concepts of Microsoft Azure. We have included approx. 60 to 70 questions which will help you check your knowledge and provide a glimpse of the Azure administration exam questions. This will help you prepare for your Azure administration exam.

In this book, we have explained how to use the Azure Active Directory and create users in the Azure subscription. We have also explained about the Azure storage account, networking component like Azure Vnet, Subnet, and how to implement the network security group to restrict the traffic to secure the Azure environments. We have also explained load balance mechanics to load balance your application. We have also explained about the Azure role-based access control which will help you fine grain the Azure subscription access. We have defined the Azure subscription usage and how to save cost management. In this book, you will also learn how to create the WebApps and Azure container/Kubernetes services which will help you to learn the same, and it's a top trending subject in the market today.

We have also covered in this chapter about the hybrid connectivity using the site to site connection and express route. We have explained what is the component which been used to create the Azure virtual machine.

Once you have all of the azure resources, then azure monitoring will also important to monitor the Azure Resources. We have nicely explained and provided the step by step solutions for Azure monitor to clear you Azure monitoring concepts. We have explained how to analysis the Azure resources etc.

The primary goal of this book is to provide information and skills that are necessary to build and deploy the Azure infrastructure in your own environment. This book contains real-life examples that will show you how to clear the Azure Administration exam as well as how to integrate an on-premises environment to Azure. You will learn the following topics in this book:

Chapter 1 Managing Azure AD Objects, introduces the Azure AD object and discusses how to create users in Azure AD, group, and so on, which will help you understand the Azure AD. This will help you in the exam as well.

Chapter 2 Implementing and Managing Hybrid Identities, discusses the Azure AD connect and how to connect on-premises AD to Azure AD and sync the users. It provides the step-by-step instructions using an actual screenshot from an Azure lab environment.

Chapter 3 Managing Role Assignments Through the RBAC Policy, discusses the Azure role-based access to control how to manage the access in the Azure subscription and defines the access level in your organization.

Chapter 4 Managing Azure Subscription and Resource Management, explains the Azure subscription and its type. It also discusses how to manage the Azure subscription and reduce the cost of your subscription.

Chapter 5 Managing and Configuring of Azure Storage Accounts, discusses, in depth, what an Azure storage account is and how to use it. It helps users to allow them to save their own data in an Azure storage account and manage the data. It also discusses how to connect the Azure storage account using the Azure Storage Explorer.

Chapter 6 Manage Data in AZURE Storage, describes how to manage the data and migrate the petabytes of the data using the Azure export and import services. It discusses the Azure databox and Azure AzCopy command-line utility to move the data from on-premise to the Azure storage account or one storage account to another.

Chapter 7 The Azure File Share, introduces the Azure file share, which is designed to integrate your on-premises systems to migrate the files to Azure automatically using the Azure file sync. It explains the core concepts of the Azure file share and how to connect to your on-premises servers.

Chapter 8 Creating and Configuring of Azure VMs, describes how to create the Azure virtual machine, explains its components, and how to configure it. It provides examples with Windows/Linux OS.

Chapter 9 Automating Deployment of VMs, describes how to create the VM automatically using the Azure Arm template.

Chapter 10 Creating and Configuring Container, describes how to create containers and configure them in Azure subscriptions.

Chapter 11 Creating and Configuring Web Apps, describes how to create and configure Azure WebApps. It describes the App services, App services plan, and so on.

Chapter 12 Configuring Virtual Networking and Integrating On-Premises to Azure Network, discusses how to configure virtual networking and integrate an on-premises to the Azure network. It explains Azure Vnet and configures Vnet-to-Vnet peering.

Chapter 13 Configuring Load Balancing Securing Access to Virtual Networks, discusses how to configure Azure load balancing and provides the Azure load balancer, Application gateway, and DNS services.

Chapter 14 Securing Access to Virtual Networks, discusses how to secure access to virtual networks using the Azure network security group and an Azure firewall. It explains Azure Bastion services.

Chapter 15 Monitoring and Troubleshooting of Virtual Networking, discusses how to monitor and troubleshoot virtual networking using the Azure network watcher.

Chapter 16 Analyzing Resource Utilization and Consumption, discusses how to analyze resource utilization using the Azure monitor and explains analyzing metrics across subscription and services health.

Chapter 17 Implementation of Azure Backup and Disaster Recovery, discusses how to implement of Azure backup and protect the Azure VMs for accidental deletion. It explains how to perform the Azure backup and restoration process.

Chapter 18 Exam Preparation Guidelines and Assessment Based on Live Questions, describes exam preparation guidelines and assessments based on live questions which will help you in your exam preparation. It covers more than 70 questions, which includes the scenario-based questions as well.

Downloading the coloured images:

Please follow the link to download the
Coloured Images of the book:

https://rebrand.ly/z8zq95n

Errata

We take immense pride in our work at BPB Publications and follow best practices to ensure the accuracy of our content to provide with an indulging reading experience to our subscribers. Our readers are our mirrors, and we use their inputs to reflect and improve upon human errors, if any, that may have occurred during the publishing processes involved. To let us maintain the quality and help us reach out to any readers who might be having difficulties due to any unforeseen errors, please write to us at :

errata@bpbonline.com

Your support, suggestions and feedbacks are highly appreciated by the BPB Publications' Family.

BPB is searching for authors like you

If you're interested in becoming an author for BPB, please visit **www.bpbonline.com** and apply today. We have worked with thousands of developers and tech professionals, just like you, to help them share their insight with the global tech community. You can make a general application, apply for a specific hot topic that we are recruiting an author for, or submit your own idea.

The code bundle for the book is also hosted on GitHub at **https://github.com/bpbpublications/Microsoft-Azure-Administrator-Exam-Prep-AZ-104**. In case there's an update to the code, it will be updated on the existing GitHub repository.

We also have other code bundles from our rich catalog of books and videos available at **https://github.com/bpbpublications**. Check them out!

PIRACY

If you come across any illegal copies of our works in any form on the internet, we would be grateful if you would provide us with the location address or website name. Please contact us at **business@bpbonline.com** with a link to the material.

If you are interested in becoming an author

If there is a topic that you have expertise in, and you are interested in either writing or contributing to a book, please visit **www.bpbonline.com**.

REVIEWS

Please leave a review. Once you have read and used this book, why not leave a review on the site that you purchased it from? Potential readers can then see and use your unbiased opinion to make purchase decisions, we at BPB can understand what you think about our products, and our authors can see your feedback on their book. Thank you!

For more information about BPB, please visit **www.bpbonline.com**.

Table of Contents

CHAPTER 1
Managing Azure AD Objects

This book will cover all the AZ-104 exam prospective study material which will help you to clear the exam. We will provide additional information in this chapter which will cover various topics and help you get an understanding of the topics in detail.

These chapters will help you understand the Azure environments easily and help you clear the AZ-104 exam.

Structure

The following topics will be covered in this chapter:

- Bulk user creation
- User creation
- Group creation
- Group management
- Guest user management
- Self-service password reset
- Azure AD Join

Objectives

In this chapter, we will explain the bulk user creation in Azure AD and group creation and management. We will discuss how to provide access to guest users and how to manage guest users. We will cover how the users can reset their passwords using the self-service password and add the devices in Azure AD using the Azure AD join tool.

Bulk user creation

Bulk user creation will help your organization in the onboarding process to be completed soon and other prospects to improve the user creation, which has been joined your organization or existing users' creation in Azure. It will reduce administrative work. If you want to create the users or bulk of users in Azure environments, you need a user administrator access in the Azure Active Directory.

Let us try and create bulk users in Azure AD. Follow the given steps to create the bulk users:

1. Go to **Azure Active Directory**.
2. Select the **Users** and click on **All users**.
3. Click on **Bulk Create**.

   Take a look at the following screenshot for bulk user creation:

Figure 1.1: Bulk User Creation

4. When you click on bulk create, it will ask you to download the CSV file.
5. Fill in the following details:
   - Provide the name, last name, and username.
   - Provide the initial password and block sign-in (Yes/No) which is a mandatory field.

- Provide the department and user location.
- Provide the job title and country code.
- Provide the official phone number, mobile number, and so on.

6. You have to put all the details in a single line as per the `.csv` file. I have changed the column to show you the properties of the CSV file. Take a look at the following screenshot for bulk user creation details:

Figure 1.2: Bulk user creation details

7. Once you fill all the details and upload the `.csv` file, click on **Submit**. It will start processing the user creation. It will take some time to create the users, and you can see all those users under the user's tab. Refer to the following screenshot:

Figure 1.3: Bulk user creation Submit

User creation

In the bulk user creation, I have explained the use of the bulk user creation, but let us say if you want to create an individual user, then *how can you create the user?*

Please follow the given steps:

1. Go to **Azure Active Directory**.
2. Select the **Users** and click on **All users**.
3. Click on the **New user**.
4. Enter the **User name.**
5. Provide the **Name, First name**, and **Last name**.
6. You can also provide the department number, location, and Job title.
7. Once you provide all the preceding details, click on **Create** and your users will be created.

Refer to the following screenshot for more details:

Figure 1.4: User creation

Group creation

If you would like to create the Azure AD group, then follow the given steps to create the Azure user's group:

1. Click on the Azure AD.

2. Select the groups from the **Manage** tab.

3. Select **All groups**.

4. Click on the **New group**.

    Please take a look at the following screenshot:

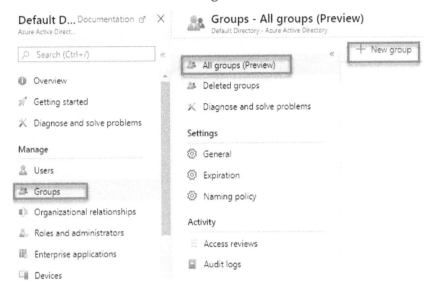

Figure 1.5: Group creation

5. **When you click on group creation, select the following group type:** Security or O365:

    • **Security Group:** It helps to manage users and computer access to shared resources for a specific group.

    • **O365 Group:** Using this group, we can provide access to users for a shared mailbox, calendar, files, SharePoint site, and so on.

6. You can assign the owner to the group administrator and then click on the membership.

7. When you click on the membership, it will ask you to select as per the given details:

    • **Assigned:** The administrator will add specific users to the group.

    • **Dynamic user:** It allows users to use dynamic membership rules and add automatically to the group.

    • **Dynamic device:** It uses the dynamic group rules to add and remove the devices automatically.

8. Please select the assigned member as default as shown in the following screenshot:

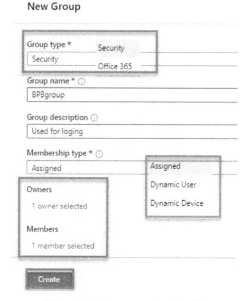

Figure 1.6: *Group creation details*

9. Once you click on create, your groups will be created successfully. Let us see how to manage the group and its properties.

Group management

Perform the following steps:

1. Once the group is created, you can click on the group and see the properties of the group like membership type, source ID, and so on.

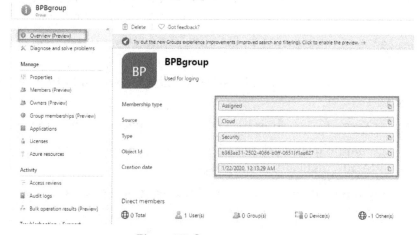

Figure 1.7: *Group management*

2. Based on the requirements, users can change the group.

3. Click on the **Members** tab and add the new members.

4. Please click on the **Owners** tab and add the multiple owners.

5. You can assign the application and see the Azure resources which have been accessed by these group members.

6. You can see the application accessed by this group and manage it.

In this section, we discussed the Azure group creation and learned how to manage the groups. We explained the Azure security group and O365 group.

We also discussed group management. Refer to the following screenshot for more details:

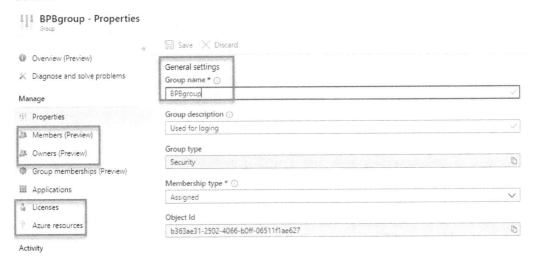

Figure 1.8: Group management general settings

Guest user management

Azure Ad supports the **Business to Customer (B2C)** and **Business to Business (B2B)** users where we can allow customers to have access to our Azure AD. The customer ID can be their organization ID, Outlook, Facebook, LinkedIn, Amazon Gmail ID, and so on. You can invite those users as guests and provide access as a request to perform the task. If you want to invite guests, the user should have the user administrator role assigned to him to invite the guest users.

Let us see how to invite guest users. Please follow the given steps:

• Go to Azure AD and click on **All users**.

• In the right pane, click on **New guest user**.

Please take a look at the following screenshot:

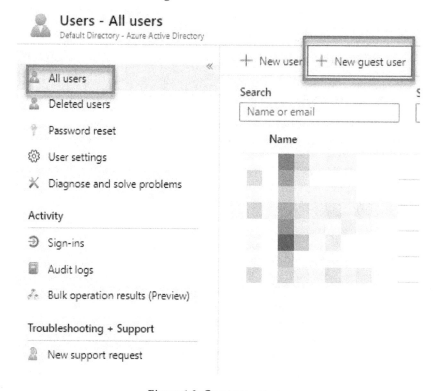

Figure 1.9: Guest user access

Select the **Invite user**.

- Provide the name and email ID of the user you want to invite.
- The rest of the fields are optional. You can then click on **Invite**.

Now, you will be able to invite all the B2B and B2C users.

Please take a look at the following screenshot:

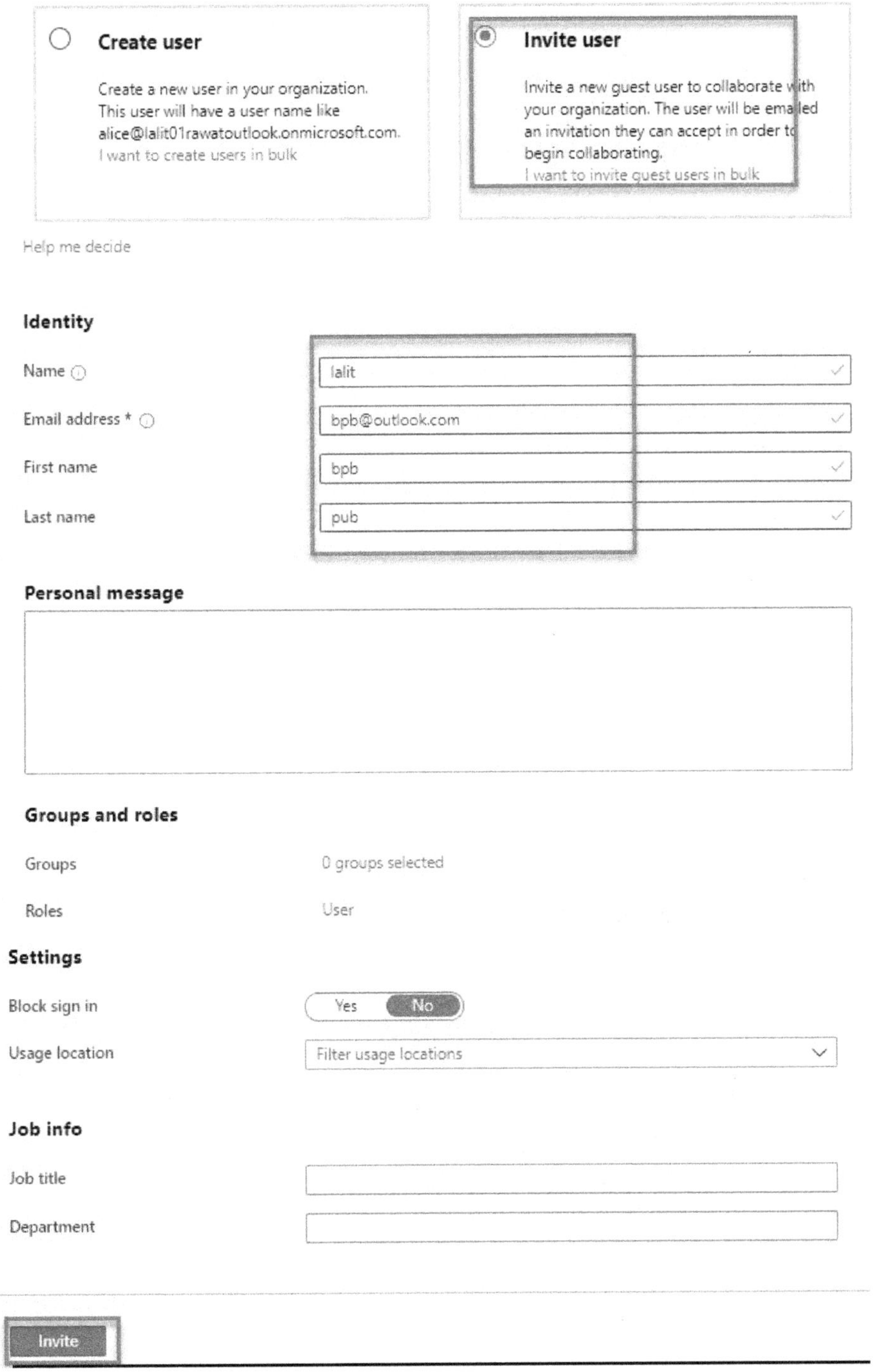

○ **Create user**

Create a new user in your organization.
This user will have a user name like
alice@lalit01rawatoutlook.onmicrosoft.com.
I want to create users in bulk

◉ **Invite user**

Invite a new guest user to collaborate with
your organization. The user will be emailed
an invitation they can accept in order to
begin collaborating.
I want to invite guest users in bulk

Help me decide

Identity

Name ⓘ	lalit	✓
Email address * ⓘ	bpb@outlook.com	✓
First name	bpb	✓
Last name	pub	✓

Personal message

Groups and roles

Groups   0 groups selected

Roles   User

Settings

Block sign in   Yes   No

Usage location   Filter usage locations   ⌄

Job info

Job title

Department

Invite

Figure 1.10: Guest User Access Invite

Self-service password reset

Azure self-service password reset will help users to reset their password without the help of a help desk administrator. If the user account is locked or if the password expires, the user can unlock/reset the password using a self-service password reset.

If you want to configure the self-service password reset, you should have global administrator rights in Azure AD.

Please follow the given steps to configure the self-service password reset:

1. Please go to your Azure AD.
2. Click on the **Password reset** tab.
3. Select the users, either All or the selected one. If you click on selected users, it will ask you to choose the group name.
4. Once you are done with this, please click on the **Save** button as shown in the following screenshot:

Figure 1.11: Password reset

Please go to Authentication method and follow the given steps:

1. Please select the authentication method as 1 or 2 as per the following methods:
    *   Mobile app code
    *   Email
    *   Phone -SMS only
    *   Mobile app notification
    *   Office phone
    *   Security question

2. Once you select the preceding method, your user will be able to reset the password using the multifactor authentication.

   Refer to the following screenshot:

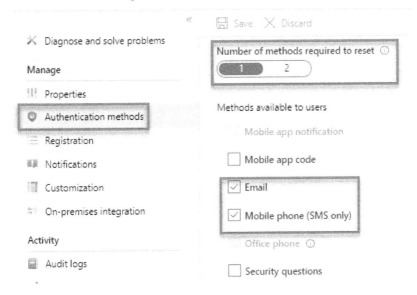

Figure 1.12: Authentication method

Once you configure this, you can go to **https://passwordreset.microsoftonline.com** to reset the password. Then, follow the given steps:

1. Please provide your user ID.

2. Enter the characters as per the image and click on the next as shown in the following screenshot:

3. Now, you will be able to reset the password.

Figure 1.13: Password reset method.

Azure AD join

Azure AD join provides the feature to register your mobile, laptop, and other devices to Azure AD with respect to the size of the device or industry. Azure Ad join works in hybrid environments as well. It enables access to both cloud and on-premises apps.

If you want to manage and configure the Azure Ad join, then you have to use the MDM and Intune solution which requires an Azure AD P2 license.

We can use the Azure AD join in the following few scenarios:

*   Windows deployment for your owned devices.

*   Access to organizational apps and resources from your device.

*   Cloud-based management of owned devices.

*   To configure the user sign in to their devices with Azure AD or synced Azure AD work or school accounts.

Conclusion

In this chapter, we discussed how to create bulk users and group management. We explained how to invite guest users and how to manage them using Azure AD. We also explained Azure AD join and learned how to set up the self-service password reset.

In the next chapter, we will discuss Azure AD connect and its installation.

We will also discuss how to manage Azure AD connect and learn how to manage the passwords of users and enable the password writeback.

References

- Create a basic group and add members using Azure Active Directory: **https:// docs.microsoft.com/en-us/azure/active-directory/fundamentals/active-directory-groups-create-azure-portal**

- Azure Active Directory B2C: **https://docs.microsoft.com/en-us/azure/active-directory-b2c/active-directory-b2c-overview**

- Guest user access in Azure Active Directory B2B: **https://docs.microsoft. com/en-us/azure/active-directory/b2b/what-is-b2b**

- Add or update a user's profile information using Azure Active Directory: **https://docs.microsoft.com/en-us/azure/active-directory/fundamentals/ active-directory-users-profile-azure-portal**

- Assign or remove licenses in the Azure Active Directory portal: **https://docs. microsoft.com/en-us/azure/active-directory/fundamentals/license-users-groups**

- Azure AD joined devices: **https://docs.microsoft.com/en-us/azure/active-directory/devices/concept-azure-ad-join**

- For more details: Azure4you Blog Post: **https://azure4you.com/**

CHAPTER 2
Implementing and Managing Hybrid Identities

In the previous chapter, we discussed how to create bulk users and group management. We also discussed how to invite the guest users.

In this chapter, we will discuss how to implement and manage hybrid identities. We will also discuss how to install and configure the Azure AD connect and how to configure the federation services with on-premises AD.

We will also cover the managed password sync, password writeback, and so on.

Structure

The following topics will be covered in this chapter:

- Azure AD Connect
- Azure AD Connect installation
- Manage Azure AD Connect
- Password writeback
- Password sync

Objectives

In this chapter, we will discuss Azure AD Connect and see how to configure and sync the on-premises identity to Azure AD. We will explain the password writeback and password sync that will help to sync the password Azure to on-premises.

Azure AD Connect

The Azure AD Connect service can be used to synchronize your on-premises active directory identities to Azure AD. It helps to connect your on-premises users to Azure and other applications to get authentication with Azure AD. It is called **hybrid connectivity.**

Integrating the on-premises identity with Azure AD provides the common identity for accessing cloud and on-premises resources. We can use the single identity to access the on-premises and cloud-based applications like **Office 365, SharePoint Online**, and so on.

It provides the following features:

- **Password hash synchronization:** It provides the **single sign-on (SSO)** method to synchronize the password of users by synchronizing the password of on-premises users to Azure AD in the hash format.

- **Pass-through authentication:** It allows users to use the same password of on-premises and cloud for signing in to applications. Only the pass-through agent gets installed, and as per the number of authentications per second, we may need more than one agent.

- **Federation integration:** Federation services can be used to configure the setup of the hybrid environment and SSO while configuring on-premises **Active Directory Federation Services (ADFS)** which require an additional server.

- **Synchronization:** It helps to create users, groups, and other objects. It verifies if the identity information of on-premises users and groups match with the cloud identity. It synchronizes password hashes as well.

- **Health monitoring:** Azure AD Connect Health provides monitoring for Azure AD Connect, and we can see Azure AD Connect health-related information/errors on the Azure portal.

Azure AD Connect services can be installed in a separate server in the on-premises AD and can be tightly integrated with Azure AD after installation and configuration. Azure sync services will sync the on-premise AD component to Azure AD. On-premises and Azure users can use the same credentials to log in to Azure and on-premises. For more details, you can refer to Azure AD Connect, which helps you to understand the components.

Please take a look the following diagram:

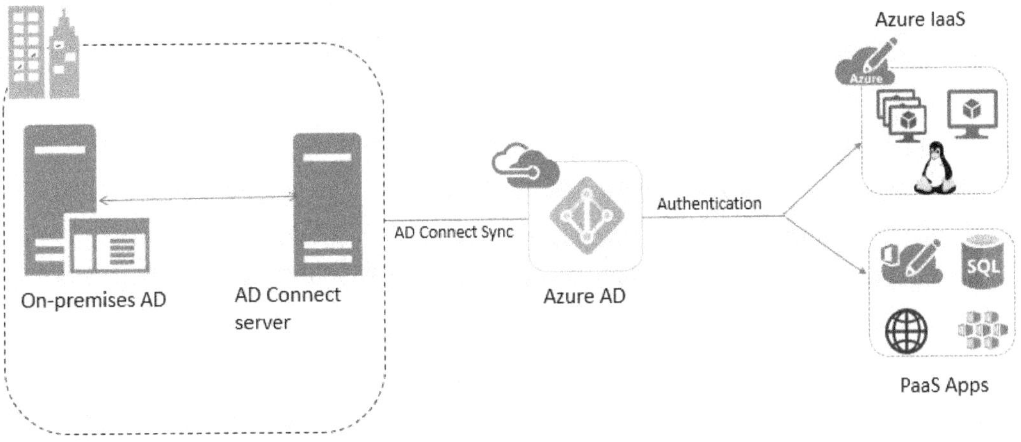

Figure 2.1: Azure AD Connect architecture

Azure AD Connect installation

Before you install the Azure AD Connect, you need to have the following pre-requisites.

Pre-requisites

You need to have the following pre-requisites; without which, you will not be able to configure the Azure AD. The following requirements are mandatory. We can see these properties been asked during configuration:

- You should have an Azure AD services/user account which has global admin rights to configure the Azure AD Connect to Azure AD.

- You should have an on-premises services/user account which has enterprise admin rights to configure the Azure AD Connect to Azure AD.

- Please download the Azure AD Connect from **https://www.microsoft.com/en-us/download/details.aspx?id=47594**.

- Whenever you configure the AD Connect, the domain name should match with a public domain name, or else you will get a warning message.

We have created lab environments for demonstration and created the VMs. We have installed the AD on this server. You can also try only for testing purpose. It's not recommended for production, but the steps of the Azure AD configuration can be performed.

Please follow the given steps to configure the Azure AD Connect:

1. Download the Azure AD Connect (**https://www.microsoft.com/en-us/download/details.aspx?id=47594**), or you can download it from the Azure portal.

2. Click on the AD Connect MSI setup and then click on **Install**. Please take a look at the following screenshot:

Figure 2.2: Azure AD Connect installation

3. Once you click on the **Install** option, the installation wizard will open.

4. Please agree to the license terms and policy and click on the **Continue** button as shown in the following screenshot:

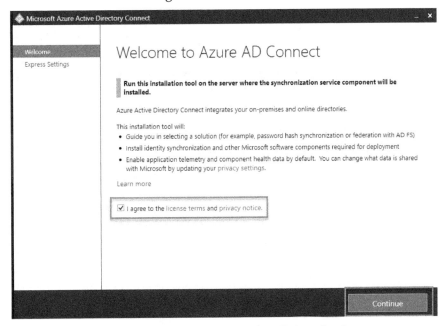

Figure 2.3: Azure AD Connect installation wizard

5. Once done, select the **Express Settings** to configure the Azure AD Connect as shown in the following screenshot:

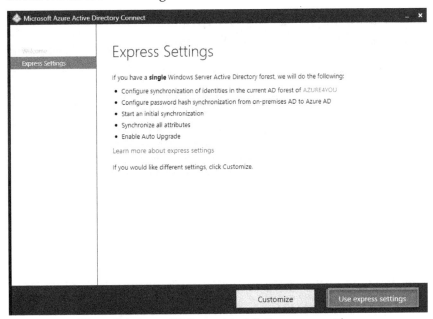

Figure 2.4: Azure AD Connect installation express settings

6. When you click on the use express settings, it will ask you to provide the global administrator credentials which have `.onmicrosoft.com` in the user ID as shown in the following screenshot.

It will connect to the Azure AD and verify the credentials before we proceed to the next step as shown in the following screenshot:

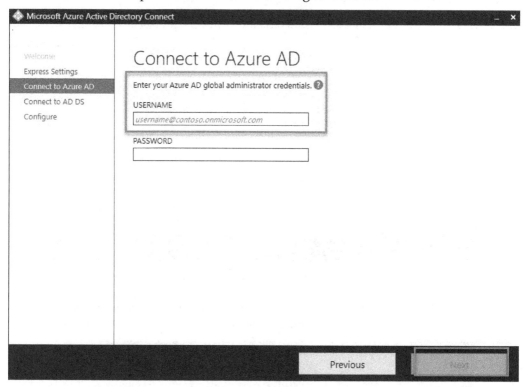

Figure 2.5: Azure AD Connect installation connect to Azure AD

7. Provide the services admin credentials which have enterprise admin rights.

8. While providing the credentials, please follow `domainname.com\userid`.

9. Once you provide the credentials, click on the **Next** button as shown in the following screenshot:

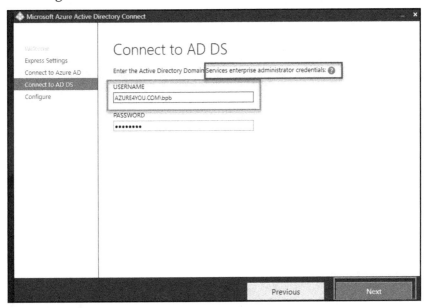

Figure 2.6: Azure AD Connect installation connect to AD DS

10. Then, it will ask you to verify the UPN suffix, but if you are doing this installation in production, then please match the UPN suffix and move forward. Please take a look at the following screenshot:

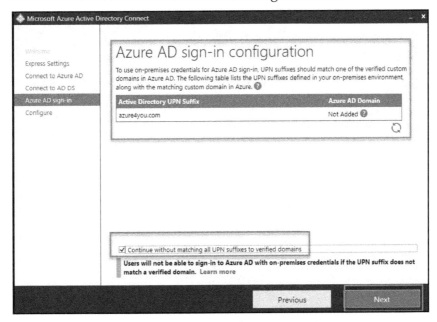

Figure 2.7: Azure AD Connect AD sign-in configuration

11. Once you click on **Next**, you are ready for configuration.

12. Start the synchronization process when the configuration is completed. But in production, it's recommended that you start the synchronization process only after the AD Connect installation.

    Please take a look at the following screenshot:

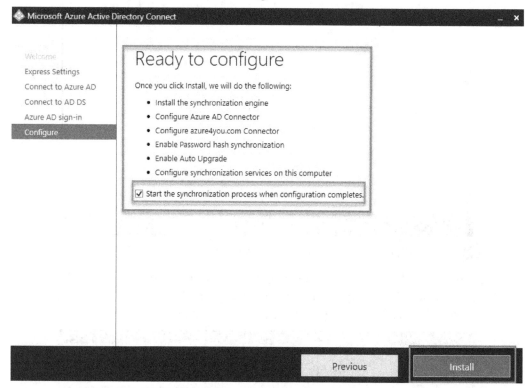

Figure 2.8: Azure AD Connect ready configuration

13. When you click on next, first it will verify the connectivity between Azure AD and on-premise. Then, it will configure the connection between Azure AD and on-premises AD.

14. It will install the sync services and verify the Azure AD.

15. Now, it will configure the Azure AD and update the sync.

16. After that, it will configure the setup to the on-premise domain.

17. After that, it will enable the password hash sync.

18. Now, it will save the sync settings.

19. After that, the final steps will be performed by the AD Connect setup to install and configure the AD Connect Health agent for sync services as shown in the following screenshot:

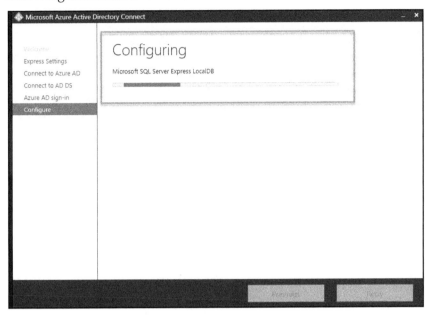

Figure 2.9: Azure AD Connect configuration

20. Now, the setup has been completed. So, exit from the setup as shown in the following screenshot:

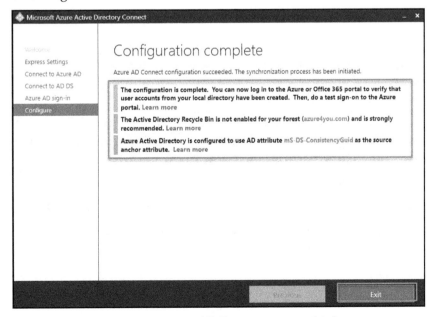

Figure 2.10: Azure AD Connect setup completed

Manage Azure AD Connect

We can manage the Azure AD Connect from the portal after installation, and we can see the configuration details of the on-premises AD. Please follow the given steps:

1. Please log in to the Azure portal.

2. Go to **Azure AD Connect** under the **Manage** tab and click on the Azure AD Connect. You will be able to see the last sync is **Less than 1 hour ago** and the sync status has been enabled as shown in the following screenshot:

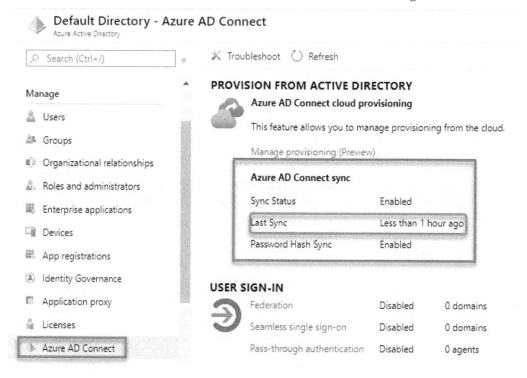

Figure 2.11: Managing Azure AD

3. We can also set up the **Federation, Seamless single sign-on**, and **Pass-through authentication** services.

4. Azure AD health services can be managed from the same portal.

5. Let us check whether the users have been synced to Azure AD or not.

6. We will go to the **Users** tab and check the on-premise users which are synced from your on-premises AD.

7. Now, in the following screenshot, you can see the user `bpb32` source is **Windows Server AD**, and if you can see Azure AD users, the sources are Azure AD:

Figure 2.12: Azure AD user verification

Password writeback

Password writeback will help you to synchronize the password which has been changed in Azure AD to on-premises AD. This feature needs to be enabled from the Azure AD Connect and provides the security mechanism to send the password from Azure AD to the on-premises AD. It provides the following features:

- **Enforcement of on-premises AD password policies:** If users reset their passwords, then it is ensured to meet your on-premises AD policy before committing it to the directory. This review process includes history, complexity, age, password filters, and other password restrictions which have been defined in your on-premises AD.

- **Zero-delay feedback:** Password writeback syncs the operations and users are notified immediately if their password doesn't meet the password policy or can't be changed for any reason.

- **Supports password changes from the access panel and Office 365:** When federated or password hash synchronized users need to change their expired or non-expired passwords, those passwords are written back to your local AD environment.

- **Supports password writeback when an admin resets them from the Azure portal:** When an admin resets a user's password in the Azure portal, if that user is federated or password hash synchronized, the password is written back to on-premises AD, but this functionality is not supported from the office admin portal.

- **Doesn't require any inbound firewall rules:** Password writeback uses an Azure service relay as an underlying communication channel and all commutation is outbound over port 443.

Enabling the password writeback from the Azure AD

Perform the following steps:

1. Log in to on-premises machines where you have installed the Azure AD.
2. Open the Azure AD Connect, and you will see the welcome wizard.
3. Click on **Configure** as shown in the following screenshot:

Figure 2.13: Password writeback

4. Click on **Customize synchronization options** to configure the password writeback. Please take a look at the following screenshot:

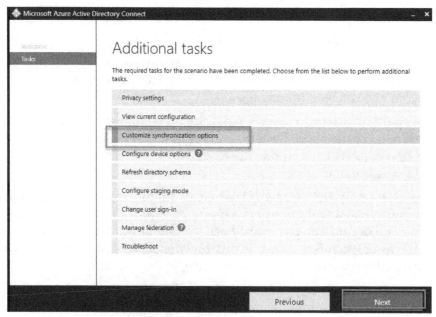

Figure 2.14: Customize the sync option

It will ask you to connect to the Azure AD and provide the credentials to configure it as shown in the following screenshot:

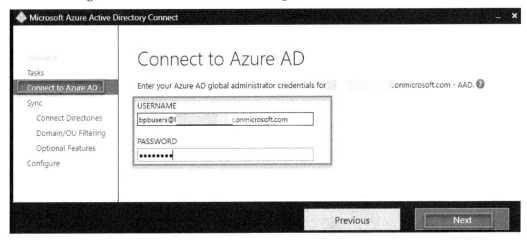

Figure 2.15: *Connect to Azure AD*

Now, please select the type of the directory and forest. Click on the **Next** button as shown in the following screenshot:

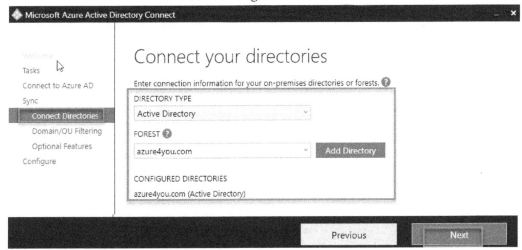

Figure 2.16: *Connect your directories*

Now, you can select **Sync all domains and OUs** and your domain as well as shown in the following screenshot:

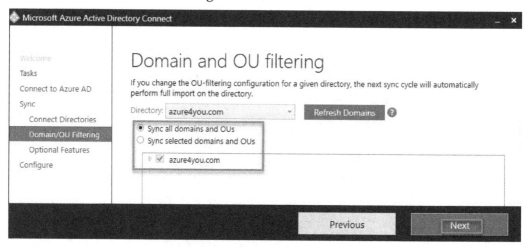

Figure 2.17: Domain and OU filtering

Please select the password writeback and click on the **Next** button as shown in the following screenshot:

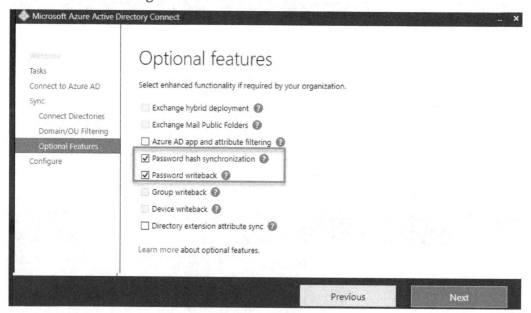

Figure 2.18: Password writeback enable

5. Once you are done with **Next**, it will verify all the settings and be ready for configuration.

6. Click on the **Configure** button. It will take a few minutes to complete the sync process and enable the password writeback. Please take a look at the following screenshot:

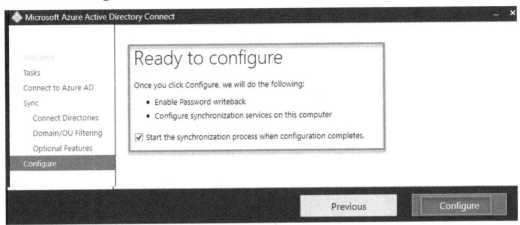

Figure 2.19: Ready to configure

In this section, we explained and demonstrated how to configure the password writeback. In the next section, we will demonstrate enabling the password writeback from the portal.

Enabling password writeback from the portal

Perform the following steps:

1. For password writeback, we need the Azure AD P1 or P2 license.
2. Go to the portal.
3. Go to Azure AD.

Under the **Manage** tab, select **Password reset** as shown in the following screenshot:

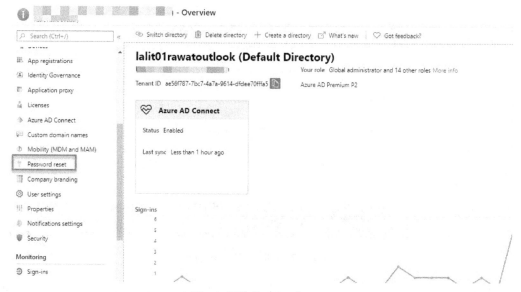

Figure 2.20: Password reset

4. In the password reset, under the **Manage** tab, please select the on-premises integration and enable the writeback password to your on-premises directory. Please take a look at the following screenshot:

Password reset - On-premises integration
lalit01rawatoutlook (Default Directory) - Azure Active Directory

✕ Diagnose and solve problems

«   🖫 Save   ✕ Discard

Manage

⌗ Properties

◉ Authentication methods   ✔ Your on-premises writeback client is up and running.

≡ Registration   Write back passwords to your on-premises directory? ⃝

▥ Notifications   (**Yes**   No)

▥ Customization   Allow users to unlock accounts without resetting their password? ⃝

⇅ On-premises integration   (Yes   **No**)

Activity

▤ Audit logs

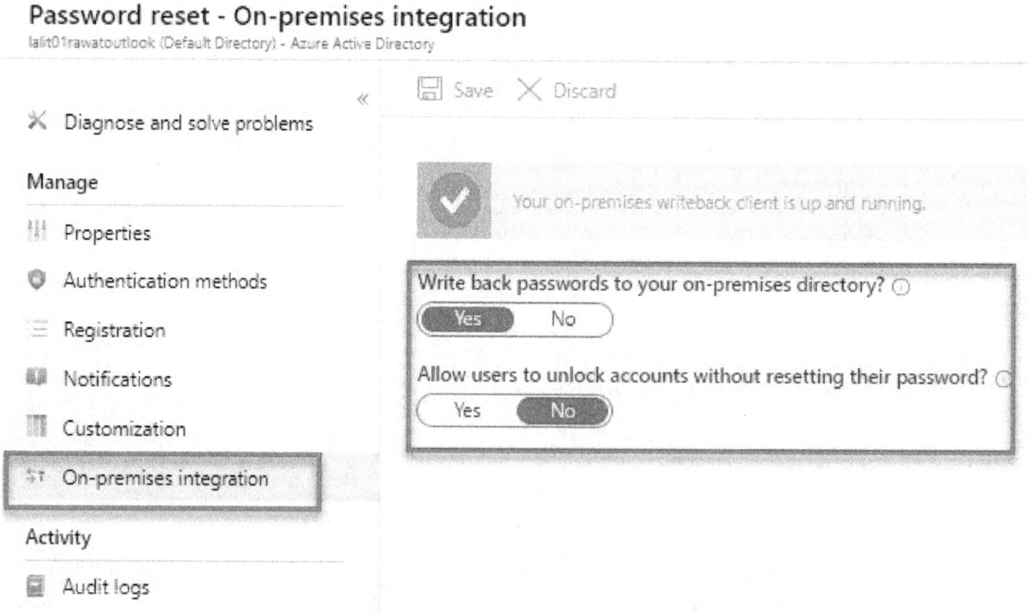

Figure 2.21: On-premises integration

Password sync

Password sync will be enabled automatically if we select the Azure AD Connect express setting installation. If you choose the custom setting, you can select the password hash sync on the user sign-in page. You can enable it.

Figure 2.22: Password Hash sync

Conclusion

In this chapter, we discussed Azure AD Connect and how to integrate it with on-premises. We covered how to enable the password writeback from Azure as well.

In the next chapter, we will learn about Azure RBAC roles and utilization of the resources and how to apply the different types of RBAC roles using various types of organization policies. We will also cover the Azure RBAC roles and custom Azure RBAC roles.

References

- Azure AD Connect: **https://docs.microsoft.com/en-us/azure/active-directory/hybrid/whatis-azure-ad-connect**

- Custom installation of Azure AD Connect: **https://docs.microsoft.com/en-us/azure/active-directory/hybrid/how-to-connect-install-custom**

- Implement password hash synchronization with Azure AD Connect sync password: **https://docs.microsoft.com/bs-cyrl-ba/azure/active-directory/hybrid/how-to-connect-password-hash-synchronization**

- User sign-in with Azure Active Directory Pass-through authentication: **https://docs.microsoft.com/en-us/azure/active-directory/hybrid/how-to-connect-pta**

- Azure AD Connect and federation: **https://docs.microsoft.com/en-us/azure/active-directory/hybrid/how-to-connect-fed-whatis**

- For more details, visit: **https://azure4you.com/**

Chapter 3

Managing Role Assignments Through the RBAC Policy

In this chapter, we will discuss Azure **role-based access control (RBAC)** roles and their utilization of the resources and how to apply the different types of RBAC roles using various types of organization policies. We will also discuss the Azure RBAC roles, custom Azure RBAC roles, and how to apply the Azure RBAC roles using PowerShell, and so on.

Structure

The following topics will be covered in this chapter:

- **Role-based access control (RBAC)**
- RBAC access configuration
- Custom RBAC role

Objective

We will discuss RBAC implementation in this chapter and see how we can use it in our organization to put control for anonymous access.

Role-based access control (RBAC)

"Role-based access control helps you to manage and provide access to your resources with the restricted manner."

Let us say in your organization the support team, application team, DB team, and so on are using the same subscription and there could be a possibility that if you allow everyone access to subscriptions, then there might be some changes mistakenly performed by any of the team members. It could result in a disruptive impact on the existing environment/subscription (production or non-production).

Hence, thinking of all such scenarios MS Azure has come up with a solution called **RBAC policy** which helps you to control the access. Let us say if you want to allow the DB team to access only DB resources which can be possible only through RBAC. The DB team can only see the DB resources and cannot make the changes to other services. So, using RBAC, you can control the access.

As per MS Azure recommendation, the best practice that you can provide is the least role access which will help the user to provide the exact access which he needs. RBAC can be applied to *groups*, *applications* or *resources*, and so on.

For any services, there are built-in RBAC roles defined as shown in the following diagram:

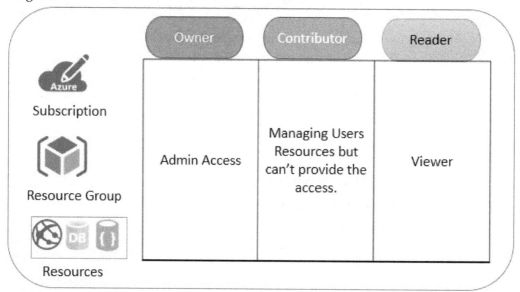

Figure 3.1: Azure RBAC role

Now, let us understand each term:

- **Owner:** The owner will have complete access of all your resources or specific resources just like the admin of your subscription.

- **Contributor:** The contributor will have equal access like the owner but cannot provide access to resources or at the subscription level. However, he can create and manage the resources.

- **Reader:** In the reader role, a user will have access to read or view permission to specific resources or subscriptions. However, he is not allowed to change or create any new resources.

- **User access administrator:** The user access administrator will help you to manage user access to Azure resources.

RBAC access configuration

RBAC access can be configured from various types like Azure resources, Azure subscriptions, and Azure resources group as well. In this section, we will see how to implement those scenarios using RBAC.

Subscription access using the RBAC policy

We will learn how to provide access to subscriptions as per the organization policy.

1. Go to the **Subscription** option.

2. Click on **Access control (IAM)** as highlighted in the following screenshot and select **Add role assignment**:

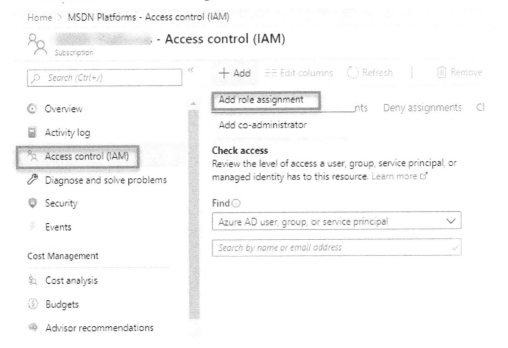

Figure 3.2: Add role assignment

3. Once you click on **Add role assignment**:

   1. Select the **Owner, Contributor**, or **Reader** role as per your requirements.

   2. Type and search the user ID for which you want to provide the access as shown in the following screenshot:

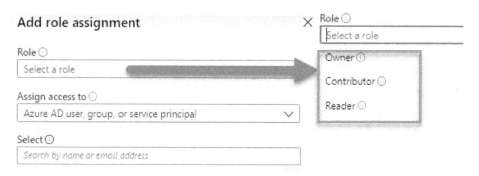

Figure 3.3: Role selection

4. When you select all the required details, your screen will look like the following screenshot. Click on the **Save** button to apply the changes.

   Once done, the user will be able to log in to the subscription and access the resources:

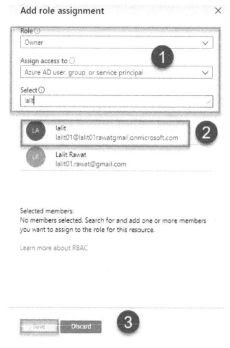

Figure 3.4: Assigning roles

In this section, we learned how to assign the RBAC roles at the subscription level.

Resource group access using the RBAC policy

We will learn how to provide access to the resources group as per the organization policy.

1. Go to the **Resource group** option.
2. Click on **Access control (IAM)** and select **Add role assignment** as shown in the following screenshot:

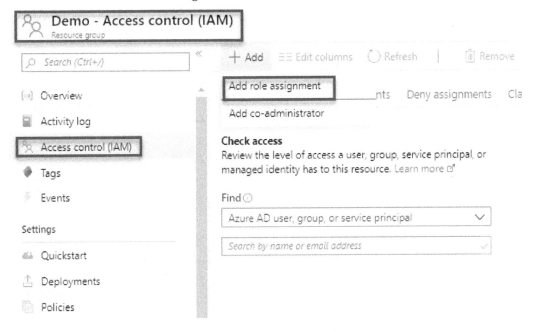

Figure 3.5: Resources group role assignment

3. Once you click on **Add role assignment**:

   1. Select the **Owner, Contributor**, or **Reader** role as per your requirements.

   2. Type and search the user ID for which you want to provide the access.

   3. Once you select all the required details, your screen will look like the following screenshot. Click on the **Save** button to apply the changes.

   4. Once done, the user will be able to see the resource group and its resources which reside in the resource group:

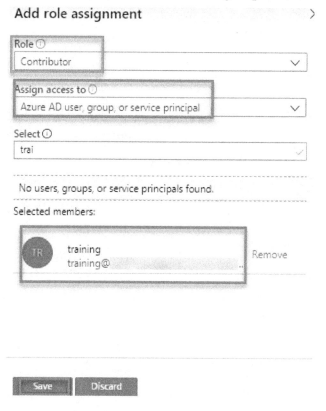

Figure 3.6: Resource group contributor role assignment

In this section, we learned how to assign the RBAC roles at the resource group level.

Resource access using the RBAC policy

We will learn how to provide access to resources like **Virtual Machines (VMs),** DB, and so on as per the organization policy.

1. Go to the resource for which you would like to provide access like VM, DB WebApps, and so on.

2. Click on **Access control (IAM)** and select **Add role assignment**:

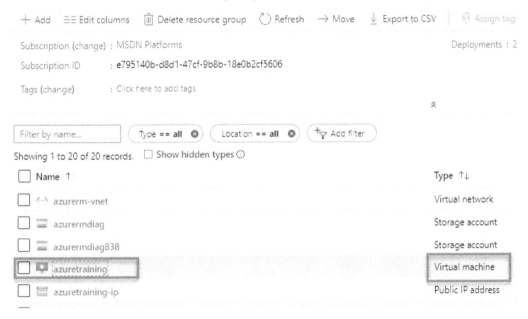

Figure 3.7: Resources role assignment

3. When you click on **Add role assignment**, select the role you want to assign the resources to:

   1. Select the **Owner, Contributor**, or **Reader** role as per your requirements.

   2. Type and search the user ID for which you want to provide the access.

   3. Once you select all the required details, your screen will look like the following screenshot. Click on the **Save** button to apply the changes.

4. Once done, the user will be able to see the resources and access the resources.

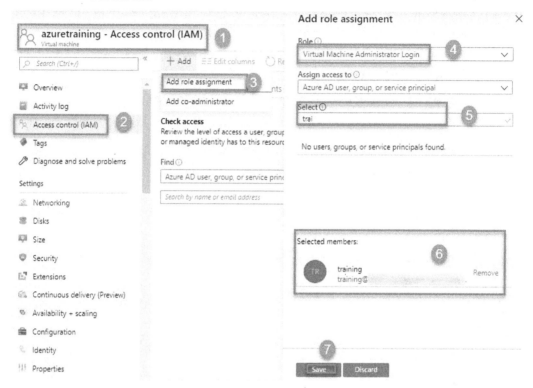

Figure 3.8: Role assignment of VM

Custom RBAC role

Custom roles come in the picture when the built-in roles do not meet your customer or organization requirements. In that case, you can create a custom role using PowerShell, **Azure Resource Manager (ARM)** template, CLI, or REST API. You can create up to 5000 custom roles in each tenant-level, but for a government cloud like, China, Germany, and so on, you can only create up to 2000 custom roles per tenant.

Creating the custom role

In this section, I will explain how to create the RBAC custom role and how to use existing built-in rules to create a new custom role.

If you want to allow any action to users, it should be listed in the `Actions` section and the deny user action can be put in the `NotActions` section while creating the custom RBAC.

If you would like to see what permission is available in the Azure contributor role, take a look at the following screenshot for the definition of the contributor role for more details:

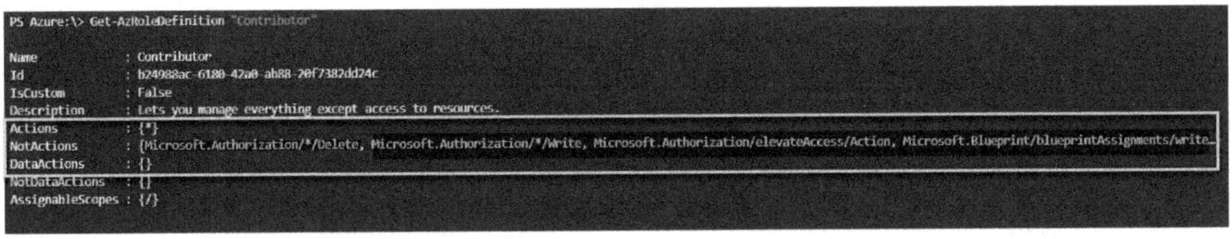

Figure 3.9: *Definition of a contributor role*

1. Please run the following command in PowerShell:

   Get-AzRoleDefinition "Contributor" | ConvertTo-Json

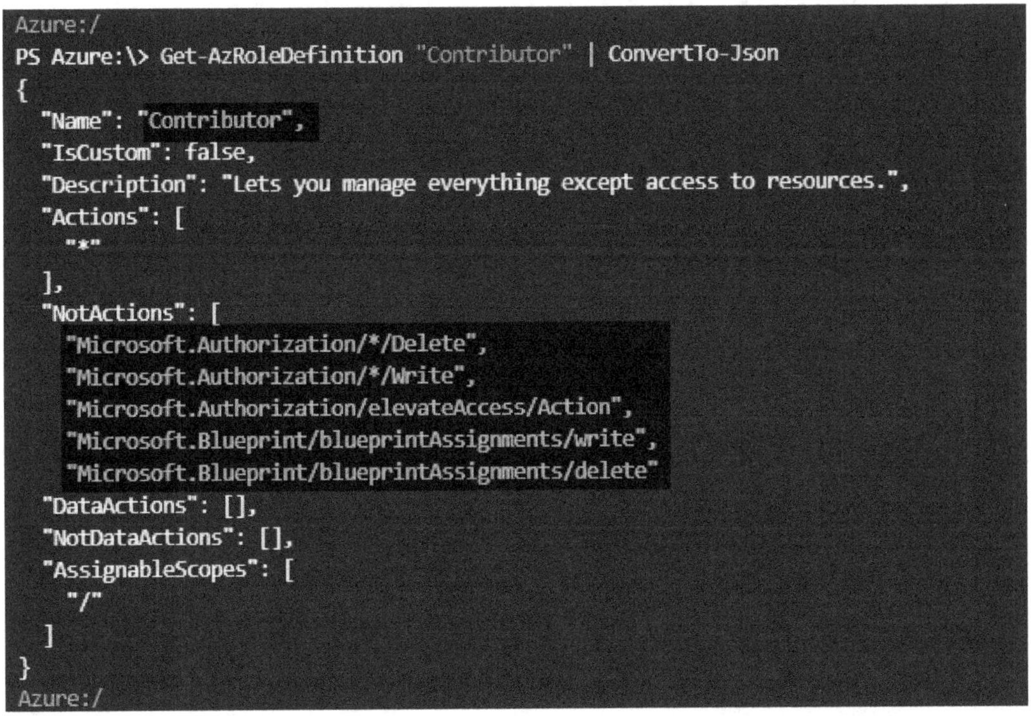

Figure 3.10: *Contributor role in JSON format*

Once you get the output, copy the file and change the action or not action rule accordingly.

I will change the NotActions rule to Actions and create a custom role.

Save the file in the **JSON** format:

```
1.   {
2.     "Name": "BPB_Contributor",
3.     "IsCustom": false,
4.     "Description": "Lets you manage everything except access
       to resources.",
5.     "Actions": [
6.       " Microsoft.Authorization/*/Delete",
7.          "Microsoft.Authorization/*/Write",        "Microsoft.
       Authorization/elevateAccess/Action",          "Microsoft.
       Blueprint/blueprintAssignments/write",       "
8.     ],
9.     "NotActions": [
10.        "
11.  "Microsoft.Blueprint/blueprintAssignments/delete"
12.     "DataActions": [],
13.     "NotDataActions": [],
14.     "AssignableScopes": [
15.       "/"
16.     ]
17.  }
```

2. Go to PowerShell and connect to the subscription using the following command:

```
Connect-AzSubscription
```

3. Please provide the user ID and password to get authenticated. Then, run the following command to create a new role:

```
New-AzRoleDefinition -InputFile "C:\Temp\BPB_Role.json"
```

Once done, you will be able to create a custom role. It will look like the following screenshot, which I had created earlier:

Figure 3.11: *Contributor role*

Conclusion

In this chapter, we covered the different types of RBAC roles and learned how to assign the RBAC custom roles in the subscription, resources group, and resources. We discussed how to create the custom role to match the organization or client requirements.

In the next chapter, we will learn about the Azure subscription and resource management. We will focus on different types of subscriptions and see how to manage Azure resources.

References

- Custom roles for Azure resources: **https://docs.microsoft.com/en-us/azure/role-based-access-control/custom-roles**

- RBAC overview: **https://docs.microsoft.com/en-us/azure/role-based-access-control/overview**

- Create a custom role for Azure resources using Azure PowerShell: **https://docs.microsoft.com/en-us/azure/role-based-access-control/tutorial-custom-role-powershell**

- Grant user access to Azure resources using RBAC and the Azure portal: **https://docs.microsoft.com/en-us/azure/role-based-access-control/quickstart-assign-role-user-portal**

- Grant user access to Azure resources using RBAC and Azure PowerShell: **https://docs.microsoft.com/en-us/azure/role-based-access-control/tutorial-role-assignments-user-powershell**

- For more details, visit: **https://azure4you.com/**

CHAPTER 4
Managing Azure Subscription and Resource Management

In this chapter, we will cover Azure subscription and resource management. We will focus on types of subscription and how to manage Azure resources. We will learn how to create a free subscription, types of subscriptions, how to manage resources using the RBAC policy. What is a quota and *how the use of the resources lock will help you from accidental deletion of resources?* Let us learn all this in this chapter.

Structure

We will cover the following topics in this chapter:
- Azure subscription
- Enterprise agreements subscription
- Subscription support plan
- Creating a free Azure subscription
- Global administrator permission
- Resources group
- Cost management
- Azure subscription policy
- Azure quota and resource tagging
- Management group

Objective

In this chapter, we will discuss Azure subscription, types of subscription. We will also discuss the step-by-step process to utilize Azure subscription, and so on. This will help all the levels of readers to get a better understanding of this topic.

Azure subscriptions

Azure subscriptions are a collection of resources known as **billing containers**. Each subscription has a unique ID that has been generated by MS automatically while creating the Azure subscription. If you need to create or access the resources, then you need a subscription access. Without the subscription access, you will not be able to access the resources under Azure subscription.

Let's take a look at the different types of subscriptions in the following section:

- **Free subscription:** MS provides this subscription. It is free for the first 30 days which includes $230 credit and free 25 services for 12 months. It is used for practical and learning purpose.

- **Pay-as-you-go subscription:** It is used widely in organizations and the pay-as-you-go subscription has a flexible payment method, and there is no limit for purpose or commitments. If a customer wants like to cancel the subscription, he/she can cancel the subscription.

- **Microsoft resellers (Cloud solution provider -CSP):** The CSP subscription is used only at the organization level where MS provides you with the access to work with partners directly to design and implement the solutions to meet your project requirements.

- **Open:** This subscription provides you with the flexibility to work with the same vendor from where you purchased the open volume license program and activated your Azure subscription.

- **Azure government customer:** This subscription is used for US government entities that are eligible to purpose Azure government services, and they can use the pay-as-you-go service.

- **Azure Germany customers:** This subscription is used for European Union or EFTA entities that are eligible to purpose Azure government services and they can use the pay-as-you-go service.

Enterprise agreement subscription

The EA (Enterprise Agreement) is designed for organizations, and in this subscription, the customer has to sign an agreement with Microsoft directly with the amount of consumption on your Azure resources. When an organization signs up for the EA agreement, a billing account is created and the billing can be done monthly, quarterly, or yearly based on the agreement.

Enterprise

It is most commonly known as Enterprise agreement, and it is only used by organizations. The EA subscription can be accessed from the Enterprise portal (**https://ea.Azure.com**) and used to create multiple departments to manage the subscription.

Departments

It is a sub-account of Azure EA subscription where we define the departments and associate a subscription to it, and it can be used by specific departments.

We can add multiple departments based on the organizational needs and assign a department owner who can manage the department and subscription under it.

It will also help us to add a cap on Azure consumption and based on the subscription utilization, we can decide the monthly or yearly budget.

Accounts

Accounts can be created by a different department and an account administrator can add new accounts to their departments to provide them access to the Azure account. Even an account administrator can create the subscription as well.

Subscriptions

As defined in the Azure subscription level, the subscription is a billing container, and all the billing for consumed resources happens at the subscription level. You can set up billing alerts of the budget spent to get an early notification if you have consumption more during a specific period. Refer to the following figure for more details:

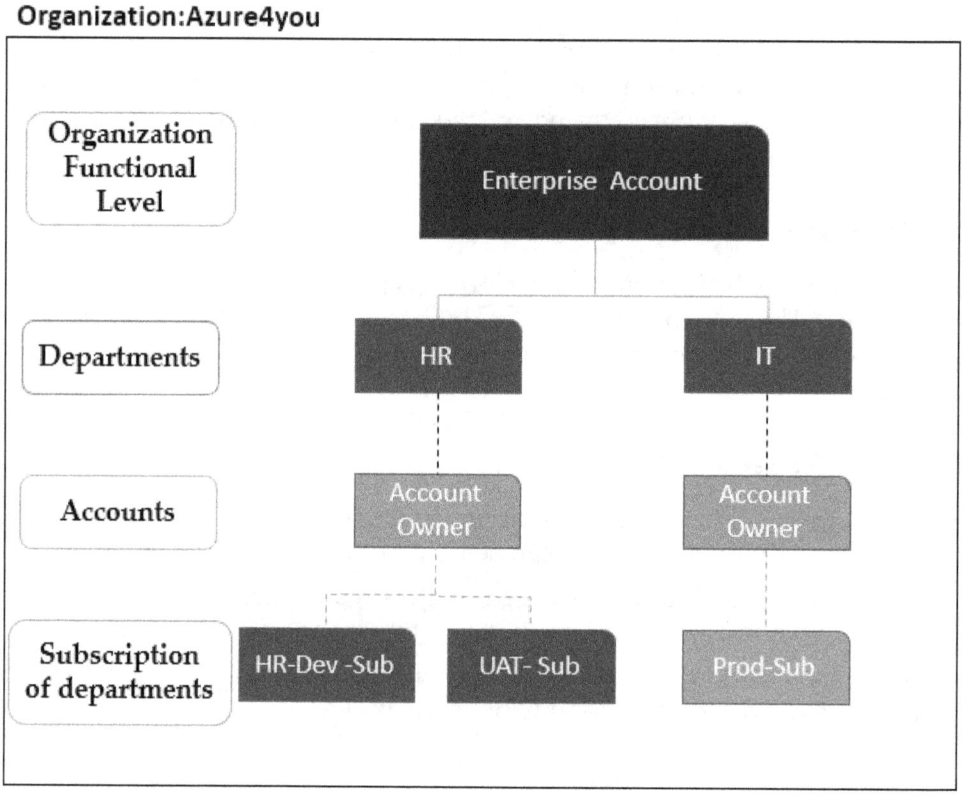

Organization:Azure4you

Figure 4.1: Enterprise subscription

Azure subscriptions support plan

Along with the subscriptions discussed earlier, we can also opt for the following support plan with a subscription which will help you to connect to the MS support team to fix or troubleshoot the issue.

Azure developer support

This kind of subscription support plan is most commonly used for Azure development/testing purposes where MS provides the discounted rates on Azure to support your ongoing development and testing activity.

Professional direct support

This subscription support plan can be used by companies where MS includes its technical, billing, and other teams to get a faster resolution and support.

Standard support

This subscription support plan can be used by companies where MS includes its technical, billing, and other teams to resolve your issues faster with 24/7 support. Most of the companies use this subscription to fix the critical dependence on the Azure subscription.

Azure tenant

An Azure tenant is nothing but Azure AD. It's a dedicated instance of Azure AD that an organization receives and authorizes the users to various cloud services. An Azure tenant can have multiple subscriptions. However, a subscription cannot have multiple tenants.

In the following diagram, you can see four 3 subscriptions and one directory. All the others are different. Once you create the subscription, the first tenant (Azure AD) will be created, and then the subscription will be associated with it. If you have a tenant, then you can create multiple subscriptions. Let's take a look at the following figure to get an understanding of how tenants work in Azure:

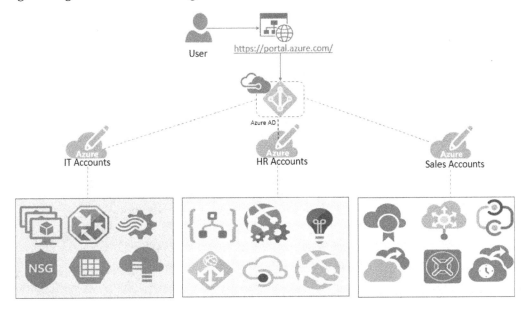

Figure 4.2: *Azure tenant*

Creating a free Azure subscription

While creating the free subscription, the following benefits are provided by MS Azure:

- 12 months of free popular services
- $200 credit to explore services within 30 days
- 25 services are always free

If you would like to create the free Azure subscription, follow the given steps:
Step: 1

1. Go the URL **https://Azure.microsoft.com/en-us/free/**.
2. Click on **Start free** as shown in the following screenshot:

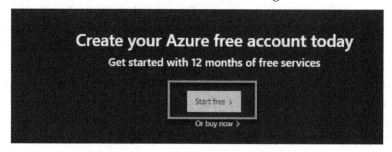

Figure 4.3: Free subscription

Step: 2

1. It will ask your login ID and password.
2. Provide your Microsoft ID like (bpb@outlook.com, bpb@live.com [reference email ID], and so on).
3. You can even log in through your organization ID like Azure4you@ mycompany.com, and so on.
4. Provide the password for the same.
5. After this, you will be able to log in to the subscriber page.
6. Provide your details as shown in the following screenshot:

Figure 4.4: Login screen

Step 3

1. Click on the free subscription.

2. Select the **Free Trial** as shown in the following screenshot:

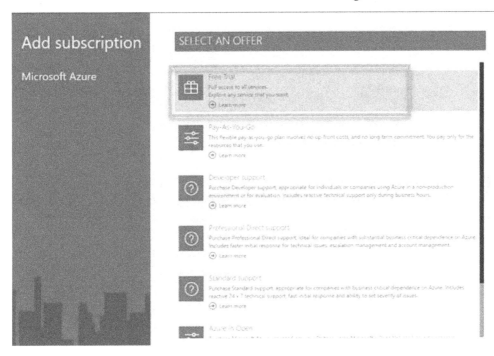

Figure 4.5: Select the subscription

Step 4:

1. Select the country code.

2. Provide the mobile number.

3. Click on **Text me** or **Call me** to get the verification code.

4. Once you get the verification code, put it in the **Verification code** section.

5. Click on the verify code.

6. Once the code is verified, you will be directed to the next tab to fill the payment information.

Take a look at the following figure for more details:

Figure 4.6: Details for subscription

Step: 5

1. Provide the cardholder name.

2. Enter the card number.

3. Provide the expiry date.

4. Type the CVV number.

5. Provide the address details and click on the **Next** button.

6. Understand the service usage and click on **Next**.

7. If you want to add MS support plans, you can do it. (It's chargeable so it's better to not add this plan.)

8. Click on the **Agreement** section and click on the **Signup** button.

9. After 10 minutes, you will receive the subscription.

10. Now, you can utilize your subscription and create the services in Azure. Provide the details as shown in the following figure:

Figure 4.7: Payment details and agreement

> Note: When you create the subscription, make sure you put all the details correctly as this has will be used for MS internal purpose. When you add your card initially, it will charge a minimal amount like Rs 2 to verify your credit card and only after that, it will allow you to create the free subscription.

Global administrator permission

Users who have global administrator permission can access all administrative services like Azure Active Directory, federate services to Azure Active Directories such as *Exchange Online, SharePoint Online,* and *Skype for Business Online.*

The first user ID who signs up for the Azure Active Directory tenant or subscription becomes a global administrator.

Only global administrators can assign other administrator roles. We can have more than one global administrator at the organization level. Global admins can reset the password for users and all other administrators.

Follow the given steps to provide the global admin access step by step:

1. Click on the **Azure Active Directory** option.

2. Go to **Manage** and click on the **Users** option.

3. Click on **All users**.

4. Select the user or search the users you want to assign the permission.

5. Select details, as shown in the following screenshot, for subscription details:

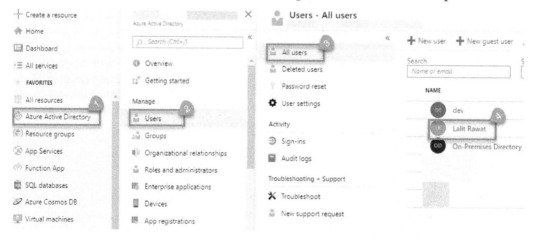

Figure 4.8: Global administrator role ·

6. Click on the user's name and then click on **Directory role**.

7. Then, click on **Add assignment**.

8. Click on **Search** and search for a `Global administrator` role.

9. Select the `Global administrator` role.

10. Click on the **Save** button, and your user will have global administrator access. Follow the steps as shown in the following screenshot:

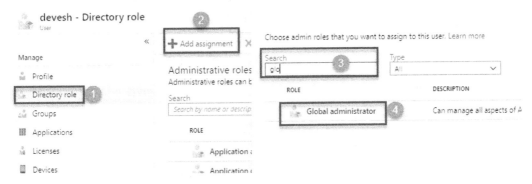

Figure 4.9: Directory: global admin role

Resources group

An Azure resource group is a logical container that contains the Azure resources in it. Resources manage the resources within the resources group together as an entity.

If you have provided the permission to a resource group, then you can also view all the resources which are available in the resource group.

You can even create or delete the resource group. If you delete the resource group, then all the resources which are present in the resource group will be deleted automatically.

For a better understanding, let's take a look at the following figure:

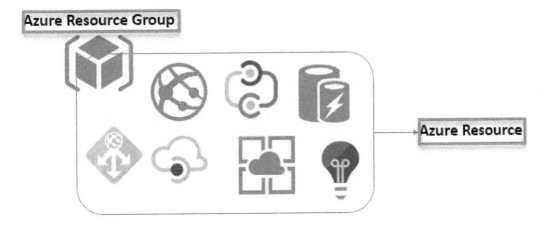

Figure 4.10: Azure resource group

Azure resource group manager

Azure Resource Manager is a deployment and management service for Azure.

It provides management layers that will help to create, update, modify, and delete the resources within the subscription. We can utilize the features like access control, lock, and tag. Refer to the following figure for more details in Azure resource group manager:

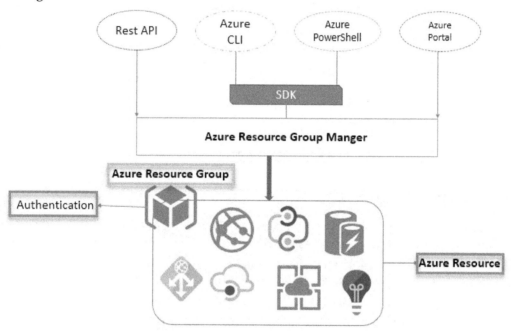

Figure 4.11: Resource group manager

Cost management

Azure cost management will help you to manage and control your cost. Organizations can utilize cost management to analyse and manage the cost. It gives you the breakup cost of each resource and resource group. It uses advanced analytics to provide a customized cost to customers. The cost will be shown based on the consumption of each service and third-party services like Red Hat, Oracle checkpoint firewall, and so on.

Exploring cost management: Cost management will add all the subscriptions which are under one tenant. To get the report of each tenant separately, you need to perform the following steps:

1. Click on the **Cost Management + Billing** option from the **FAVORITES** item or search on the Azure portal.

2. Click on **Overview** that will help you to get all the subscription accounts under your tenant.

3. Then, you will be able to view how much you have spent every month. For a detailed analysis, use the cost management tool and follow the steps performed as shown in the following screenshot:

Figure 4.12: Exploring cost management

Cost management tools will help you to get more details of resource services costs. It will help you to set up an alert for your Azure account, and you can define the budget as well. Follow the given steps to configure the same:

4. Click on **Cost analysis**:

   • You can see the graphical view of the cost analysis.

   • You can see the usage of each service, region.

   • If you want to go deeper, then click on each resource and you will get more details.

   • You can export the data in CSV or Excel file for your reference or telly purpose.

The following screenshot displays a sample report:

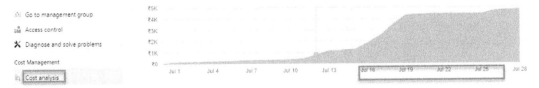

Figure 4.13: Cost management graphical view

- The following screenshot displays a sample report which is shown in cost view models:

Figure 4.14: Cost management- cost separation into services

Configuration of the budget alerts

The configuration of the budge alerts will help you get the alerts when your subscription cost gets utilized beyond the limit, and you can set an account spending limits as well. Perform the following steps to configure the budget alerts:

1. Click on the **Budgets** option in the left pane.
2. Once you click on the budget, you will get a window to provide the information.
3. Provide the alert name or budget name.
4. Reset the period month/years/weeks.
5. Provide the start date and end date of your budget.
6. Provide the number of your budget.
7. Once this is done, click on the **Next** button to create the alert.
8. Click on **Alert conditions** and set the alert % number based on your budget. Let us say your total budget is 5K. Once you have spent up to 60% (3000 INR), you will get an alert. You can change this setting as well.

9. Provide the email ID of your users or IT team to get the budget alert.

10. Click on **Create** and your alert will be created soon.

11. Perform the following steps as shown in the following screenshot:

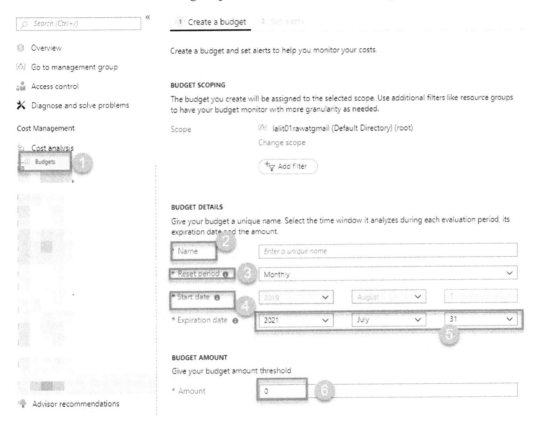

Figure 4.15: *Alerts creation*

12. Add the conditions as shown in the following screenshot:

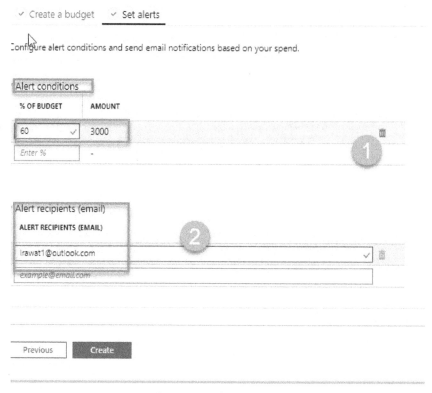

Figure 4.16: Alert condition

Azure subscription policy

The Azure subscription policy or Azure policy is used to achieve the compliance of your organization. It helps you to control the Azure environments as per your organization's compliance prospects.

You can create, manage, modify, and assign the policy based on your organization standards. It will also help you to identify the non-compliance resources in your subscription.

- Let us take an example that your organization needs to deploy a specific VM (Virtual Machine) instance size (VM size) in your subscription, and you want to disallow the rest of them, then you can achieve this using the subscription policy.

- The second example would be if your company resides in Asia or the US region with few states. If you want to allow access, users can create the resources in the specific region and then you can choose the allow location policy and allow only specific locations. All the other locations can be denied automatically. The allow location policy will help health care, financial, government services, and so on to achieve compliance specific to the location.

Azure policy creation, configuration, and assignment

In this section, we will learn how to implement, manage, and implement the policy. For the Azure policy configuration, follow the given steps:

1. Login to Azure portal (**https://portal.Azure.com**).

2. Click on search or on the left-hand side of the page in the **FAVORITES** section. Then, select the **Subscriptions** option.

3. In the **Subscriptions** section, click on the settings and select policies and follow the steps as shown in the following screenshot:

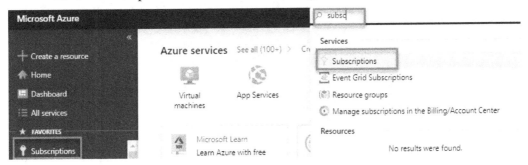

Figure 4.17: Select subscription

4. When you click on the **Policies**, you will be able to see the assigned policy in your subscription.

5. As you can see, I have applied a couple of policies in the subscription, and you can see the compliance level of the subscription. Follow the steps as shown in the following screenshot:

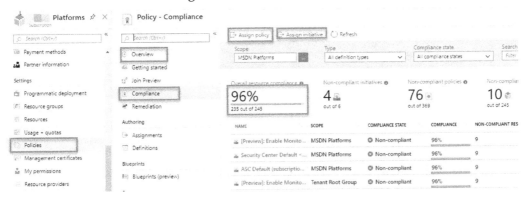

Figure 4.18: Azure policy

6. If you want to create the new policy, click on **Assigned policy**.

7. It redirects you to a new screen, and here we can create a new policy.

8. You can provide the following values in your Azure policy. The policy will be created for a specific region:

Scope: Provide the subscription as shown in the following screenshot:

Figure 4.19: Policy compliance

- **Exclusions**: This option can be used if you want to exclude the resources from the policy. If you want to apply to the entire subscription, then do not select any resources in the exclusion policy.

- **Policy definition**: Policy definition will help you to choose the defined policy from the policy gallery to control your resources. Follow the steps as shown in the following screenshot:

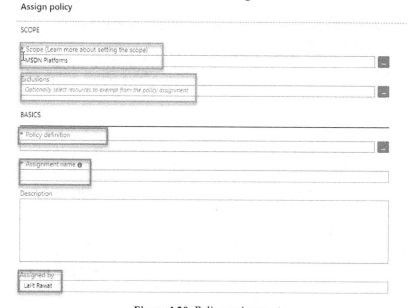

Figure 4.20: Policy assignments

- If you are planning to have the resources in a specific location, then click on the **Allowed locations** policy.

- If you want to allow a specific SKU, then you can achieve this by using the Azure policy.

- Take a look at the following specific policy. You can search and apply the policy based on your organization's standard policy. Refer to the following screenshot:

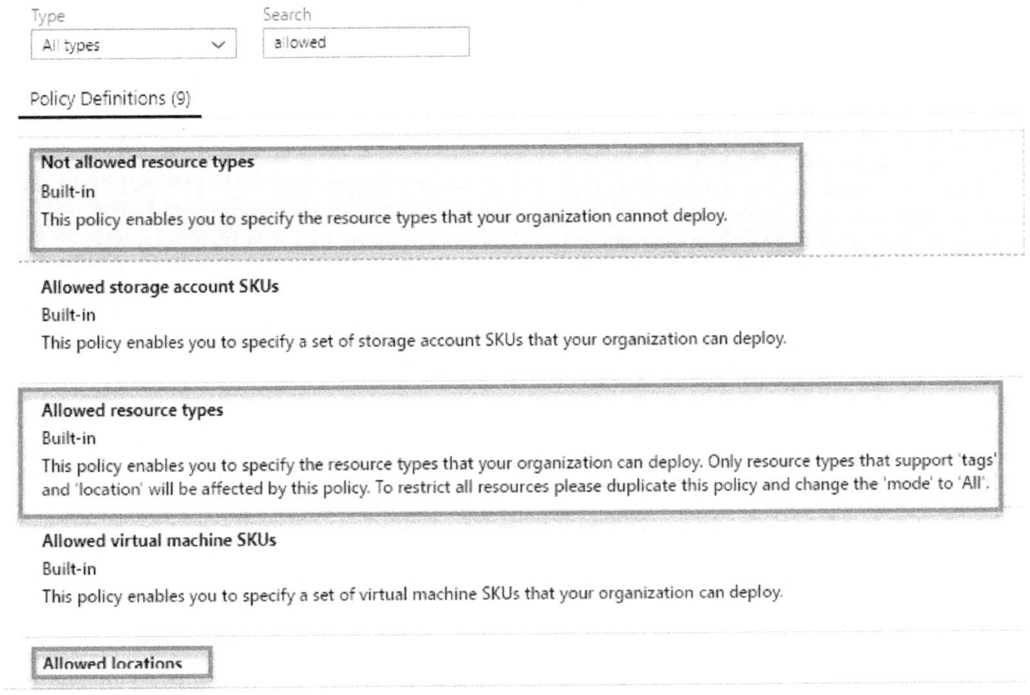

Type
All types ∨

Search
allowed

Policy Definitions (9)

Not allowed resource types
Built-in
This policy enables you to specify the resource types that your organization cannot deploy.

Allowed storage account SKUs
Built-in
This policy enables you to specify a set of storage account SKUs that your organization can deploy.

Allowed resource types
Built-in
This policy enables you to specify the resource types that your organization can deploy. Only resource types that support 'tags' and 'location' will be affected by this policy. To restrict all resources please duplicate this policy and change the 'mode' to 'All'.

Allowed virtual machine SKUs
Built-in
This policy enables you to specify a set of virtual machine SKUs that your organization can deploy.

Allowed locations

Figure 4.21: Azure policy type

- Once you select the policy allowed location, choose the location you want to allow such as *East US, Central India,* and so on.

- Choose the **Assigned by** option.

- Click on the **Assign** button.

- Once done, you will be able to assign the policy successfully. Follow the instructions as shown in the following screenshot:

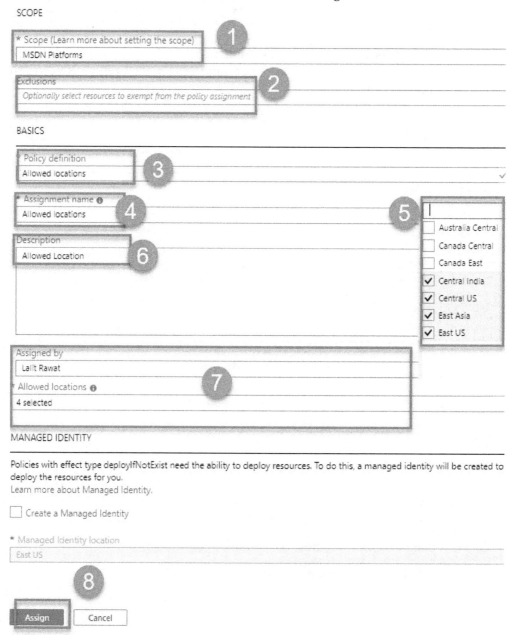

Figure 4.22: *Azure policy configuration*

Finally, we have successfully implemented the policy.

Azure quota

An Azure quota is nothing but the limitation of a specific subscription of how many resources can be deployed. Generally, a quota is of two types:

- **Soft limit:** Default resources available in the subscription can be increased by raising the request with the MS team.

- **Hard limit:** Maximum resources can be deployed within the subscription and even raising the request with the MS team cannot be increased.

If you want to see the usage limit and quota of your subscription, then click on the subscription. In the **Settings** section, click on **Usage + quotas**, and you will be able to view the available services in your subscription and see the quota as well.

You can see the details of the subscription limitation in the following screenshot:

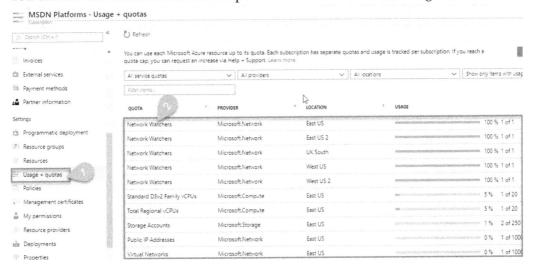

Figure 4.23: Usage and quota limitation

Resource tag

We can use the Azure resource tag to add the extra fields to identify the resources and it can be used for billing purposes. Every tag contains the following fields:

- **Name: Production Application**
- **Owner: Lalit Rawat**
- **Department: IT**
- **Bill to: IT**

Note: The preceding resource tags are just examples that can be changed based on your organization's policy. Based on that, you can define the tags and associate specific resources.

Usage of the resource tag

Let us say if you are a big organization and have deployed 4,000 applications, then *how you can understand which resources group belongs to which app and who is the owner? Who to bill the usage of services which is presented in the resources group?*

Hence, to identify the billing purpose, resource group tags can be used, and they are very helpful in the long term for a structured organization. Perform the following steps:

1. Click on **Resource groups**.

2. Under the **Overview** tab, click on the **Tags** option.

3. Provide the resource name, application, owner, database, and so on.

4. Then, provide the values, where values is your application name like **Tomcat, Apache, SQLDB**, and so on.

5. Click on **Save** as shown in the following screenshot:

Figure 4.24: Resources tag

Configuration of a resource lock

The resource lock will help you with your accidental deletion of resources.

Administrators can lock the resources to prevent others from deleting the resources.

In the subscription, you can find two types of locks:

- **Delete:** This lock prevents resources from users deleting the resource. However, users can still read and modify the resource.

- **Read-only:** This lock provides access to read-only resources; in that case, users cannot modify or change the resources. However, they can still see the resources.

Take a look at the following screenshot:

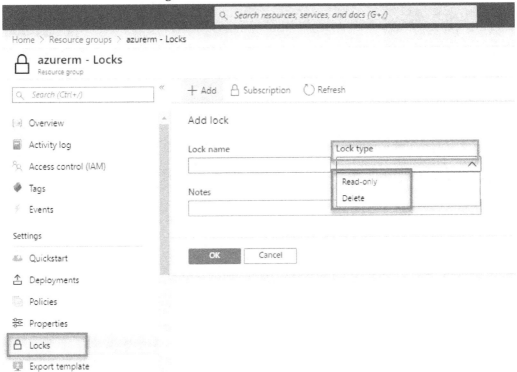

Figure 4.25: Resources lock

If you want to apply a lock on your resource group, follow the given steps.

1. Log in to the Azure portal by opening **https://portal.Azure.com**.

2. Select **Resource groups**.

3. Under the resources group, click on **Locks**.

4. Create a lock.

5. After the lock creation, you can deploy the lock-in resource group successfully.

6. Perform the following steps as shown in the following screenshot:

Figure 4.26: Resources lock creation

7. If you try to delete the resources, you will get the message that *the resources group has been locked and cannot be deleted* as shown in the following screenshot:

Figure 4.27: Resources lock

Resources movement from one resource group to another

If you are planning to move the resource group resource (VMs and so on) to another resource group, then this can be done easily.

You can also migrate the resources between subscriptions under the same tenant, and this can be done using the portal.

If you want to move the resources, perform the following steps:

1. Click on the resources group in which you want to move the resources.

2. Select the **Move** button at the top-right corner of the screen as shown in the following screenshot:

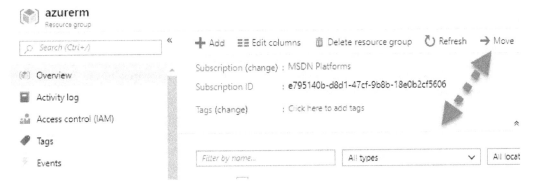

Figure 4.28: Resources move

3. Select the resources you want to move from once resources group to another.

4. Click on **OK**.

5. It will take 45 to 20 minutes based on the size of the resource to complete the task.

6. Follow the given steps as shown in the following screenshot and click on **Move** to move to the new resources group.

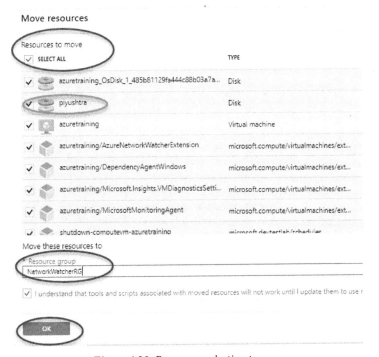

Figure 4.29: Resources selection to move

7. When you click on your resources, the resources will be migrated to a new resources group.

Removing a resource group

A resource group can be removed by clicking on the delete resource group. This can be done through the Azure portal, CLI, PowerShell, and so on. Take a look at the following screenshot:

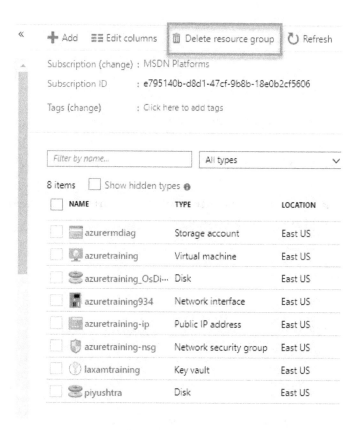

Figure 4.30: Resource group deletion

Perform the following steps:

1. Click on the delete resources group.

2. Provide the resource group name.

3. Once you provide the resources group name, click on the **Delete** button.

4. Once done, the resources will be deleted automatically.

Take a look at the following screenshot for more details:

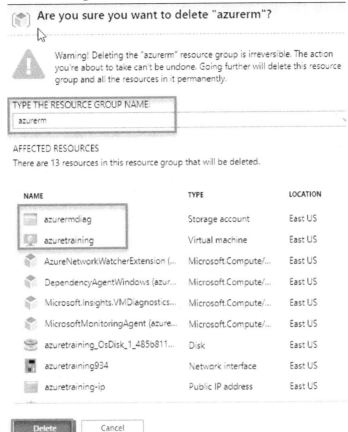

Figure 4.31: Resource group deletion confirmation

Creating and configuring the management groups

The management group will help you to manage multiple subscriptions in a single tenant. We can efficiently manage the access, policies, and compliance for these subscriptions.

We can apply the single policy within the tenant group. The first management group will act as a tenant, and the policy that applies on this subscription will be inherited to other subscriptions as well.

If you want to create and configure the management group, follow the given steps:

1. Click on all services.
2. Type management in the search box.

3. Click on the **Management groups** option, as shown in the following screenshot:

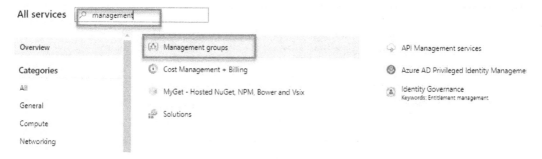

Figure 4.32: Management group

4. Once you click on the management group:

   • Click on **Create new**.

   • In **Management group ID (Cannot be updated after creation)***, provide the name.

   • Provide the management group display name.

   • Click on **Save** as shown in the following screenshot:

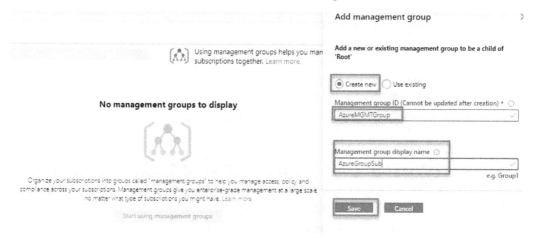

Figure 4.33: Management group creation

5.   Once you click on **Save**, it will start creating the first management group which might take up to 15 minutes. Refer to the following screenshot:

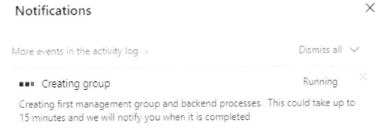

Figure 4.34: Group creation

6.   Once the management group is created, you will see the following screen as shown in the following screenshot:

Figure 4.35: Management group view

7.   If you want to create another management group, then click on the **+ Add management group** and create another group as shown in the following screenshot:

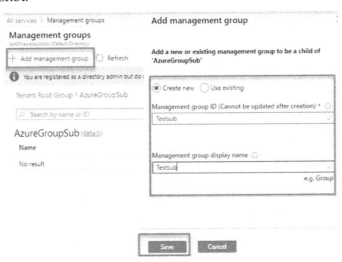

Figure 4.36: Add management group

8. Once the management group is created, you need to assign the subscription to the management group so that when you apply the policy, it should be inherited to the subscription associated with the management group. You can configure it as shown in the following screenshot:

9. Now, we will complete this step to configure the management group and associate it with the subscription:

Figure 4.37: Add subscription to the management group

Conclusion

In this chapter, we learned how to create the free Azure subscription, subscription management, and how to assign the policy. If you want to allow the resources from the Azure policy, configure the Azure resources group tags and implement the resource lock. We covered the types of subscriptions. In the next chapter, we will cover how to monitor resources in Azure subscription.

In the next chapter, we will also learn about the management and configuration of Azure storage and its types, storage account replication, and so on.

References

- Free subscription creation: **https://azure.microsoft.com/en-us/free/**
- Associate or add an Azure subscription to your Azure Active Directory tenant: **https://docs.microsoft.com/en-us/azure/active-directory/fundamentals/ active-directory-how-subscriptions-associated-directory**
- Activate Azure subscriptions and accounts with Cloudyn: **https://docs. microsoft.com/en-us/azure/cost-management-billing/cloudyn/activate- subs-accounts**
- Cloudyn service : **https://docs.microsoft.com/en-us/azure/cost- management-billing/cloudyn/overview**
- Azure cost management: **https://docs.microsoft.com/en-us/azure/cost- management-billing/cloudyn/overview**
- Azure resource manager: **https://docs.microsoft.com/en-us/azure/azure- resource-manager/management/overview**
- Azure4you-blog: **https://azure4you.com/**

CHAPTER 5
Managing and Configuring of Azure Storage Accounts

In this chapter, we will cover how to manage and configure the Azure storage account. In this chapter, you will learn about different types of Azure storage accounts, the use of storage accounts, and creation and configuration of Azure storage accounts which will help you to understand how the storage accounts work in Azure. We will explain how to secure your storage account using the Azure firewall configuration and integrate it with a virtual network. *What is the use of the Azure storage explorer and how to manage the Azure storage account access key?* Monitoring Azure storage account using log analytics will help you understand if you need to troubleshoot your storage account if anything goes wrong. We will cover more about replication, how this replication will work, and how your data can be synced to a different region.

Structure

The following topics will be covered in this chapter:

- Azure storage account
- Generate and manage the shared access signature
- Managing storage account access keys
- Installation and configuration of the storage explorer

Objective

In this chapter, you will learn how to configure the storage account and how to store data in Azure. We will provide you with step-by-step instructions of how to create and configure the Azure storage account, how to connect to the Azure storage account using the Azure storage explorer, and how to use the Azure storage key.

Azure storage account

An Azure storage account is a cloud-based solution for storing structural and unstructural data.

It is also used to store the data disk of VMs, files, and so on. It is highly available, durable, and secure. It can be accessed by HTTP/HTTPS from anywhere. You can take a look at the following diagram for more details to understand about the storage account data structure:

- **Storage for VMs data:** This kind of data will be stored in a blob storage account under the page blob which stores the **Virtual Hard Disk (VHD)** file of VMs.

- **Structured data:** It is a commonly used cosmos DB, table, and so on where the data will be stored structurally and it can give the results easily.

- **Unstructured data:** Unstructured data can be used to store the data log file, image, movie or archival data, and so on, which is used to dump the data. This does give results faster as this is not stored in a format or structural way. Please take a look at the following diagram for more details:

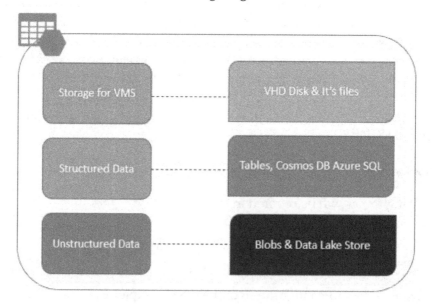

Figure 5.1: Azure storage account data

Azure storage accounts consist of the following three types:

1. **Blob storage account:** Blob storage accounts are used for unstructured data like backup, JPEG, AVI files, and so on. A blob storage account offers three kinds of accounts: **cool storage, hot storage**, and **archive**.

   - **Access tiers:** Access tiers have the functionality to determine how frequently data can be accessed. Based on the tiers, your storage account bill will be charged:

     o **Hot storage:** This type of storage account can be used when you need to access the data frequently such as day-to-day operations.

     o **Cool storage:** This type of storage account can be used for data that is infrequently accessed and stored for a minimum of 30 days. Let us say if you have an older backup or file you just want to store to a storage account, and you need to access it monthly once or twice.

     o **Archive storage:** This type of storage account is used to store the data which has been accessed rarely and stored for at least 180 days such as an older backup with more than 5 or 10-year compliance data.

Please see the following screenshot for more details:

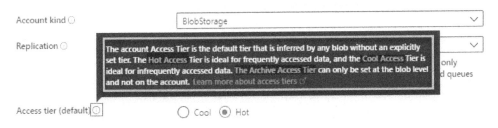

Figure 5.2: Azure blob storage account tier

2. **General purpose V1:** GPv1 storage accounts are legacy accounts and they have been used for blobs (name changed to a container), files queues, and tables. They are most commonly used and support replication like LRS, GRS, and RA-GRS. Please take a look at the following screenshot:

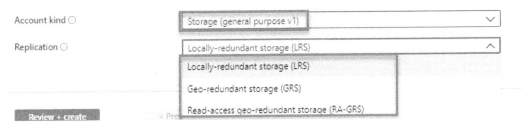

Figure 5.3: Azure GPv1 account

3. **General purposeV2:** GPv2 storage accounts are recommended to use as they are upgraded versions. They are used for blobs (name changed to a container), files queue, and tables. They support replication like LRS, GRS, RA-GRS, and ZRS. They also have the feature for cold/hot storage account which you can get only in the blob storage account.

    Recently, MS Azure has released new replications like **GZRS-zone** redundant storage and **read-access geo-zone-redundant storage (RA-GZRS).** It is in the preview feature. Please take a look at the following screenshot:

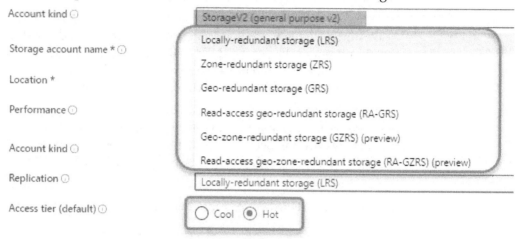

Figure 5.4: GPv2

4. **Premium storage accounts:** Premium storage accounts use the SSD disk and provide high performance and low latency disk support. The premium storage account is mainly used for mission-critical applications or production environments. 1 TB disk provides the 7500 IOPS and 250 MB throughput for the disk. Please take a look at the following screenshot:

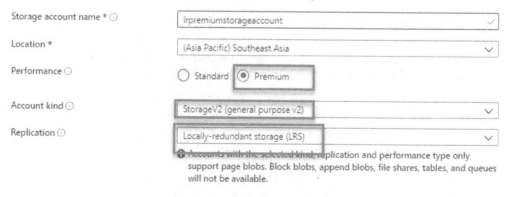

Figure 5.5: Premium storage account

Azure storage account creation and configuration

If you want to create a storage account, follow the given steps:

1. Please click on **Create a resource**.

2. Search for **Storage account**.

3. Click on the **Create** button to create a storage account as shown in the following screenshot:

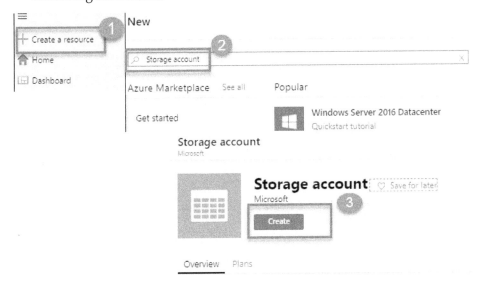

Figure 5.6: Storage account creation

4. Please select the subscription for which you want to create the Azure storage account.

5. Please create the new resources group or use an existing resources group from the drop-down menu.

6. Provide the Azure storage account name (name will only be in lowercase and in numbers).

7. Select the region you want to deploy the storage account.

8. Performance type can either be **Standard** or **Premium** as per customer requirements.

9. For the account kind, you can select: GPv1, GPv2, or blob storage account. I have selected GPv2 as its latest version.

10. For replication, you can select the default RA-GRS but based on the requirements, you can change to GRS, LRS, or ZRS (if available in your region).

11. Select the access tier: **Hot** or **Cool**. In my case, I have selected **Hot**.

12. Click on **Next: Networking >** for further configuration as shown in the following screenshot:

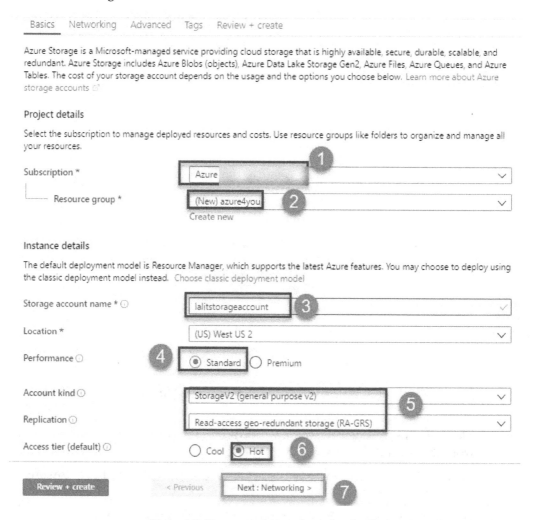

Figure 5.7: Storage account configuration details

13. Based on the requirements, you can only enable the following endpoints:

   • **Public endpoint (all network):** Open to all networks.

   • **Public endpoint (selected networks):** For a selected network.

- **Private endpoint:** Integrate the VNet and make it available for your network only as shown in the following screenshot:

Figure 5.8: Storage account networking configuration

- Please click on the **Advanced** tab, and here, you can set the security like secure transfer required and data protection settings, etc. For more details, take a look at the following screenshot.

- Please click on **Tags** and assign the tags for billing purposes as shown in the following screenshot:

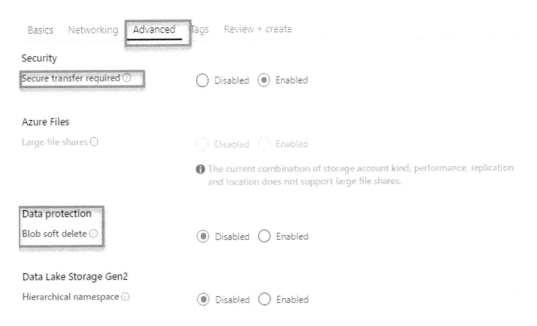

Figure 5.9: Storage account advance settings

14. Once the validation is complete, you will see the green mark.

15. Please verify the details one more time and click on **Create** to create the account.

16. After that, the deployment will start and your storage account will be created within 5 to 10 minutes. Please take a look at the following screenshot:

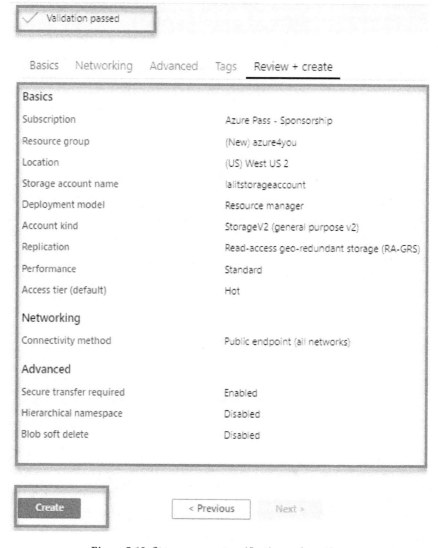

Figure 5.10: Storage account verification and creation

In this session, I have explained the Azure storage account data type and its usage.

I have briefly explained how to create the storage account and so on. Now, you will be able to understand and create the storage account.

Implement Azure storage replication

In Azure storage replication, we have replication policies as part of the storage account replication. It helps us to maintain the compliance part and secure the data on it:

- **Locally redundant storage (LRS) account:** It maintains three copies of your data within a single datacenter in a single region. Its usage data can be reconstructed, and it help in your complincae for regional governance requirements.

- **Zone redundant storage (ZRS):** It maintains three copies of your data within 2 or 3 datacenters in a single region or across the region. Data will be replicated across the three-storage clusters in a single region. It is not available in Azure of the region.

- **Geo redundant storage (GRS) account:** It maintains six copies of the data and data that has been replicated three times within the primary region and three times in the secondary region 100 miles away from the primary region. Data will be available to read-only during a failure.

- **Read-only geo-redundant storage (GRS) account:** It maintains six copies of the data and works in the same way as your GRS, but it provides the read access to your secondary region even without the failover.

If you would like to implement or change the replication, then you need to follow the given steps:

1. Please select the Azure storage account.

2. Go to **Configuration**.

3. Select the appropriate replication from the **Replication** drop-down menu.

4. Click on **Change**. If you click on change, the changes might be applicable based on the replication you select.

5. Click on **Save** as shown in the following screenshot:

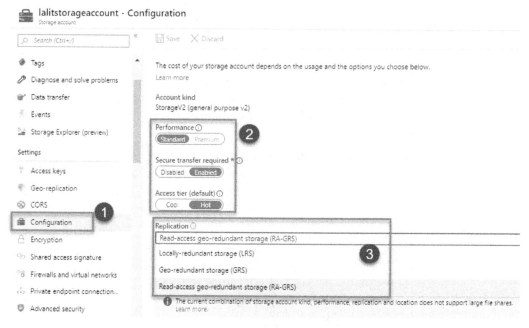

Figure 5.11: Storage account replication

6. Once you change the replication, click on `Geo-replication`.

7. In this section, you will able to see the primary and secondary regions where your data has been copied as shown in the following screenshot:

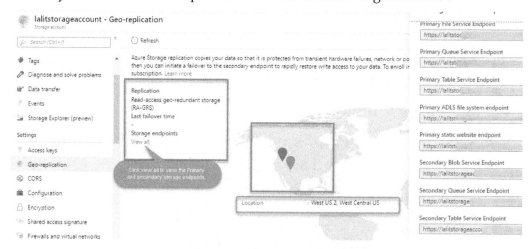

Figure 5.12: Storage account replication with a secondary endpoint

Generate and manage the shared access signature

A shared access signature will help you to provide the restricted access to the storage account if any developer or any one requests to gain access to the storage account. You can provide access with time limitation, and after the set duration, the access will get expired. You can generate the SAS access using your primary storage account key or secondary storage account key.

If you need to generate the SAS key, select the **Shared access signature** tab under **Settings**:

1. Please select the allowed services like **Blob, File, Table**, or **Queue**.

2. Select the allowed resource types like **Service, Container**, or **Object**.

3. Allow permission like **Read, Write**, and so on based on the requirements.

4. You can select the specific IP to allow your storage account.

5. Select the HTTP or HTTPS selection.

6. Click on the **Generate SAS and connection string** button.

7. After a few seconds, keys will be generated, and the user can access the key. Please take a look at the following screenshot:

Figure 5.13: Generating shared access signature

Managing the storage account access key

The Azure storage account key is used to access the storage account from the storage explorer or if you want to access it publicly. It is just like a storage account password which you can change any time while clicking on the *Refresh* button.

- You will have a primary and secondary key.

- While clicking on the Refresh button, you can generate the new key which is marked in a red circle as shown in the following screenshot:

- You can use the connection string to connect to the storage account:

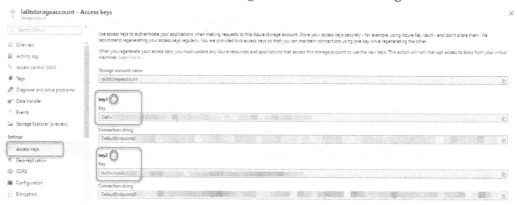

***Figure 5.14:** Managing the Azure storage account key*

Configure network access to the storage account

Enabling the VNet to the Azure storage account will provide an additional layer of security to your storage account which has your critical data. After integration, the storage account can be accessed within VNet not publicly until the public endpoint or public IP is not added:

1. Please select the storage account for which you want to enable the VNet.

2. Select **Firewalls and virtual networks** under **Settings**.

3. Select the network and click on the **Add new virtual network** option, or you can add the existing network as well as shown in the following screenshot:

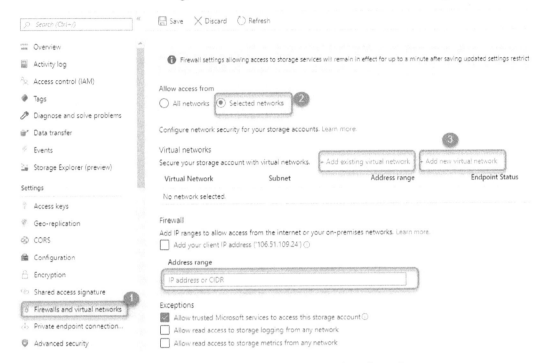

Figure 5.15: *Azure Storage account network configuration*

4. Once you select the existing VNet or create a new VNet, click on ok.

5. Please provide the VNet name and range of IP.

6. Provide the resources group and region.

7. Provide the subnet name and range of IP.

8. Provide the location and click on **Create**. Please check out the details in the following screenshot:

Figure 5.16: Azure storage account-VNet creation

Once the Vet is associated with a storage account, click on the **Save** button to save the configuration. After that, you will be able to successfully configure the network with a storage account. Please take a look at the following screenshot:

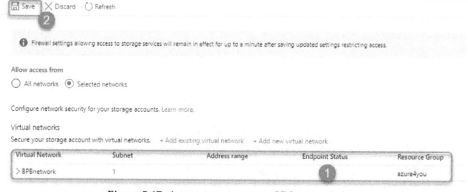

Figure 5.17: Azure storage account VNet association

Installation and configuration of the storage explorer

The Azure storage explorer is an application that will help you to connect to storage accounts and move the data from an on-premises system to the Azure blob, file, queue, and table storage account.

You can easily upload, download, and manage Azure blobs, files, queues, and tables storage account, Azure Cosmos DB, and Azure Data Lake Storage data. It is easy to manage and access from your system. You can access virtual machine disks from the ARM or classic storage accounts.

If you want to install the Azure storage explorer, then follow the given steps:
1. Please go to **https://Azure.microsoft.com/en-in/features/storage-explorer/ to download the Azure storage explorer**.
2. Please select the OS (**Windows/Linux** or **MAC**) from the drop-down menu based on the requirements. Please take a look at the following screenshot:

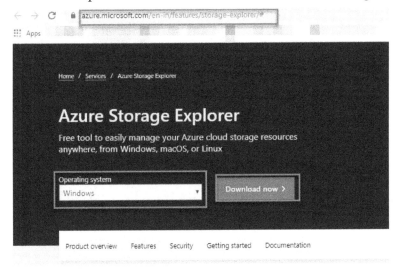

Figure 5.18: Azure storage explorer

3. Once you download the storage account file, double click on it and follow the instructions.
4. Once done, you will be able to successfully install the storage explorer.
5. Please open the Azure Storage Explorer.
6. Click on the *User* icon.
7. Click on **Add an account**… as shown in the following screenshot.
8. Log in with the Azure account, connection string or SAS URI, or any other option mentioned in the following screenshot.

9. Click on **Next**:

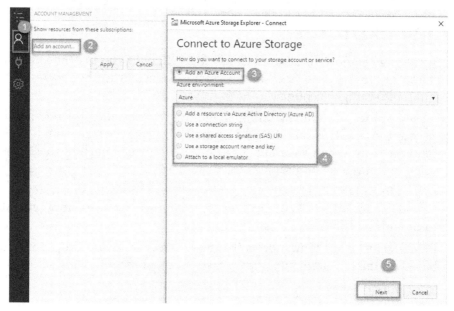

Figure 5.19: Azure storage explorer sign in

10. Now, you can copy and paste the storage account strings as shown in the following screenshot.

11. For **Connection string**, please check the topic managed access key.

12. Once done, you will be able to log in successfully to the storage account:

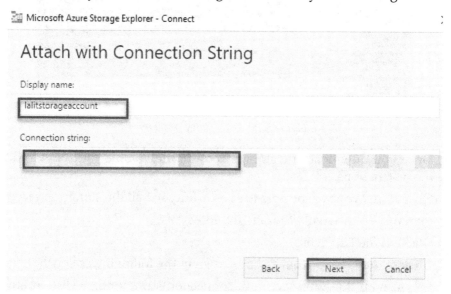

Figure 5.20: Azure storage explorer login method

Now, you will successfully be able to log in to the Azure storage explorer as shown in the following screenshot:

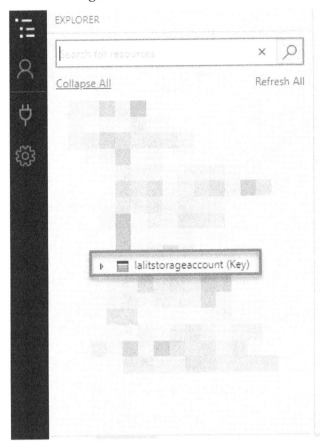

Figure 5.21: Azure storage in explorer

13. Now, you can upload the data to the Azure blob storage accounts.

14. You can create the container.

15. Now, you can upload the data using the **Upload** option.

16. You can download the data by clicking on the **Download** option.

17. Create a new folder if required.

18. You can select all the documents and update the necessary changes.

19. The same storage account can work for your file storage, and you can create the queue and table as well. For more details, refer to the following screenshot:

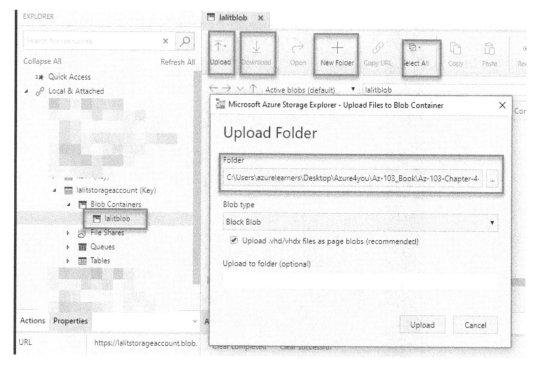

Figure 5.22: *Azure storage in explorer usage*

Conclusion

In this chapter, we covered the different types of storage accounts and how to use those storage accounts. We explained the replication policy and learned how it can help you in your compliance with the data or to replicate the data. We learned how to create the storage account and what are the GPv1 and GPv2 storage accounts. We covered the premium storage account and its usage.

In the next chapter, we will discuss how to import and export data and how to move the data using the Azure AzCopy command-line utility.

References

- Azure storage account overview: **https://docs.microsoft.com/en-us/azure/storage/common/storage-account-overview**

- Blob storage accounts: **https://docs.microsoft.com/en-us/azure/storage/blobs/storage-blobs-introduction**

- Blob file-disk: **https://docs.microsoft.com/en-us/azure/storage/common/storage-introduction**

- Storage scalability and performance: **https://docs.microsoft.com/en-us/azure/storage/common/scalability-targets-standard-account**

- For more details, visit: Azure4you blog post: **https://azure4you.com/**

CHAPTER 6

Manage Data in AZURE Storage

In this chapter, we will discuss how to migrate large data to the Azure storage account using the *Azure import and export services*. We will also discuss the Azure Data Box and configuration of Azure AD authentication for the storage account usage. We will cover how to use the `Azcopy` command which will help you to move the data from on-premises to the Azure storage account.

Structure

The following topics will be covered in this chapter:

- Import and export jobs in Azure
  - o Configuring Azure Blob storage
  - o Creating the import and export jobs in Azure storage
- Azure Data Box
  - o Configuring Azure AD authentication for a storage account
  - o Copy data using **AzCopy**

Objectives

The objectives of this chapter is to explain how to migrate the petabytes of the data using the Azure export/import utility and Azure Data Box solutions and how to transfer the data to a blob storage account using the AzCopy command-line utility.

Import and export jobs in Azure

We can create the import and export jobs using the Azure storage account which requires a blob storage account where we can keep the data. Import and export jobs can be used to send large data to Azure Blobs; for example, terabytes or petabytes of data.

If you require a data disk to copy the data and configure the services, then data will need to be shipped to Microsoft, and Microsoft will copy the data to Azure Blob as per the customer's request, and the data will be encrypted end to end using BitLocker while the configuration of import and export jobs.

Configuring Azure Blob storage

In *Chapter 5, Managing and Configuration of Storage Accounts*, I have explained about the blob and its usage. If you want to create the blob (container) under the storage account, follow the given steps:

1.   Log in to the portal.

2.   Select the storage account for which you want to create the blob storage (container).

3.   Click on **Containers**.

> **Note: The blob storage name has been changed recently to container due to new modifications made by Microsoft Azure, but the terminology and usage are the same. Take a look at the blob creation in the storage account in the following screenshot.**

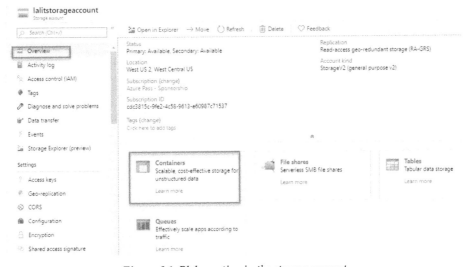

Figure 6.1: Blob creation in the storage account

4. Click on the **Container** button.

5. Provide the name of the container.

6. For **Public access level:** Select any of the following based on the requirements:

    - **Private(no anonymous access)**
    - **Blob (anonymous read access for blobs only)**
    - **Container (anonymous read access for containers and blobs)**

The following screenshot shows the container creation:

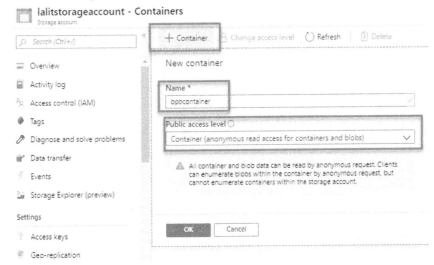

Figure 6.2: Container creation

7. Once your container is created, you will be ready to configure the import and export jobs. You can also upload the data directly. Take a look at the container configuration:

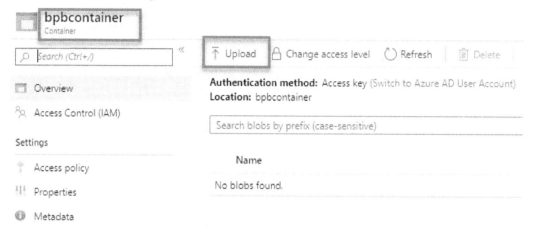

Figure 6.3: Container configuration

Creating the import and export job in Azure Storage

If you want to create an import job, follow the given steps:

1. Login to subscription.

2. Go to **All services** and search for **Import/export jobs**.

   Take a look at the following screenshot:

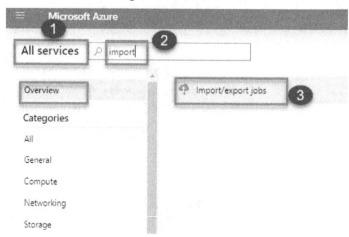

Figure 6.4: Import and export search

3. Once done, you can provide the basic configuration setting.

4. Select the **Import into Azure** option.

5. Provide the subscription and resource group name. Take a look at the following screenshot:

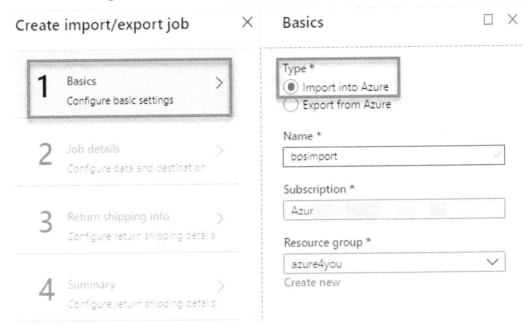

Figure 6.5: Import basic configuration

6. Click on **Job details**.

7. Download and install the WAImportExport tool to generate the .jrn file.

8. Now, you can upload the JRN or XML file.

9. Once it is uploaded, select the storage account.

10. The location will be the default.

11. Click on the **OK** button and provide the return shipping information and configure the return shipping details.

12. Click on **OK** and your import jobs will be created.

Take a look at the following screenshot:

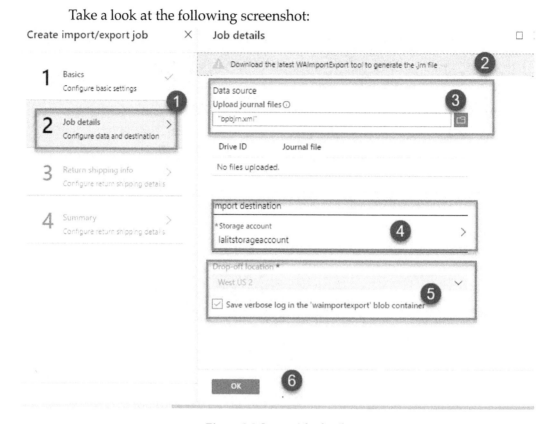

Figure 6.6: Import jobs details

After creating the import job, I will now explain how to create an export job in Azure. Now, you need to follow the same steps you followed in the import job. In the configuration, you can export the job rather than import the job:

1. After you create the job, you can provide the basic configuration setting.

2. Select the **Export tab from the Azure** option.

3. Provide the subscription and the resource group name.

Take a look at the following screenshot:

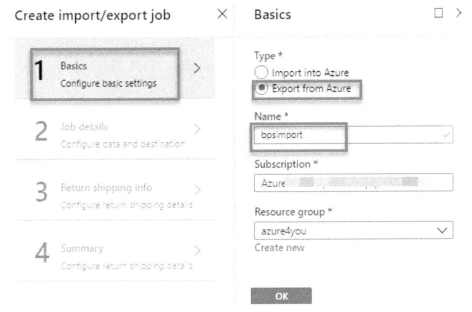

Figure 6.7: Export basic configuration

4.　Select the data source and select the storage account.

5.　Click on **Export all, Selected containers and blobs**, or **Export from the blob list file (XML format)** based on the requirements.

Take a look at the following screenshot:

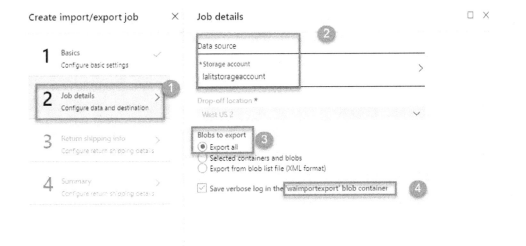

Figure 6.8: Export job details

6. Provide the courier name such as `Blue Dart, DHL, FedEx`, and so on.

7. Then, add the name, address, phone number, and other details as shown in the following screenshot:

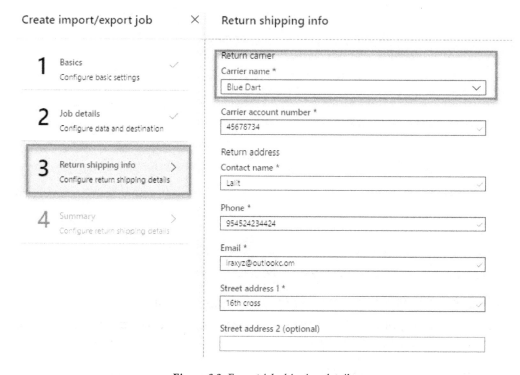

Figure 6.9: Export job shipping details

Now, you are successfully able to create the export job, and the courier guys will pick up the courier and sent it to your data center to recover the data. You can securely transfer the data using the data box. Each data box has the storage capacity of 80 TB data.

Azure data box

Azure Data Box will help you to migrate the terabytes of data to Azure quickly, and it is a less expensive and reliable solution. It is a Data Box device (hardware) that needs to be set up and configured.

It is used for different scenarios:

- **One-time migration:** If you have a large amount of on-premises data and you want to move to Azure:
  - o You can move the media library from your on-premises and backup tapes.

o   It will help if you want to migrate your VM, SQL Server, and applications to Azure.

o   If you want to move historical data from on-premises to Azure for in-depth analysis, and so on.

- **Initial bulk transfer:** Initial bulk transfer is done using Data Box (seed), and it provides incremental transfers over the network.

- **Periodic uploads:** If your organization generates a large amount of data periodically and if it needs to be moved to Azure, then the Data Box will help you do this.

The Data Box supports a large amount of data to migrate to Azure. It is a Microsoft device that can be configured in your on-premises data center and connected to the Azure Data Box solution.

Configuring Azure AD authentication for a storage account

In this section, we will discuss how to configure the authentication of Azure AD users for a storage account. Follow the given steps to configure it.

It helps to manage a single identity to access the blob storage account and provide access to it, so you do not have to depend on the storage account key and provide the granular access using Azure AD authentication.

1.   Go to the storage account and then click on **Containers**.

2.   Select the container and click on the container as shown in the following screenshot:

Figure 6.10: Azure AD authentication to the storage account

3.   One you get an insight into the Azure storage container, click on the Access control (IAM) in *figure 6.11* and select the appropriate role as follows. It can also be done from the storage account IAM as well.

- **Storage Blob Data Owner:** It is used to set ownership and manage access control for **Azure Data Lake Storage Gen2** and the storage account.

- **Storage Blob Data Contributor:** It is used to grant read/write/delete permissions to blob storage resources.

- **Storage Blob Data Reader:** It is used to grant read-only permissions to blob storage resources.

- **Storage Queue Data Contributor:** It is used to provide the read/write/delete permissions to Azure queues.

- **Storage Queue Data Reader:** It is used to provide read-only permissions to Azure queues.

- **Storage Queue Data Message Processor:** It is used to grant peek, retrieve, and delete permissions to messages in Azure storage queues.

- **Storage Queue Data Message Sender:** It is used to provide the permissions to messages in Azure storage queues.

4. Once you select the roles to assign, click on **OK** to provide the access as shown in the following screenshot:

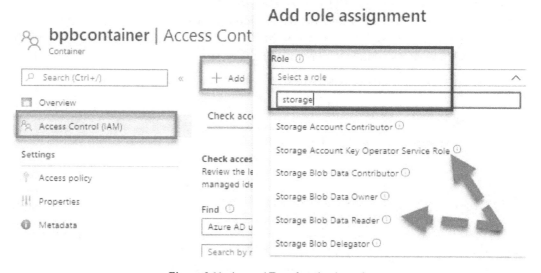

Figure 6.11: Azure AD authentication role

Once you provide the permission, the user will have a specific role and will be able to access the data or storage account as per the associate role.

Now let us learn how to enable the **Active Directory Domain Services (ADDS)** in the Azure storage account to access an Azure file share.

1. Click on **Storage account**.

2. In the storage account, click on **Configuration**.

3. Select **Identity-based access for file shares**.

4. Click on **Enabled** and save the settings as shown in the following screenshot:

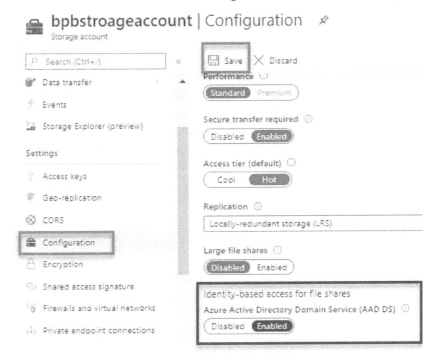

***Figure 6.12:** Identity-based access for a file share*

Copying data using AzCopy

AzCopy is a command-line utility that is designed to copy the data from the Azure Blob, file, and table storage account. It uses the Azure AD or SAS-based authentication to connect to the Azure storage account.

We can use the utility in Windows, Mac, or Linux OS. It can also be used if you want to move or copy your blob storage account from one storage account to another.

Let us see how we can run these command-line utilities to make sure we copy the data from the blob storage or upload the data in the blob storage. You can download the utility from **https://docs.microsoft.com/en-us/azure/storage/common/storage-use-azcopy-v10**.

1. Use the following command to log in to your Azure AD tenant:

   "azCopy login --tenant-id=aeXXXX-XXXX-XXX"

2. Then, click on **Enter**.

3. Once the URL comes up in the command line, select and press *Enter* to copy the URL (**https://microsoft.com/devicelogin**). Go to the URL and browse it and provide the code which comes with the URL as shown in the following screenshot:

Figure 6.13: AzCopy login

4. Provide the authentication code as shown in the following screenshot:

Figure 6.14: AzCopy login auth-code

5. Once you enter the auth-code, you will be able to log in to the Azcopy console as shown in the following screenshot:

Figure 6.15: AzCopy login successful

6. Use the following command to copy the data to the blob storage account:

```
azCopy copy 'C:\bpbfolder\bpbTextFile.txt' 'https://bobstorage.
blob.core.windows.net/bpb/bpbTextFile.txt'
```

7. Once you click on Enter, you will be able to copy the data and make sure you use the correct blob storage account and destination to copy the data.

Conclusion

In this chapter, we discussed the use of the import and export services and how to migrate the petabytes of data to Azure. We also discussed the Azure AD authentication which will help you to define the fine-grained access to the Azure storage account. Using the Azure AzCopy command utility, you can transfer the data from one blob storage account to another and you can transfer from on-premises systems as well.

In the next chapter, we will discuss Azure file configuration and see how to access the Azure file share. We will learn about the Azure file sync as well and the details of usage and configuration in the next chapter.

References

- Azure storage account overview: **https://docs.microsoft.com/en-us/azure/ storage/common/storage-account-overview**

- Azure storage introduction: **https://docs.microsoft.com/en-us/azure/ storage/common/storage-introduction**

- Azure Blob storage: **https://docs.microsoft.com/en-us/azure/storage/blobs/ storage-blobs-overview**

- Azure Data Lake Storage: **https://docs.microsoft.com/en-us/azure/data- lake-store/data-lake-store-overview**

- For more details, visit: **beginning-modern-c-and-net-development- scorm2004_4-7OiO-Aea.zip**

Chapter 7

The Azure File Share

In this chapter, we will discuss Azure file share and how to create the Azure File share and map a network drive. We will use the Azure File sync services and see how to troubleshoot them. We will also discuss the different types of Azure File sync groups.

Structure

The following topics will be covered in this chapter:

- Azure File share
    - o Creating and configuring the Azure File share
    - o Configuring the Azure File sync
    - o Azure File sync group
- Azure File sync troubleshooting

Objectives

In this chapter, we will explain the Azure File share and how to create the Azure File share. The Azure File share can be used as a network drive, and you can map it to your servers and sync the on-premises files to Azure. We will explain the Azure File sync and Azure File sync will help customers transfer the on-premises files to Azure. It provides flexibility, performance, and compatibility.

Azure File share

The Azure File share can be used for network sharing just like your map network drives. It works on SMB port 445 port, and it can be used to keep the data with regards to Virtual Hard Disk (VHD), backup, and sharing the data. You can keep a maximum of 5 TB data per file share. If you want to keep more data in it, then you must create more file share storage account to keep the data.

There is a limitation in the Azure File share, not Azure storage account. In one storage account, you can create multiple file shares and keep the data and apply different kinds of security policies.

The Azure File share helps us to provide the storage space without adding any additional storage on-premises.

Creating and configuring the Azure File share

In *Chapter 5, Managing and Configuration of Storage Accounts,* I have explained how to create a storage account, its type, and its usage. If you want to create the file share in the storage account, follow the given steps:

1. Log in to the portal.

2. Select the storage account for which you want to create the Azure File share.

3. Click on the **File shares** option.

   Take a look at the Azure File share created in the storage account as shown in the following screenshot:

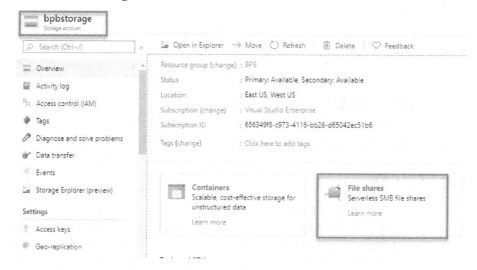

Figure 7.1: Azure File share creation in a storage account

4. Click on the **File share** button.

5. Provide the name as shown in the following screenshot.

6. Set the quota limit as per the customer's requirements.

7. Click on the **Create** button.

   Let's take a look at the following screenshot:

Figure 7.2: File share creation

8. You can create the file share up **5** TB each and this is a limitation from MS Azure end. Let's take a look at the following screenshot:

Figure 7.3: Azure File share limitation

9. Once the file share is created, it will look like the following screenshot:

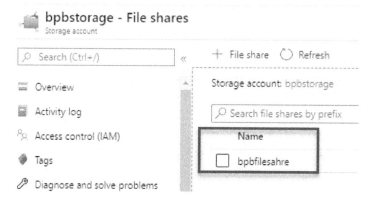

Figure 7.4: Azure File share

10. Once you click on the folder, you will get the option to upload the data.

11. Click on the **Upload** tab.

12. Select the file and browse the folder to upload the documents.

13. Once done, click on the **Upload** button to upload the documents:

- **Add directory:** User for folder creation or use to add folder in the file share.

- **Refresh:** If the data is not reflecting, you can refresh the button.

- **Delete share:** This can be used to delete the complete share folder.

- **Quota:** This will help increase or decrease the quota limit.

- **View snapshots:** This can be used to see a snapshot of your file share.

- **Create Snapshot:** This can be used to create the backup of your file share or create the snapshot within a storage account.

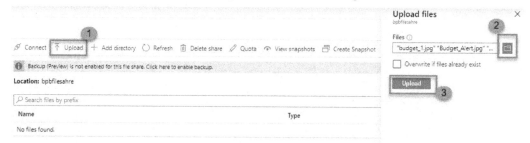

Figure 7.5: Azure File share file upload

Now, I will show you how to connect the file share with your on-premise machine or local desktop PC:

1. Click on the **Connect** option.

2. Once done, it will ask you to copy the path and run it in PowerShell.

3. The Azure File share supports Windows, Linux, and Mac OSes to connect to the file share.

4. Based on the OS, you can copy the command line and follow the instructions to connect.

5. Make sure you allow **445** port from your Firewall and NSG to connect to the file share.

Let's take a look at the following screenshot:

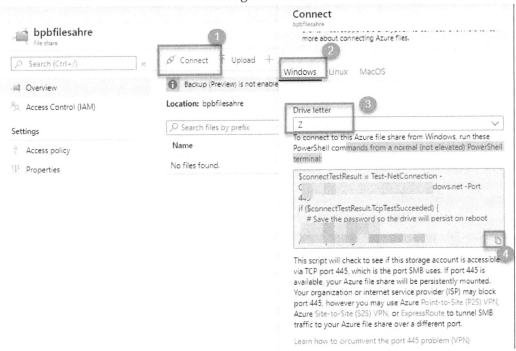

Figure 7.6: Azure File share connect

Now, you can connect the Azure File share and upload the data which will automatically sync to an Azure File share.

Configuration of Azure File sync

Azure File sync will help you manage the documents centralized just like your network share. It provides flexibility and high performance with your on-premises file server. It supports protocols like SMB, NFS, and FTPS to access your data locally and provides the cache to the Azure File share.

Note: For now, it supports only Windows Server and no other platform as per the MS documentation. Please take a look at the documentation for more clarification on Azure File sync support and features.

If you want to create the Azure File share, follow the given steps to create the Azure File sync:

1. Go to **Marketplace** and search for **Azure File Sync**.
2. Select the services.
3. Provide the name of the file sync services.
4. Click on create Azure File sync.
5. Select the resources group.
6. Click on **Review + Create**.
7. Once done, you will be able to create file sync services.

    Let's take a look at the following screenshot:

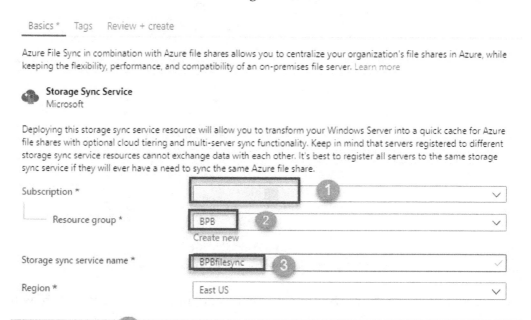

Figure 7.7: Azure File sync creation

8. Now, you can create the Azure File sync.

Next, we will create the Azure File sync group.

Azure File Sync group

Azure File sync provides a set of sync topology to a set of files to keep the data syncing through the endpoint which has been created during the Azure File sync group creation. The sync group helps to sync files from multiple endpoints to keep syncing.

To create the sync group, let's follow the given steps:

1. Select the Azure File sync.

2. Go to the **Sync** tab and click on the **Sync group** option.

Let's take a look at the following screenshot:

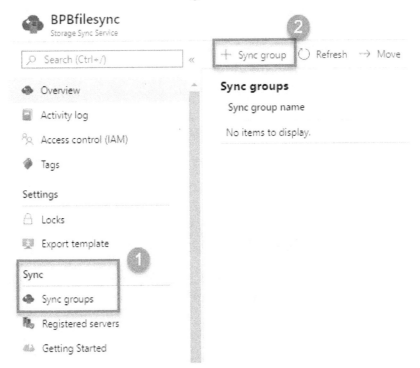

Figure 7.8: Sync group creation

3. Provide the sync group name.

4. Select the subscription.

5. Click on the storage account and select the Azure storage account, and then you can select the Data Box as well for the same solution.

6. Select the Azure File share from the drop-down menu.

7. Click on **Create**. Once done, your sync group will be created. Let's take a look at the following screenshot:

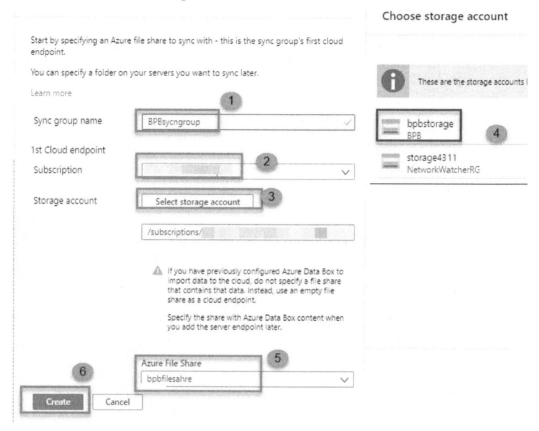

Figure 7.9: Sync group creation steps

Now, you can create the Azure sync group. Once the sync group is created, please register the servers you want to transfer the data to:

1. Click on the **Sync** tab.

2. Click on **Registered servers**.

3. Click on the **Download Azure File Sync agent and install it on all servers you want to sync** option.

4. Once the agent is installed, your servers will be shown to register servers.

5. You will be able to transfer the files and folders automatically. Let's take a look at the following screenshot:

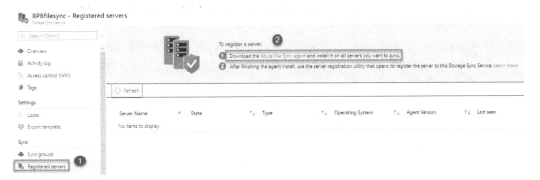

Figure 7.10: Registered servers

Azure File sync troubleshooting

Azure File sync troubleshooting will help you to figure out the common issues you face to connect to the Azure File share. You might have a problem deleting the files from the Azure File share or agent installation. You might have an issue with registered servers' addition or removal process.

I sometimes face an issue of the server been already added and had to troubleshoot and fix the issue. Sometimes, you might face the issue of the sync group not working or MgmtServerJobFailed.

For all these issues, Microsoft Azure has written a wonderful documentation (**https:// docs.microsoft.com/en-us/azure/storage/files/storage-sync-files-troubleshoot?tabs =portal1%2Cazure-portal**), so follow this documentation to fix the issue.

Conclusion

In this chapter, we explained the usage of the Azure File share and how to connect and transfer the files in the Azure File share. We also explained the limitation of the Azure File share. We discussed the Azure File sync configuration and explained the components as well. In Azure File sync, we discussed about the sync group and how to register the servers. If you get stuck on some issues, then you can use the Azure File sync troubleshooting steps to fix the issue.

In the next chapter, we will discuss the implementation of the Azure virtual machine and how to create and configure the Azure virtual machine.

We will discuss the high Azure availability and disk encryption and how to redeploy the Azure VM and its usage.

References

- Azure File share: **https://docs.microsoft.com/en-us/azure/storage/files/storage-files-introduction**

- Create and manage Azure Files share with Windows virtual machines: **https://docs.microsoft.com/en-us/azure/storage/files/storage-files-quick-create-use-windows**

- Enable and create large file shares: **https://docs.microsoft.com/en-us/azure/storage/files/storage-files-how-to-create-large-file-share**

- Deploy Azure File sync: **https://docs.microsoft.com/en-us/azure/storage/files/storage-sync-files-deployment-guide?tabs=azure-portal**

- Azure File sync proxy and firewall settings: **https://docs.microsoft.com/en-us/azure/storage/files/storage-sync-files-firewall-and-proxy**

- Troubleshoot Azure File Sync: **https://docs.microsoft.com/en-us/azure/storage/files/storage-sync-files-troubleshoot?tabs=portal1%2Cazure-portal)**

- For more details, visit: **https://azure4you.com/**

CHAPTER 8

Creating and Configuring of Azure VMs

In this chapter, we will be discussing the use of Azure VMs, how to configure the high availability, and how to monitor the Azure VMs usage of the Azure storage and what kind of disk required while creating the VMs. I will be explaining about the Azure scale set as well. How to scale-in the Azure environments using Azure scale set. We will be discussing how to choose the Azure VM size and much more stuff.

Structure

The following topics will be covered in this chapter:

- Azure **Virtual Machine (VM)**
- Azure VM scale sets
- Configure Azure disk encryption
- Redeploy VM

Objectives

We will be explaining in this chapter, creating the Azure Windows and Linux VM in Azure subscription which can be used for your test, development, and production environments. Configuring the high availability will help you to reduce the downtime of the Azure VMs. We have also explained how to set up the monitoring, storage, VM size, and configure the disk encryption in Azure VM, which will help to encrypt the disk and secure the disk data.

Azure virtual machine

The Azure VM provides flexibility in virtual environments without buying on-premise hardware or software licenses. It provides high availability, and we can use it as on-premise servers. You can even perform tasks like software installation patching and other tasks as per the customer's requirements.

Azure VMs are mainly used for application testing, development work, or hybrid cloud scenarios. If you need to extend your on-premises environments to Azure, you can do that as well. Microsoft Azure supports Windows, Linux, and another custom OS version as per marketplace standards. Microsoft Azure supports the various types of VM sizes so that customers can deploy the VMs based on their required configuration. It also supports high level of VM sizes for SAP and SAP HANA as well.

Virtual machine components

If you are planning to create a VM, then you need to follow the given steps and complete a few pre-requisites. Please follow the given steps to create VMs.

Pre-requisites

First, I will explain a few of the components under the pre-requisite section. Once you understand the components, it will be easy for you to create the VMs:

- **Subscription:** You need to select the correct subscription where you want to deploy the VMs.

- **Resource group:** Please select the correct resources group for which you want to deploy the VMs. For more details, refer to *Chapter 4, Resource Group Management.*

- **Virtual machine name:** Follow your organization naming convention or get the details from your customer/project. Provide the machine name.

- **Region:** The region is equal to your Azure data center location. If your customer is from the US, you can choose a location like **East US, East US2, West US**, or **Central US**. Based on the customer location, you can choose the region which will help to reduce the latency.

- **Availability set:** The availability set is a logical grouping of your Azure VMs which provides high availability of your VMs in case of unexpected hardware failure, unplanned hardware or software maintenance, and if there is any planned maintenance from Microsoft Azure.

o **Fault Domain:** Fault domain shares the common power sources and physical network switch. This means that if anything happens in the hardware or network layer, then it will help your VMs to keep alive.

o **Update Domain:** Update domain will help you in case of any planned or unplanned software maintenance from Microsoft Azure. It ensures your application VMs reboot at the time within the availability set. Take a look at the following diagram:

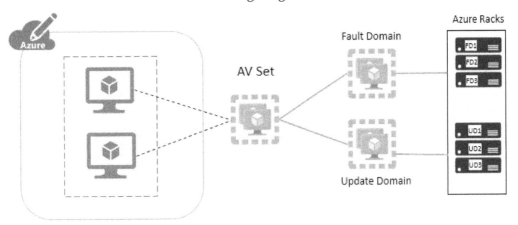

Figure 8.1: Azure availability set

• **Availability zone:** The availability zone is another option that provides high availability in case of data center failure within the zone. The zone has been designed with one more data center; which provides the resiliency and availability of your data and application services. Please take a look at the following diagram:

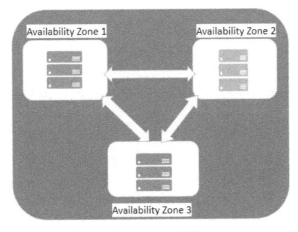

Figure 8.2: Azure availability zone

- **Image:** Images are nothing, but your operating system that you can choose while creating the VMs. Images can have Windows, Linux, Ubuntu, and customized images that are available in the Azure marketplace. Please take a look at the following screenshot:

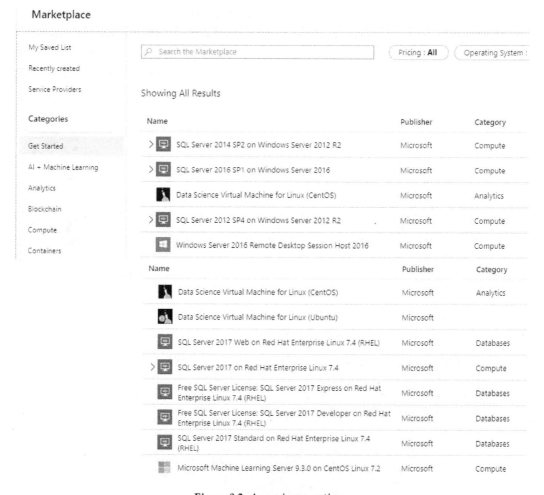

Figure 8.3: Azure image options

- **Administrator accounts:** The administrator account is used to log in locally in the VMs. You can use the VM credentials that will help you to connect the VMs to the **Remote Desktop Protocol (RDP)** or **Secure Shell (SSH).**

- **Disk type:** The disk type is where your data and OS are stored. It consists of the following types:

  o **HDD:** Hard disk drive is backed by a magnetic disk and it provides *500 IOPS/1TB.* It is used for any workload based on the customer's requirements.

- o **SSD:** It is also called a premium disk which is backed by the solid-state drive and provides *7500 IOPS/1TB*. It is mainly used for production workload.

- o **Standard SSD:** It is a combination of SSD and HDD disk, which provides faster performance and provides *500 IOPS/1TB*. It can be used for development and UAT environments.

- **Azure VMs size:** Azure VMs size is a collection of the capacity (memory, disk, IOPS, and so on) and features supported by your Azure VMs instance like 2 GB RAM with 120 GB disk space as your on-premises hardware. You can choose based on the requirements. It supports large instance sizes which can be used for GPU-based systems or SAP VMs. Please take a look at the following screenshot:

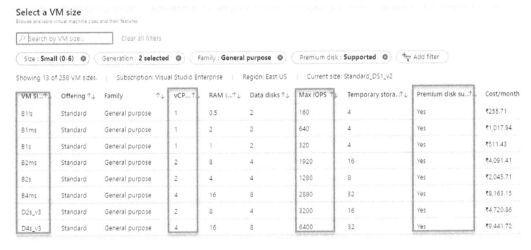

Select a VM size
Browse available virtual machine sizes and their features

Search by VM size...   Clear all filters

(Size : **Small (0-6)** ⊗) (Generation : **2 selected** ⊗) (Family : **General purpose** ⊗) (Premium disk : **Supported** ⊗) (⊹ Add filter)

Showing 13 of 258 VM sizes. | Subscription: Visual Studio Enterprise | Region: East US | Current size: Standard_DS1_v2

VM Si...↑↓	Offering ↑↓	Family ↑↓	vCP...↑↓	RAM (...↑↓	Data disks ↑↓	Max IOPS ↑↓	Temporary stora...↑↓	Premium disk su...↑↓	Cost/month
B1ls	Standard	General purpose	1	0.5	2	160	4	Yes	₹255.71
B1ms	Standard	General purpose	1	2	2	640	4	Yes	₹1,017.94
B1s	Standard	General purpose	1	1	2	320	4	Yes	₹511.43
B2ms	Standard	General purpose	2	8	4	1920	16	Yes	₹4,091.41
B2s	Standard	General purpose	2	4	4	1280	8	Yes	₹2,045.71
B4ms	Standard	General purpose	4	16	8	2880	32	Yes	₹8,163.15
D2s_v3	Standard	General purpose	2	8	4	3200	16	Yes	₹4,720.86
D4s_v3	Standard	General purpose	4	16	8	6400	32	Yes	₹9,441.72

Figure 8.4: Azure instance size

- **Network component:** Azure network components are mainly used to connect your VMs/services to your network. For example, while creating VMs, you need to select the virtual network and subnet which define the network boundary of your VMs.

- **Public IP:** A public IP address is used if you want to connect your VMs to the internet or access and connect applications publicly.

- **NSG (inbound and outbound port):** The network security group defines the rules for ports that need to be allowed or denied and based on the requirements, you can allow the ports.

- o **Inbound port:** The traffic which you want to allow from the internet to your VMs.

- o **Outbound port:** The traffic which you want to allow from your VMs to the internet.

- **Boot diagnostics:** It is used to capture the console output and help you to provide the screenshots of the VM running on a host in case of an occurrence of an issue.

- **OS guest diagnostics:** It helps to collect the metrics of your virtual machine. So, you can use and create alerts to update your teams.

- **Diagnostic accounts:** The diagnostics account is nothing but your storage account where you want to store the diagnostics logs for further troubleshooting.

- **Auto shutdown configuration:** It helps to shut down the VMs after your business hours automatically. It is recommended that you do not use this option for your production environments.

- **Dedicated host:** It is a new feature that is launched by Microsoft Azure and allows a dedicated host in the Azure data center to provision the VMs within a dedicated host. It provides isolated environments and helps in any maintenance initiated by Microsoft Azure. However, it is not necessary to choose the same.

- **Proximity placement group:** It allows users to group Azure resources physically closer together within the same region.

- **Resource group tag**: It is used for billing purposes and you can tag your resources based on your requirements like a cost center, application name, product team, and so on.

- **Review and create:** Finally, you will see all the required details in this tab, and you can review and create the VMs.

As I have explained all the components, let us understand and create the Azure VMs.

Creating a Windows virtual machine

To create the Windows VM, perform the following steps:

1. Provide the following-required details:

   - **Subscription:** Provide the subscription name.

   - **Resource group:** Provide the resources group name based on the organization standards.

   - **Virtual machine name:** Provide the VM name.

   - **Region:** Provide the location you want to deploy the VM to.

   - **Availability set:** Provide the availability set based on the requirements.

- **Availability zone:** Provide the availability zones based on the requirements.
- **Image:** Select the image Windows, Linux, or custom image.

Look at the following screenshot:

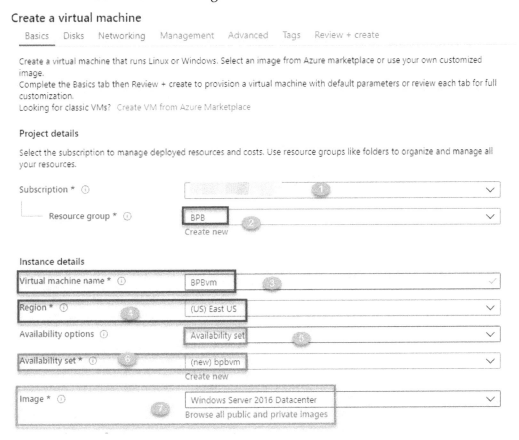

Figure 8.5: Azure VM details

2. Then, add the following details:
    - **Administrator account:** Provide the admin account username and password.

- **Size:** Provide the size of the VMs based on the requirements. Please take a look at the following screenshot:

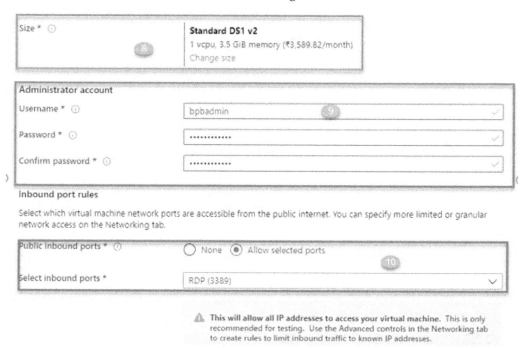

Figure 8.6: Azure VMs credentials

3. Specify the disk based on the requirements like **Premium SSD, Standard HDD,** or **Standard SSD**.

4. You can add an additional disk using advance options. Take a look at the following screenshot:

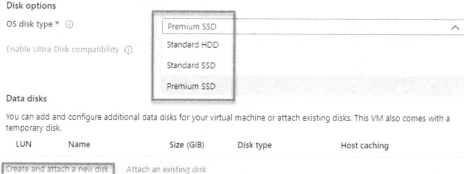

Figure 8.7: Azure VMs disk specification

5. Select the virtual network name and subnet.

6. If you need **Public IP**, then click on **Create new** and provide the name.

7. Select the ports you want to allow to connect to VMs like **3389** or **22**, and so on.

Take a look at the following screenshot:

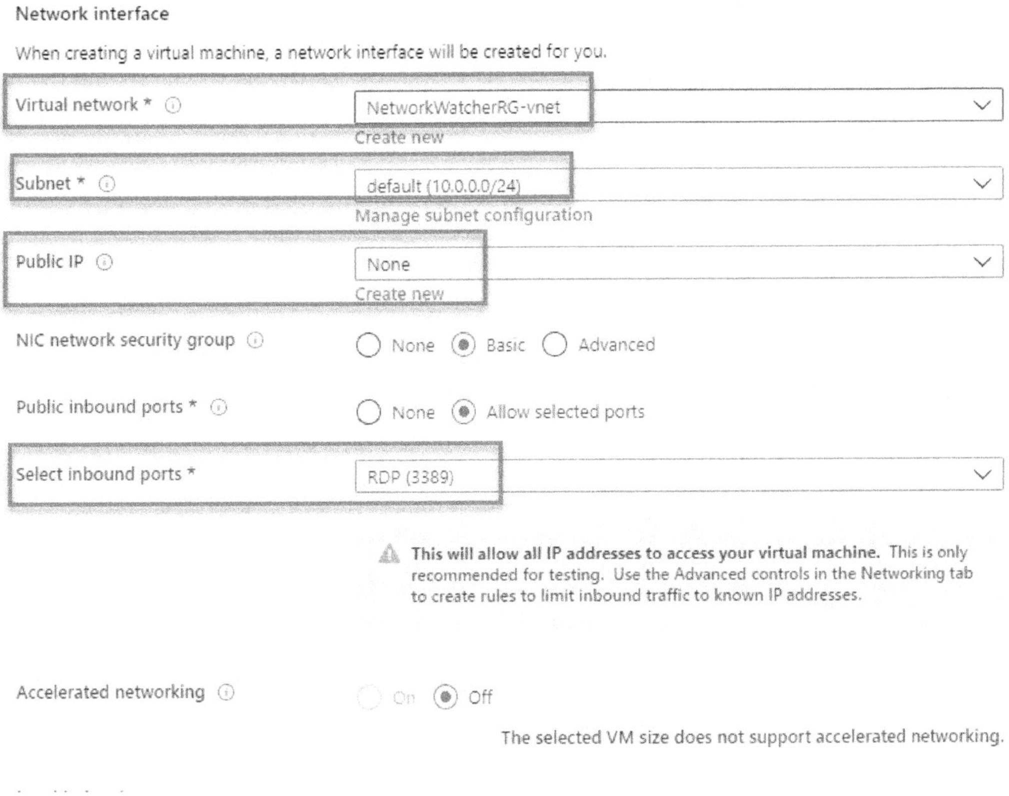

Network interface

When creating a virtual machine, a network interface will be created for you.

Virtual network * ⓘ	NetworkWatcherRG-vnet	⌄
	Create new	
Subnet * ⓘ	default (10.0.0.0/24)	⌄
	Manage subnet configuration	
Public IP ⓘ	None	⌄
	Create new	
NIC network security group ⓘ	○ None ⦿ Basic ○ Advanced	
Public inbound ports * ⓘ	○ None ⦿ Allow selected ports	
Select inbound ports *	RDP (3389)	⌄

⚠ **This will allow all IP addresses to access your virtual machine.** This is only recommended for testing. Use the Advanced controls in the Networking tab to create rules to limit inbound traffic to known IP addresses.

Accelerated networking ⓘ	○ On ⦿ Off	

The selected VM size does not support accelerated networking.

Figure 8.8: Azure VMs network configuration

8. Provide the boot and OS diagnostics accounts.

9. Select the **Diagnostic storage account** from the drop-down menu.

10. Enable the auto-shutdown option for VMs that are not production VMs.

11. Provide the email ID and time zone and so on. Take a look at the following screenshot:

Configure monitoring and management options for your VM.

Azure Security Center

Azure Security Center provides unified security management and advanced threat protection across hybrid cloud workloads.
Learn more

✅ Your subscription is protected by Azure Security Center standard plan.

Monitoring

Boot diagnostics ⓘ	◉ On ○ Off

OS guest diagnostics ⓘ	○ On ◉ Off

Diagnostics storage account * ⓘ	bpbstorage ⌄
	Create new

Identity

System assigned managed identity ⓘ   ○ On ◉ Off

Auto-shutdown

Enable auto-shutdown ⓘ	◉ On ○ Off
Shutdown time ⓘ	7:00:00 PM
Time zone ⓘ	(UTC) Coordinated Universal Time ⌄
Notification before shutdown ⓘ	◉ On ○ Off
Email * ⓘ	lalit

Backup

Enable backup ⓘ   ○ On ◉ Off

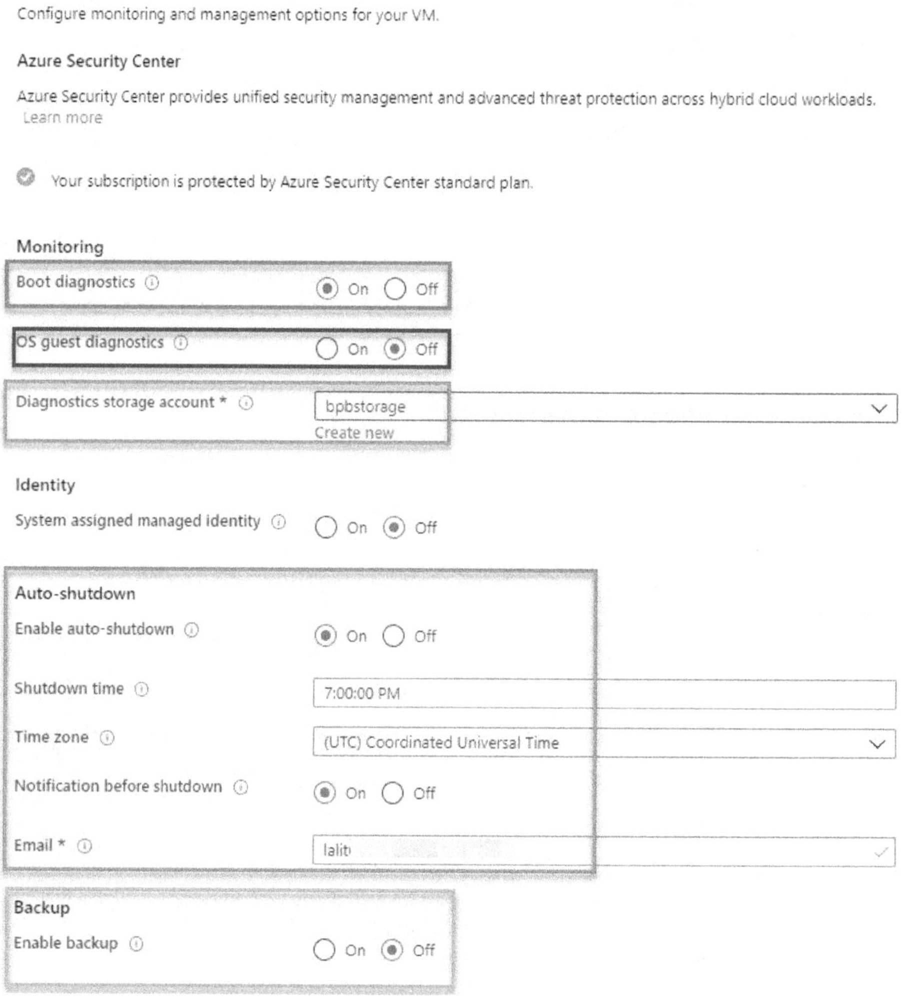

Figure 8.9: Azure VMs diagnostics configuration

12. Select the **Advanced** tab and click on **Next** to select the **Tags** option. Take a look at the following screenshot:

Tags are name/value pairs that enable you to categorize resources and view consolidated billing by applying the same tag to multiple resources and resource groups. Learn more about tags ⌐

Note that if you create tags and then change resource settings on other tabs, your tags will be automatically updated.

Name ⓘ	Value ⓘ	Resource
Project	: ITS	All resources

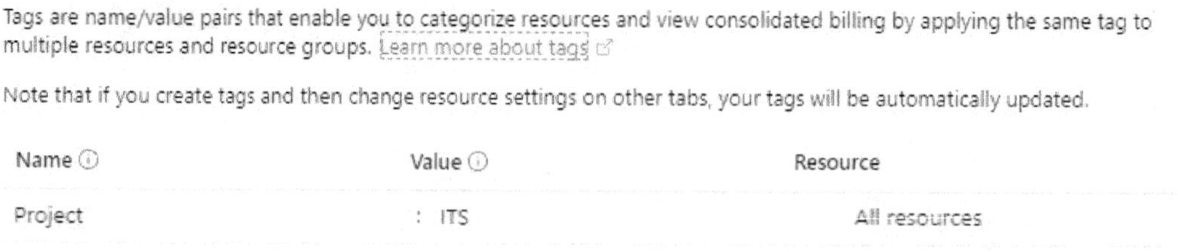

Figure 8.10: Azure VMs resources tag

13. Verify **Review + create** the VMs. It will take 8 to 10 minutes to create the VMs. Now, the VM creation process is complete. Take a look at the following screenshot:

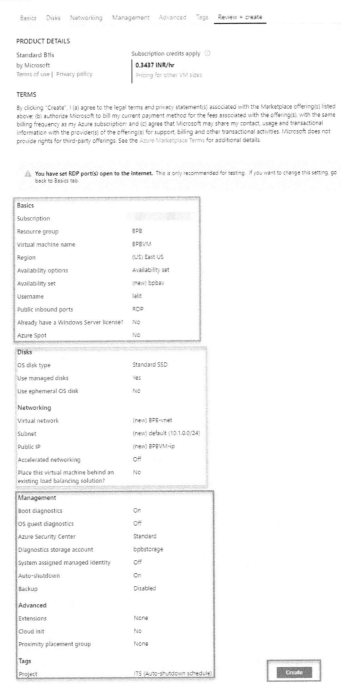

Figure 8.11: Azure VMs creation review

Now, you will be able to create the Windows VM, and I will show you how to take care of the Linux VMs.

Creating Linux VMs

If you need to create the Linux VMs, please change the image name to Linux, Red Hat Enterprise, and so on, followed by the preceding steps as provided for the Windows virtual VM creation:

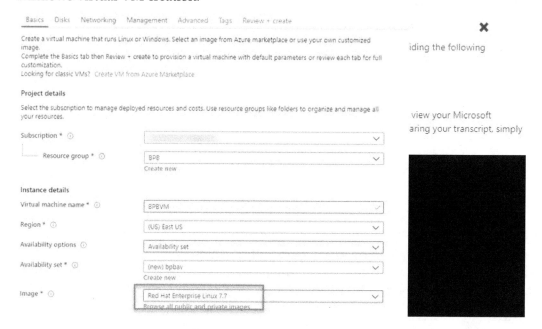

Figure 8.12: Azure Linux VMs

Once you complete all the steps, click on Create and your Linux VM will be created. You can refer to the VM creation section to get more details.

Azure virtual machine scale set creation

The Azure scale set helps you to create a group of VMs and manage them. It is automatically managed to increase or decrease the VMs based on the CPU usage or other rules which you have to define in a scale set. It provides high availability of your application while auto-scaling the VM based on the required configuration. It provides redundancy and improves the performance of your applications which is distributed across multiple instances.

It is easy to create a scale set and high availability and application resiliency. You can scale the instance based on application demands.

1. Let us configure and deploy the scale set and follow the given steps:
   - **Virtual machine scale set name:** BPBScaleset
   - **Operating system disk image: Windows Server 2016 Datacenter**
   - **Subscription:** Select a subscription.
   - **Resource group: BPB**
   - **Location: (US) East US**
   - **Availability zone:** Select if required or leave it to default.
   - **Username:** BPBuser
   - **Password:** Provide the password.

     Please take a look at the following screenshot:

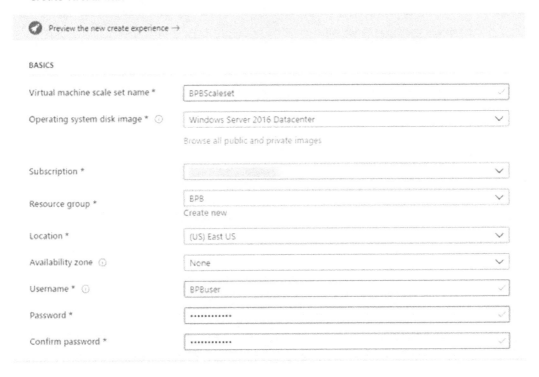

Figure 8.13: Azure scale set configuration

- **Instance count:** The default value is 2 and based on the requirement, you can increase the count.
- **Instance size:** Standard B1S
- **Use managed disks:** Select Yes, if it is required.

- Enable the scale set while creating or you can select after creating it as well.

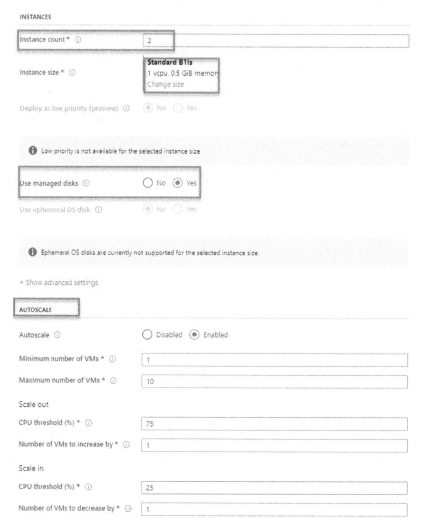

Figure 8.14: *Azure scale set auto-scale configuration*

2. If you want to select the application gateway, please select the same.
3. Select the virtual network.
4. Select Public IP if required.
5. Public inbound ports are required.
6. Enable the boot diagnostics.
7. Click on the **Create** button.

Take a look at the following screenshot:

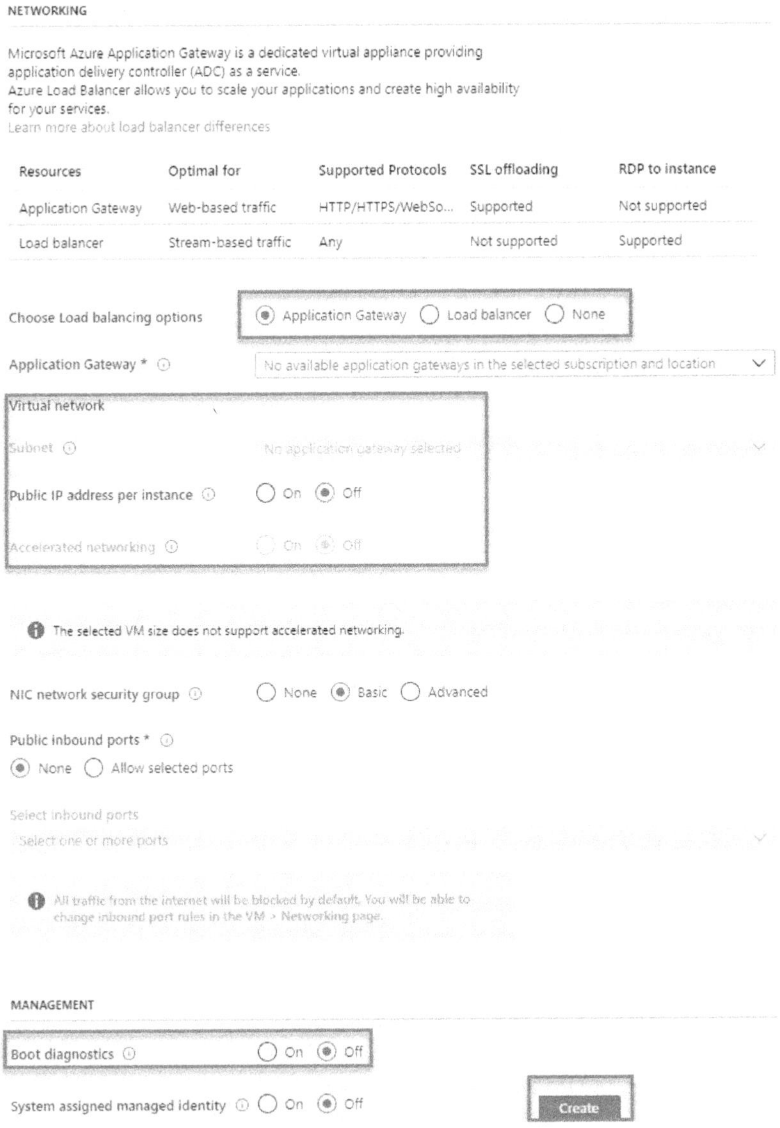

NETWORKING

Microsoft Azure Application Gateway is a dedicated virtual appliance providing
application delivery controller (ADC) as a service.
Azure Load Balancer allows you to scale your applications and create high availability
for your services.
Learn more about load balancer differences

Resources	Optimal for	Supported Protocols	SSL offloading	RDP to instance
Application Gateway	Web-based traffic	HTTP/HTTPS/WebSo...	Supported	Not supported
Load balancer	Stream-based traffic	Any	Not supported	Supported

Choose Load balancing options   ⦿ Application Gateway   ◯ Load balancer   ◯ None

Application Gateway * ⓘ   No available application gateways in the selected subscription and location   ⌄

Virtual network

Subnet ⓘ   No application gateway selected   ⌄

Public IP address per instance ⓘ   ◯ On   ⦿ Off

Accelerated networking ⓘ   ◯ On   ⦿ Off

ⓘ The selected VM size does not support accelerated networking.

NIC network security group ⓘ   ◯ None   ⦿ Basic   ◯ Advanced

Public inbound ports * ⓘ
⦿ None   ◯ Allow selected ports

Select inbound ports
  Select one or more ports   ⌄

ⓘ All traffic from the internet will be blocked by default. You will be able to
change inbound port rules in the VM > Networking page.

MANAGEMENT

Boot diagnostics ⓘ   ◯ On   ⦿ Off

System assigned managed identity ⓘ ◯ On ⦿ Off   **Create**

Figure 8.15: Azure scale set network configuration

Configure Azure disk encryption

The Azure disk encryption will use a BitLocker feature to enable the full disk
encryption of the Windows OS and data disk. We can configure the Azure disk
encryption using the Azure portal, PowerShell, and Azure CLI. The Azure key vault
is integrated with Azure encryption to help you to manage the access and control
the encrypted disk.

For Linux, the Azure VM uses a DM encrypt feature to provide the volume encryption to the OS and data disk of the Linux VM. The Azure key vault is integrated with the Azure encryption to help you to manage the access and control the keys and secrets.

It supports the follows OSes:

- Windows 8 and later OS version
- Servers 2008 R2 and later OS version
- Red Hat, Ubuntu, and so on as per Linux OS disk encryption supported

Let us just see how to configure the disk encryption:

1. Go to the VM to which you want to enable the disk encryption.
2. Under **Settings**, click on the **Disks** option.
3. On the right-hand side of the tab, click on **Encryption** as shown in the following screenshot:

Figure 8.16: Azure disk encryption

4. Once you click on **Encryption**, it will open another tab to provide the details to encrypt the disk. Follow the given details:

- Select the following disk option from the drop-down menu:
  - **None**
  - **OS disk**
  - **OS and data disks**

- Once you select this option, you need to select the key vault, key, and key version as shown in the following screenshot:

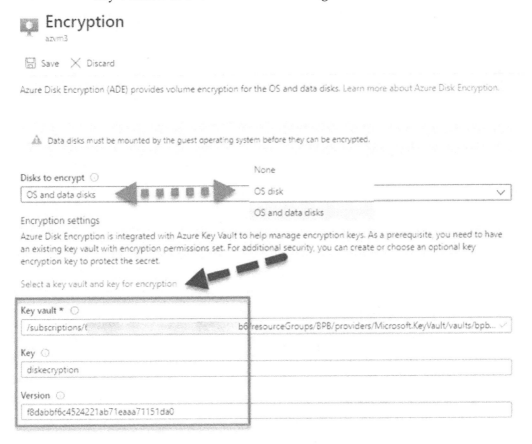

Figure 8.17: Azure disk encryption settings

5. Once you fill all the parameters, click on **Save** at the top to encrypt the disk. It will pop up the message the VM might reboot, and you need to reboot the VM.

6. Click on **Yes** and your disk will start encrypting as shown in the following screenshot:

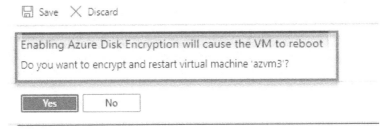

Figure 8.18: Azure disk encryption save

7. Once you log in to your system, you will observe that you have enabled the disk encryption. Then, you will see that the disk has a lock sign which is a BitLocker encryption symbol. Hence, your disk has been encrypted as shown in the following screenshot:

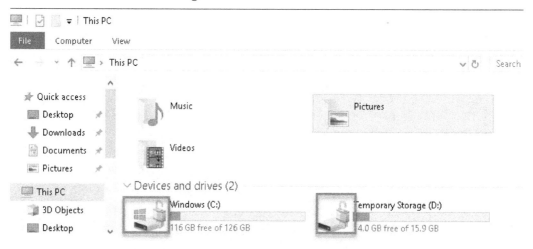

Figure 8.19: Azure disk encryption verification

Now, we have successfully verified that the Azure disk encryption is done and understands the whole process.

Redeploy a VM

Azure VM redeploy can be used if you are facing an RDP connection troubleshooting issue or application connectivity issue in the Azure VM. Azure redeploy will help you to move them to a new node, and in this process, the VM will be shut down and retain the entire configuration, including your data disk, but the temporary disk data will be deleted.

Let us see how to process with the Azure virtual machine redeploy VM option.

1. Go to the VM for which you want to perform the Azure VM redeploy option.

2. Go to **Support + troubleshooting**.

3. Then, click on the **Redeploy** option as shown in the following screenshot:

Home > Virtual machines >

Virtual machines
(alit01rawatoutlook (Default Directory)

+ Add   🕒 Reservations   ···

Filter by name...

☐ Name ↑↓

☐ 🖥️ azvm3   ···

🔨 **azvm3 | Redeploy**
Virtual machine

🔍 Search (Ctrl+/)

Support + troubleshooting

💗 Resource health

🖥️ Boot diagnostics

📊 Performance diagnostics (Pre...

🔑 Reset password

🔨 Redeploy

🛠️ Maintenance

🖥️ Serial console

🖥️ Connection troubleshoot

👤 New support request

Figure 8.20: Azure VM redeploy

4. Once you click on the **Redeploy** option, click on the **Redeploy** button and the process will start and then you can go through the instruction as shown in the following screenshot:

Can't connect to your virtual machine?

Try redeploying your virtual machine, which will migrate it to a new Azure host. If you continue, the virtual machine will be restarted and you will lose any data on the temporary drive. While the redeployment is in progress, the virtual machine will be unavailable.

Learn more 🗗

Redeploy

Figure 8.21: Azure VM redeploy instruction

It will take up to 15 to 20 minutes to complete the process. Once this is complete, you can see your VM up and running fine and you can connect to apps or VMs.

Conclusion

In this chapter, we discussed the Azure virtual machine and its usage. We described the Azure virtual machine and scale set components in detail. We also discussed how to implement the Azure disk encryption and encrypt your disk and how to troubleshoot the issue using the Azure VM redeploy option.

In the next chapter, we will discuss how to deploy the Azure virtual machine automatically using the Azure template. We will also discuss how to use the ARM template and modify the same.

References

- Compute-optimized virtual machine sizes: **https://docs.microsoft.com/en-us/azure/virtual-machines/linux/sizes-compute**

- Sizes for Linux virtual machines in Azure: **https://docs.microsoft.com/en-us/azure/virtual-machines/linux/sizes**

- Create a Linux virtual machine in an availability zone with the Azure CLI: **https://docs.microsoft.com/en-us/azure/virtual-machines/linux/create-cli-availability-zone**

- What are availability zones in Azure: **https://docs.microsoft.com/en-us/azure/availability-zones/az-overview**

- Deploy VMs to dedicated hosts using the portal: **https://docs.microsoft.com/en-us/azure/virtual-machines/windows/dedicated-hosts-portal**

- Manage the availability of Windows virtual machines in Azure: **https://docs.microsoft.com/en-us/azure/virtual-machines/windows/manage-availability**

- For more details, visit: **Azure4you**

CHAPTER 9

Automating Deployment of VMs

In this chapter, we will discuss the automation of Azure VMs, how to deploy the VMs using the ARM template, how to configure the location of VMs, how to configure the ARM template, and how to save the template and deploy the VMs.

Structure

The following topics will be covered in this chapter:

- Azure ARM template
- Modifying the ARM template
- Template deployment

Objectives

In this chapter, we will learn about the ARM template and how to create the Azure VM using the template. We will also learn how to generate and deploy the ARM template in an Azure subscription

Azure ARM template

The Azure ARM template defines an automated way to deploy the Azure infrastructure like the Azure virtual machine storage account, and so on. This is managed by the API, called the **ARM API** or resource manager, and used to deploy the infrastructure code. You can use the Azure portal, PowerShell, or CLI, by calling the API directly and by creating ARM templates.

We can create the ARM template in the JSON format, and we can use it for the repeated deployment of your resources. It can also be used to deploy resources across the subscription environments.

> **Note: Many templates are available in the GitHub and Microsoft documentation which can be used and modified for your deployment. Refer to the ARM GitHub at https://github.com/Azure/azure-quickstart-templates.**

Modifying the ARM template

In this section, I will deploy an Azure virtual machine and you will see how to use the ARM template deployment from the template. You will understand how to generate and modify the Azure template.

If you need to create the template, follow the given steps:

1. Log in to the portal.
2. Select the virtual machine and provide the parameters.
3. Select the subscription.
4. Select the Resources group name:
    - VM name
    - Azure disk
    - VNet
    - Subnet

5. Once the process is complete, download the template as shown in the following screenshot:

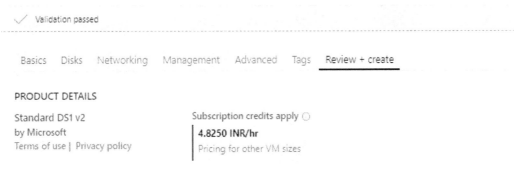

Figure 9.1: Resources template Create

6. Once you click on **Download a template for automation**, you will get multiple options as follows:

    *   Download the template
    *   Add to ARM library
    *   Deploy using the same template

7. You can see the template been created in the JSON format. It has strings and values in the template.

8. If you need to edit the template, then you will have certain edit parameters such as `$schema`, `contentVersion`, `Parameters`, `Variables`, `Resources`, and `Output`. Once you set all these parameters, your template is ready for deployment.

   Let's take a look at the following screenshot:

Figure 9.2: Resources template download

The template will be downloaded in the ZIP folder, and you can open it in the ARM editor software.

9. Now, you can see the template parameters, and you can even set the value that could be required for further template deployment, and so on. You can see the following values:

   • Location
   • RDP
   • Ports

Let's take a look at the following screenshot:

```
Template    Parameters    Scripts

3       "contentVersion": "1.0.0.0",
4       "parameters": {
5          "location": {
6             "value": "eastus"
7          },
8          "networkInterfaceName": {
9             "value": "bpbvm1358"
10         },
11         "networkSecurityGroupName": {
12            "value": "BPBVM1-nsg"
13         },
14         "networkSecurityGroupRules": {
15            "value": [
16               {
17                  "name": "RDP",
18                  "properties": {
19                     "priority": 300,
20                     "protocol": "TCP",
21                     "access": "Allow",
22                     "direction": "Inbound",
23                     "sourceAddressPrefix": "*",
24                     "sourcePortRange": "*",
25                     "destinationAddressPrefix": "*",
26                     "destinationPortRange": "3389"
27                  }
28               }
29            ]
30         },
```

Figure 9.3: Resources template parameter

10. Search for the deployments and select the **Deploy a custom template** option. Take a look at the following screenshot:

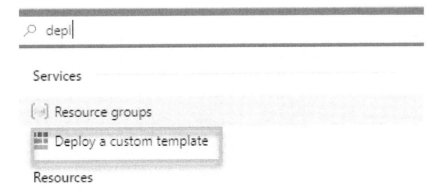

Figure 9.4: Resources template custom deployment

11. Once you select the template, you will get an option to edit the template. You can choose the template from the GitHub directly and click on edit. Please take a look at the following screenshot:

Figure 9.5: Template editor deployment

12. Once you click on **Edit template**, you will be directed to the next section. Then, select the **Load file** option and try and upload the file:

Figure 9.6: ARM template load file

13. Once you add the template, it will add your parameters, and you need to verify the parameters. Then, click on **Save**:

Edit template
Edit your Azure Resource Manager template

+ Add resource   ↑ Quickstart template   ↑ Load file   ↓ Download

```
                                    1   {
      ▶ ▩ Parameters (22)           2       "$schema": "https://schema.management.azure.com/schemas/2015-01-01/deploymentParamete
        ▩ Variables (0)             3       "contentVersion": "1.0.0.0",
        ▩ Resources (0)             4       "parameters": {
                                    5           "location": {
                                    6               "value": "eastus"
                                    7           },
                                    8           "networkInterfaceName": {
                                    9               "value": "bpbvm1358"
                                    10          },
                                    11          "networkSecurityGroupName": {
                                    12              "value": "BPBVM1-nsg"
                                    13          },
                                    14          "networkSecurityGroupRules": {
                                    15              "value": [
                                    16                  {
                                    17                      "name": "RDP",
```

Figure 9.7: ARM template edits

Template deployments

To deploy the template, perform the following steps:

1. Once you click on **Save**, it will automatically go to the deployment screen.

2. Provide all the parameters as per your requirements.

3. Once you are done with the parameters, click on **Purchase** and you will be able to deploy the VMs.

4. It will take 10 to 15 minutes to deploy the VMs. After this, your deployment will be completed. Take a look at the following screenshot:

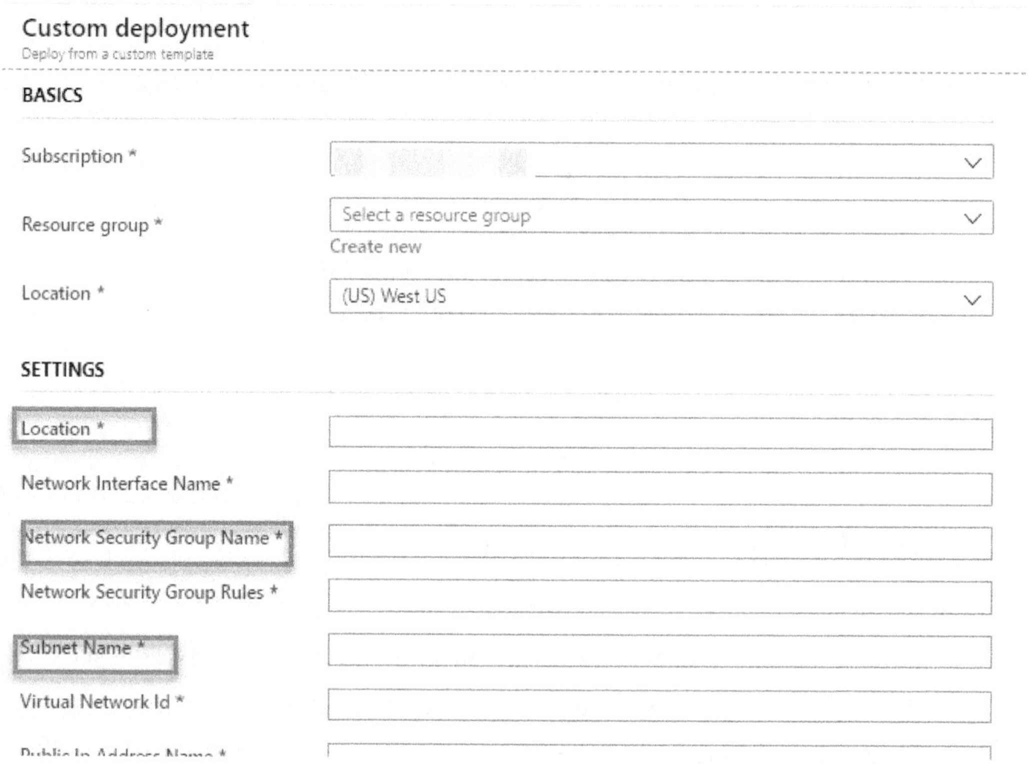

Custom deployment
Deploy from a custom template

BASICS

Subscription *

Resource group *
Create new

Location *
(US) West US

SETTINGS

Location *

Network Interface Name *

Network Security Group Name *

Network Security Group Rules *

Subnet Name *

Virtual Network Id *

Public Ip Address Name *

Figure 9.8: ARM template deployment

Conclusion

In this chapter, we discussed how to deploy the Azure virtual machine using the ARM automation, which will help you to deploy your big infrastructure quickly and save your time.

In the next chapter, we will discuss how to create and configure the Azure containers and use of the Kubernetes services. We will give you step-by-step instructions on how to deploy the Kubernetes and container services in an Azure subscription.

References

- GitHub ARM template: **https://github.com/Azure/azure-quickstart-templates**

- Azure Resource Manager templates overview: **https://docs.microsoft.com/en-us/azure/azure-resource-manager/template-deployment-overview**

- Create and deploy Azure resource manager templates by using the Azure portal: **https://docs.microsoft.com/en-us/azure/azure-resource-manager/resource-manager-quickstart-create-templates-use-the-portal**

- Azure resource manager templates for management features code samples: **https://docs.microsoft.com/en-us/azure/azure-resource-manager/template-samples**

- For more details on Azure4you blog post, visit: **https://azure4you.com/**

CHAPTER 10
Creating and Configuring Container

In this chapter, we will learn about the Azure Container and Kubernetes services and how to create these services and their usage. We will also discuss an Azure Container and its uses.

Structure

The following topics will be covered in this chapter:

- Azure Container
  - o   Use of an Azure Container
  - o   Create a container
- Azure Kubernetes
  - o   Create Azure Kubernetes

Objective

The objective of this chapter is to create and configure **Azure Container Instances (ACI)** and **Azure Kubernetes Service (AKS).**

Azure Container

An Azure Container is a standard package of software which helps you to package the code, dependencies, and configuration of a particular application. Containers help to split the monolithic applications into individual services which make up the solution.

Use of an Azure Container

The following are the uses of an Azure container:

- It is used to scale up the application.
- It provides the lightweight and immutable infrastructure for packaging the application and deployment.
- It provides better performance and removes the OS, versions, and dependencies.

Create a container

Let us see how to create the container services using the following steps:

1. Click on **Create a resource**.
2. Search for **Container Instances**.
3. Click on **Create** for creating the container instance:

Figure 10.1: *Container instance create*

4. Provide the following details:
   - The subscription and the resources group name.
   - The region for which you want to create the container.
   - Select the image sources from any of the following options:
     - o **Quickstart images**
     - o **Azure Container Registry**

        o **Docker Hub or other registry**

- Select the size of the container instance.

5. Click on the **Next: Networking >** button as shown in the following screenshot:

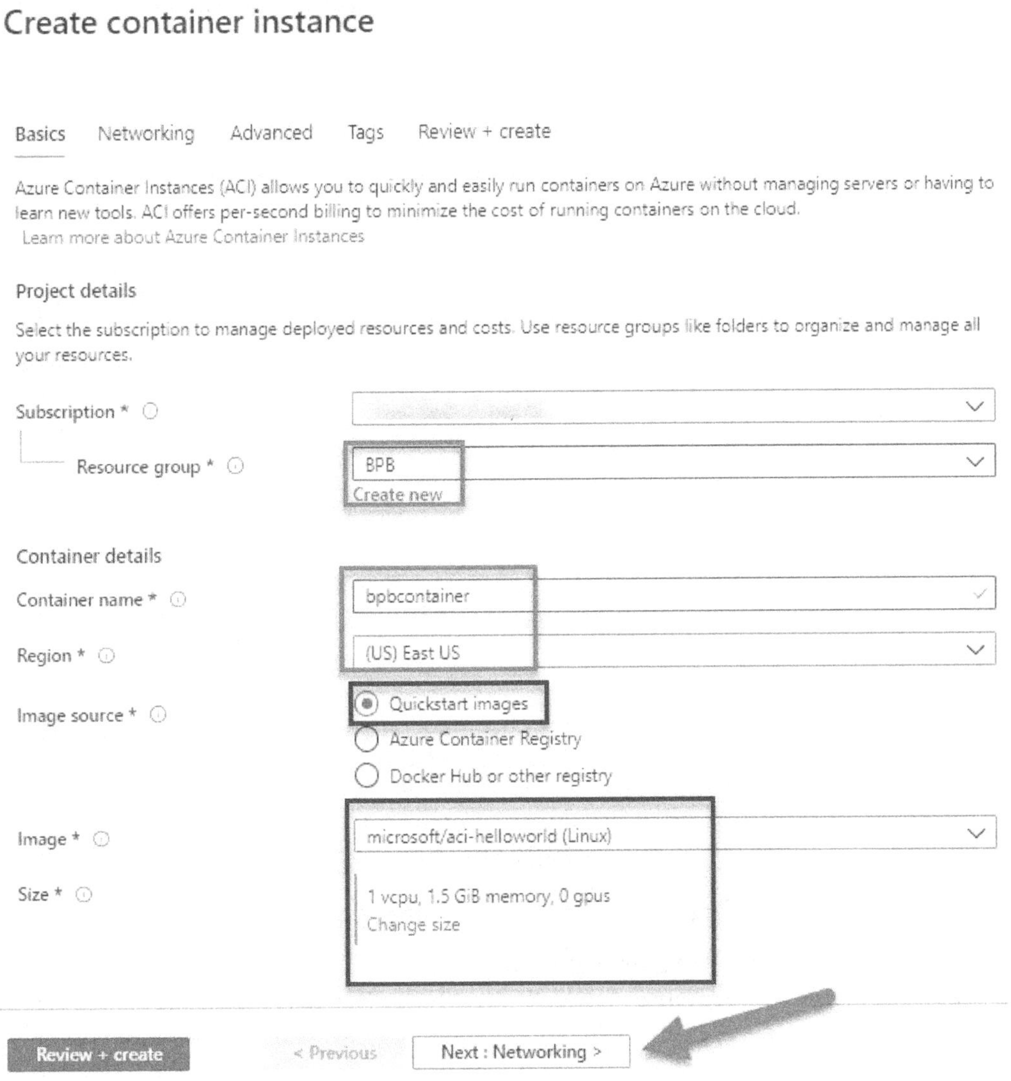

Create container instance

Basics   Networking   Advanced   Tags   Review + create

Azure Container Instances (ACI) allows you to quickly and easily run containers on Azure without managing servers or having to learn new tools. ACI offers per-second billing to minimize the cost of running containers on the cloud.
  Learn more about Azure Container Instances

Project details

Select the subscription to manage deployed resources and costs. Use resource groups like folders to organize and manage all your resources.

Subscription * ⊙

      └── Resource group * ⊙   BPB
                                            Create new

Container details

Container name * ⊙   bpbcontainer

Region * ⊙   (US) East US

Image source * ⊙   ⦿ Quickstart images
                        ◯ Azure Container Registry
                        ◯ Docker Hub or other registry

Image * ⊙   microsoft/aci-helloworld (Linux)

Size * ⊙   1 vcpu, 1.5 GiB memory, 0 gpus
                          Change size

Review + create   < Previous   Next : Networking >

Figure 10.2: Container instance details

6. In the **Networking** tab, provide the following details:
   - Select the networking type from the following options:
     - o **Public:** It will create a public IP address and assign it to the container for public access.

    o **Private:** If you want to integrate a VNet with the container, select this option.

   • Provide the DNS custom name.

   • Verify the port number.

7. Once done, click on the **Next: Advanced >** button as shown in the following screenshot:

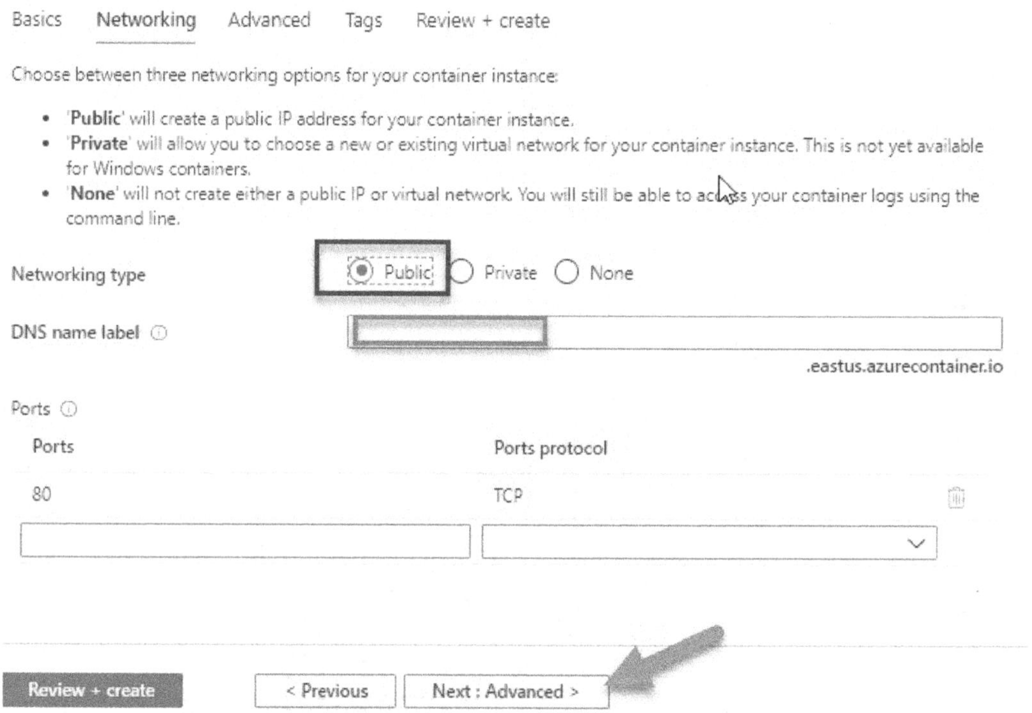

Basics Networking Advanced Tags Review + create

Choose between three networking options for your container instance:

- 'Public' will create a public IP address for your container instance.
- 'Private' will allow you to choose a new or existing virtual network for your container instance. This is not yet available for Windows containers.
- 'None' will not create either a public IP or virtual network. You will still be able to access your container logs using the command line.

Networking type	⦿ Public ◯ Private ◯ None
DNS name label ⓘ	

.eastus.azurecontainer.io

Ports ⓘ

Ports	Ports protocol	
80	TCP	🗑
		⌄

Review + create   < Previous Next : Advanced >

Figure 10.3: Container networking

8. In the **Networking** tab, follow the given steps:

   • Click on any of the restart policy:

    o **On failure**

    o **Always**

    o **Never**

   • Set up the environment variable if you want to set up the container.

   • You can set a command line to override if required.

Let's take a look at the following screenshot:

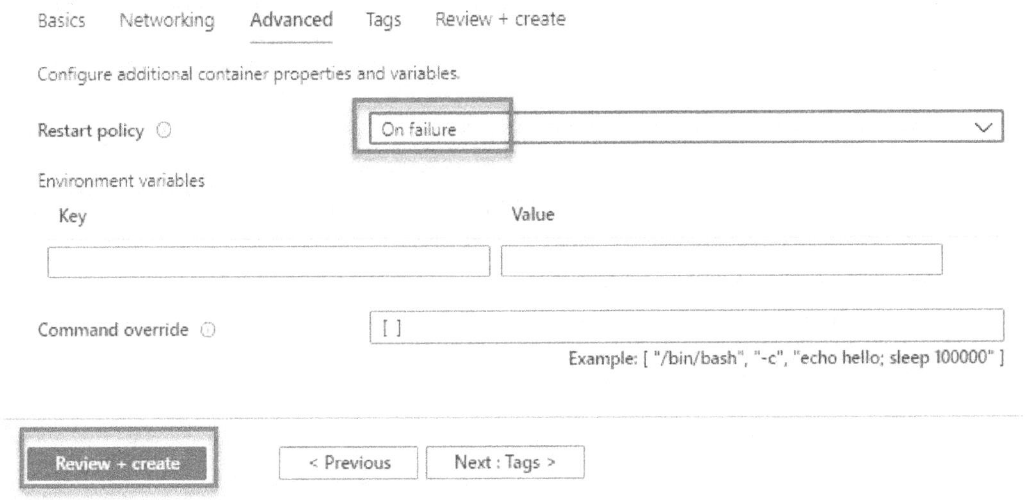

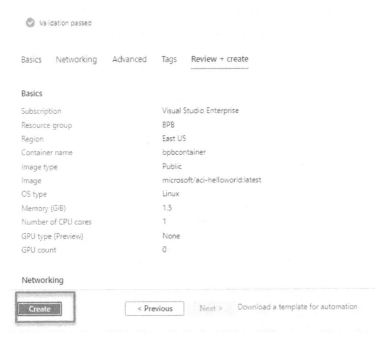

Figure 10.4: Container advance settings

9. Click on **Create** after the validation of the container services as shown in the following screenshot:

Figure 10.5: Container instance creation

The container will be created in a few minutes after performing these steps, and you can make use of it.

Azure Kubernetes

Kubernetes is an open source portable platform for automatic deployment, scaling, and management of containerized workload. It is managed and orchestrated by the container in difference compute environments. This orchestration platform provides the ease of use and flexibility with PaaS and IaaS environments.

Create Azure Kubernetes

Let us see how to create Azure Kubernetes by following the given steps:

1. Click on **Create a resource**.
2. Search for **Kubernetes Service**.
3. Select the service and click on **Create**:

Figure 10.6: Kubernetes services

4. Once you click on create the Kubernetes services, it will ask you to fill the following details:
   - **Subscription**
   - **Resource group**
   - Provide the cluster details as follows:
     o **Kubernetes cluster name:** Set of node machines called Kubernetes for running containerized applications.
     o **Region** You want to deploy the services.
     o The version of Kubernetes services you want to deploy.
   - **Node:** A node is a physical or virtual machine that depends on the cluster configuration. Provide the node size and node count.
   - You want to add an additional Kubernetes cluster.

Take a look at the following screenshot:

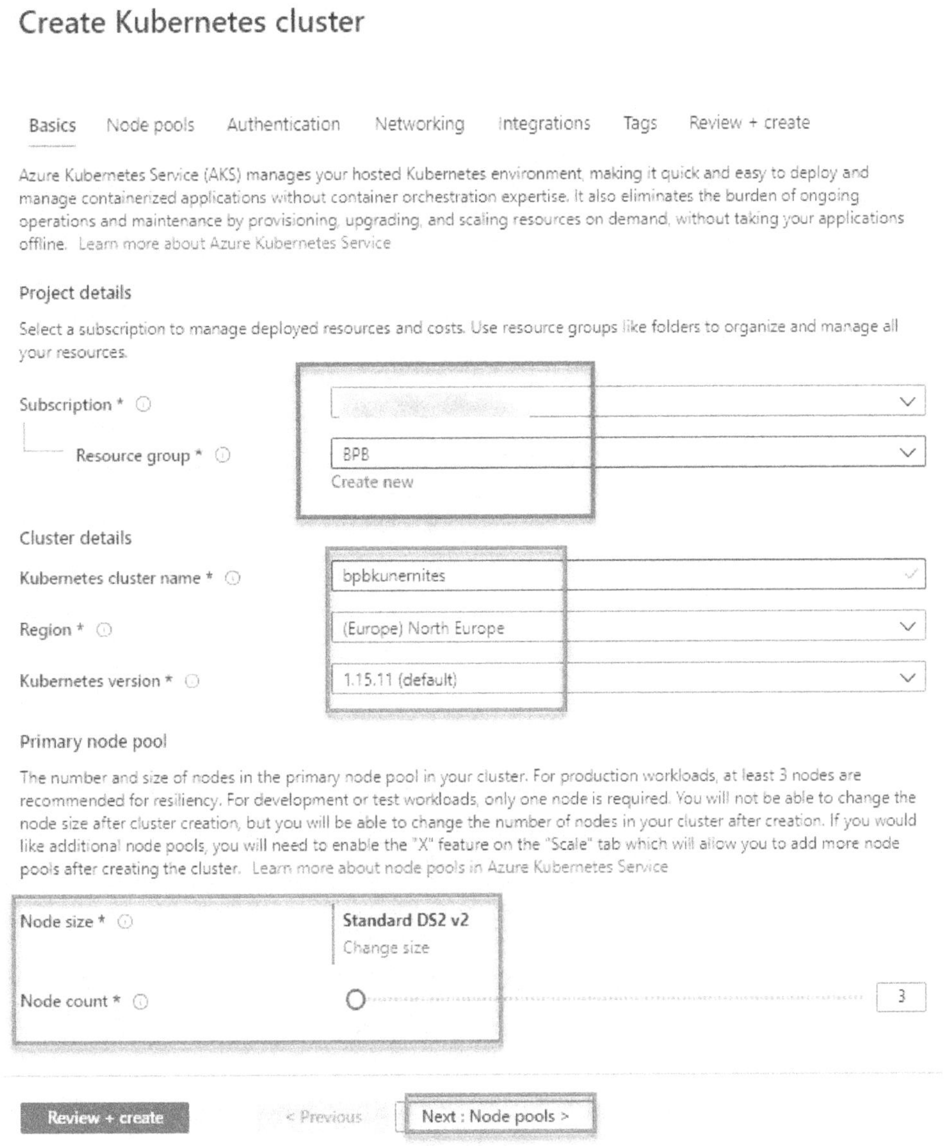

Create Kubernetes cluster

Basics   Node pools   Authentication   Networking   Integrations   Tags   Review + create

Azure Kubernetes Service (AKS) manages your hosted Kubernetes environment, making it quick and easy to deploy and manage containerized applications without container orchestration expertise. It also eliminates the burden of ongoing operations and maintenance by provisioning, upgrading, and scaling resources on demand, without taking your applications offline. Learn more about Azure Kubernetes Service

Project details

Select a subscription to manage deployed resources and costs. Use resource groups like folders to organize and manage all your resources.

Subscription * ⓘ	[ ] ⌄
└─ Resource group * ⓘ	BPB ⌄
	Create new

Cluster details

Kubernetes cluster name * ⓘ	bpbkunernites ✓
Region * ⓘ	(Europe) North Europe ⌄
Kubernetes version * ⓘ	1.15.11 (default) ⌄

Primary node pool

The number and size of nodes in the primary node pool in your cluster. For production workloads, at least 3 nodes are recommended for resiliency. For development or test workloads, only one node is required. You will not be able to change the node size after cluster creation, but you will be able to change the number of nodes in your cluster after creation. If you would like additional node pools, you will need to enable the "X" feature on the "Scale" tab which will allow you to add more node pools after creating the cluster. Learn more about node pools in Azure Kubernetes Service

Node size * ⓘ	**Standard DS2 v2** Change size
Node count * ⓘ	◯ ·· [3]

[Review + create]   < Previous   [Next : Node pools >]

Figure 10.7: Kubernetes services details

5. Once you are done with the preceding configuration, go the **Node pools** section and provide the following details:

    • Add the node pool and its instance size with the OS.

    • Select the virtual node to be enabled or disabled.

    • Select the VM scale set to be enabled.

6.   Go to the **Authentication** tab as shown in the following screenshot:

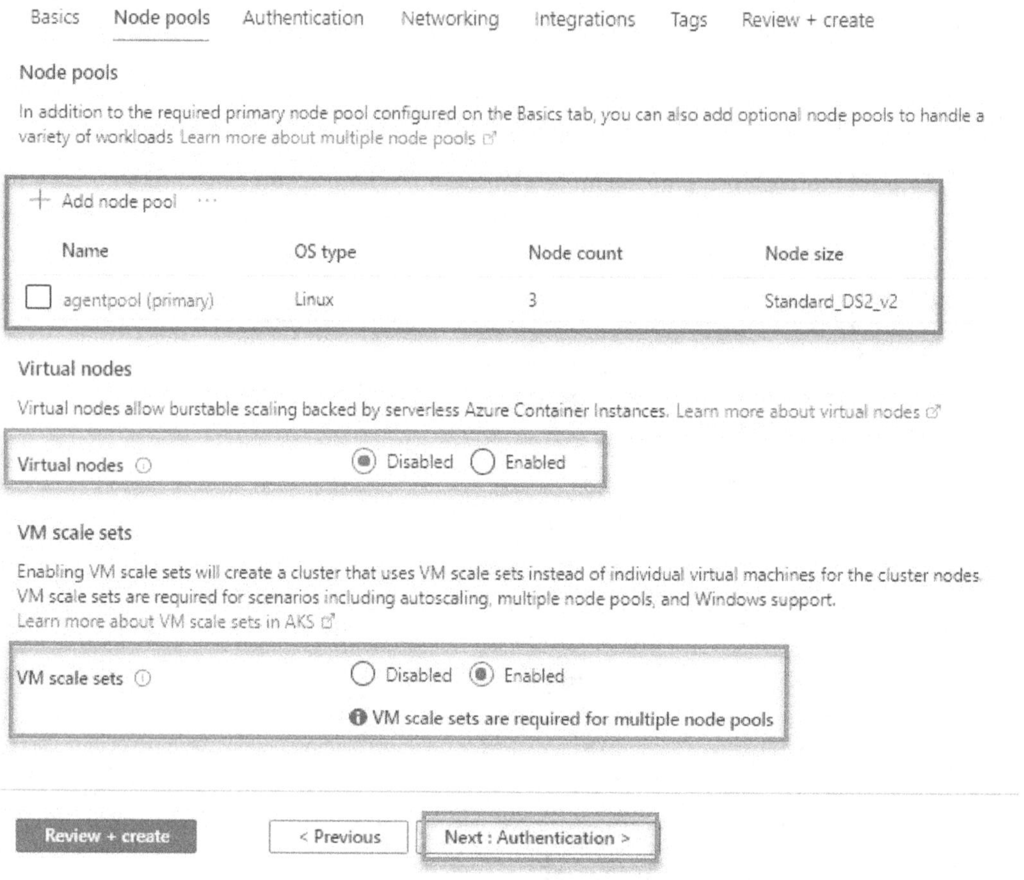

Basics   Node pools   Authentication   Networking   Integrations   Tags   Review + create

Node pools

In addition to the required primary node pool configured on the Basics tab, you can also add optional node pools to handle a variety of workloads Learn more about multiple node pools ☐

+ Add node pool   ...

Name	OS type	Node count	Node size
☐ agentpool (primary)	Linux	3	Standard_DS2_v2

Virtual nodes

Virtual nodes allow burstable scaling backed by serverless Azure Container Instances. Learn more about virtual nodes ☐

Virtual nodes ☐   ⦿ Disabled   ◯ Enabled

VM scale sets

Enabling VM scale sets will create a cluster that uses VM scale sets instead of individual virtual machines for the cluster nodes. VM scale sets are required for scenarios including autoscaling, multiple node pools, and Windows support. Learn more about VM scale sets in AKS ☐

VM scale sets ☐   ◯ Disabled   ⦿ Enabled

                          ❶ VM scale sets are required for multiple node pools

Review + create   < Previous   Next : Authentication >

Figure 10.8: Kubernetes services node pool

7.   In the **Authentication** tab, select the following details:

   •   Select the authentication method **Service   Principal** or **system-assigned managed identity.**

   •   In Kubernetes authentication and authorization, enable the RBAC role.

   •   Select the encryption type as default.

8. Click on the **Networking** tab as shown in the following screenshot:

Basics   Node pools   Authentication   Networking   Integrations   Tags   Review + create

Cluster infrastructure
The cluster infrastructure authentication specified is used by Azure Kubernetes Service to manage cloud resources attached to the cluster. This can be either a service principal ☑ or a system-assigned managed identity ☑.

| Authentication method | ◉ Service principal ◯ System-assigned managed identity |

| Service principal * ⓘ | (new) default service principal |
| | Configure service principal |

Kubernetes authentication and authorization
Authentication and authorization are used by the Kubernetes cluster to control user access to the cluster as well as what the user may do once authenticated. Learn more about Kubernetes authentication ☑

| Role-based access control (RBAC) ⓘ | ◉ Enabled ◯ Disabled |

Node pool OS disk encryption
By default, all disks in AKS are encrypted at rest with Microsoft-managed keys. For additional control over encryption, you can supply your own keys using a disk encryption set backed by an Azure Key Vault. The disk encryption set will be used to encrypt the OS disks for all node pools in the cluster. Learn more ☑

| Encryption type | (Default) Encryption at-rest with a platform-managed key ⌄ |

Review + create   < Previous   Next : Networking >

Figure 10.9: Kubernetes services authentication

9. Once you click on the **Networking** tab, provide the following details:
   - Select the network configuration: **Basic** or **Advanced**
   - **DNS name prefix**
   - **Load balancer**
   - **Private cluster: Enabled or Disabled**
   - **Network policy**
   - **HTTP application routing: Yes** or **No**

Go to the next tab as shown in the following screenshot:

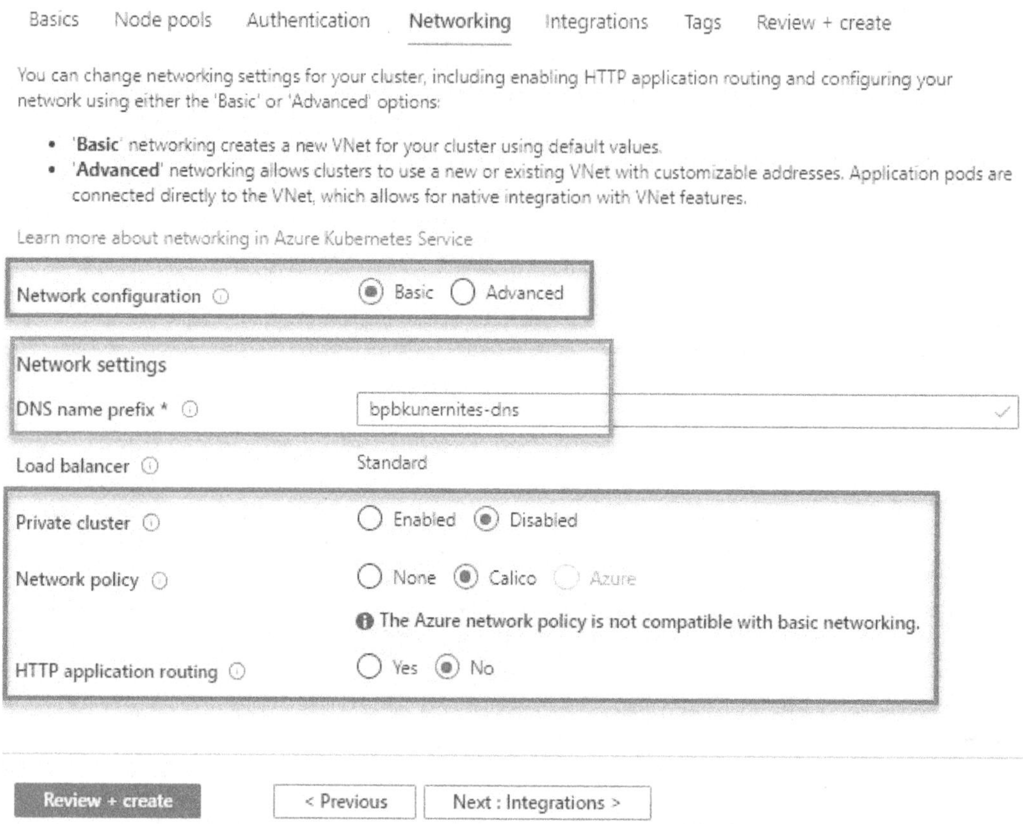

Figure 10.10: Kubernetes services networking

10. Once you click on the **Integration** tab, select the **Log Analytics workspace** under the **Azure Monitor** section.

11.   Click on the **Next: Tags>** button as shown in the following screenshot:

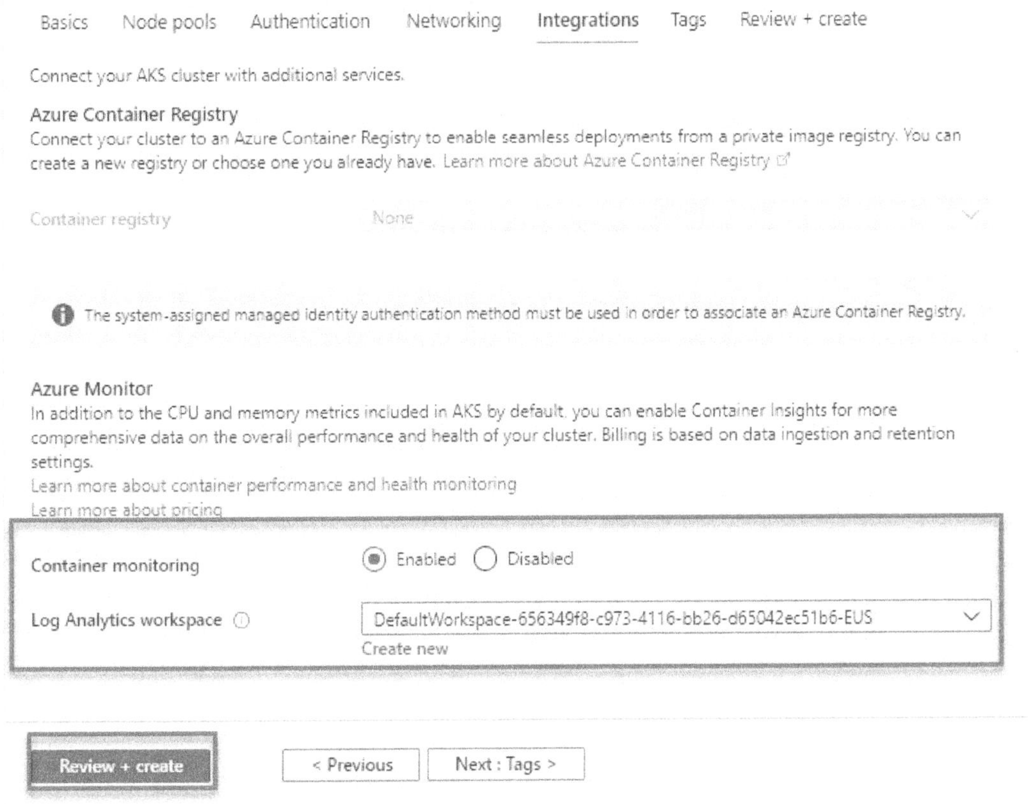

Basics   Node pools   Authentication   Networking   Integrations   Tags   Review + create

Connect your AKS cluster with additional services.

Azure Container Registry
Connect your cluster to an Azure Container Registry to enable seamless deployments from a private image registry. You can create a new registry or choose one you already have. Learn more about Azure Container Registry ✎

Container registry   None   ⌄

ℹ The system-assigned managed identity authentication method must be used in order to associate an Azure Container Registry.

Azure Monitor
In addition to the CPU and memory metrics included in AKS by default, you can enable Container Insights for more comprehensive data on the overall performance and health of your cluster. Billing is based on data ingestion and retention settings.
Learn more about container performance and health monitoring
Learn more about pricing

Container monitoring   ◉ Enabled   ○ Disabled

Log Analytics workspace ⓘ   DefaultWorkspace-656349f8-c973-4116-bb26-d65042ec51b6-EUS   ⌄
                                 Create new

Review + create   < Previous   Next : Tags >

Figure 10.11: Kubernetes services integration

12. Here, provide the tag name and click on create the Kubernetes services. After the validation, click on next to create the Kubernetes services as shown in the following screenshot:

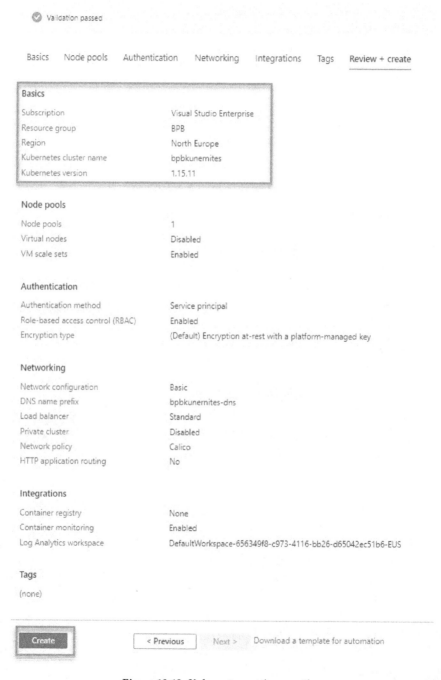

Figure 10.12: Kubernetes services creation

It will take 10 to 15 mins to create the Kubernetes services. After this, we will be able to use the services as per our requirements.

Conclusion

In this chapter, we discussed the creation and configuration of Azure Container and Kubernetes. We also covered the Kubernetes resources, how to set up and configure the container and Kubernetes, and how it will help you and the customer to manage the larger applications.

In the next chapter, we will discuss Azure app services and see how to create and deploy the app services in your Azure environments. We will also discuss the configuration part on WebApps which will help you to learn the WebApps services more easily.

References

- Container: **https://azure.microsoft.com/en-in/overview/what-is-a-container/**

- Kubernetes: **https://docs.microsoft.com/en-us/azure/aks/intro-kubernetes**

- Container services: **https://azure.microsoft.com/en-in/product-categories/containers/**

- Kubernetes services: **https://docs.microsoft.com/en-us/learn/modules/intro-to-azure-kubernetes-service/2-what-is-azure-kubernetes-service**

- Deploy an Azure Kubernetes Service (AKS) cluster using the Azure portal: **https://docs.microsoft.com/en-us/azure/aks/kubernetes-walkthrough-portal**

CHAPTER 11
Creating and Configuring Web Apps

In this chapter, we will discuss the benefits of Azure app services, how to create the app services, and how to configure the app services plan. We will also discuss the Azure apps services components and how to use the web apps slot and custom domain configuration. We will discuss how to secure your Azure web apps.

Structure

The following topics will be covered in this chapter:

- App services
- Create and configure app services
    - o   Custom domain configuration
    - o   App service security
    - o   App service backup

Objectives

The main objective of this chapter is to learn about Azure app services and its use cases. We will discuss the properties of its app services and see how to create and configure the app services using the Azure portal. So, the customer can utilize the Azure app services based on their requirements.

App service

Azure app services are HTTP-based services which are used to host the application similar to your on-premise IIS server. We can develop our application using .NET, .NET Core, Java, Ruby, Node.js, PHP, or Python language. The app services automatically manage the patches, OS, and language framework.

App services plan

The app services plan defines the SKU/size of the Azure app services instance based on the app services plan. You will be able to utilize the features like custom domain, VNet-integration, load balancing, and size of app services such as 2 GB and 100 ACU, and so on.

Let us see how to create the app services plan:

1. Click on the **+ Create a resource** option.
2. Search for **App Service Plan**.
3. Click on **Create** as shown in the following screenshot:

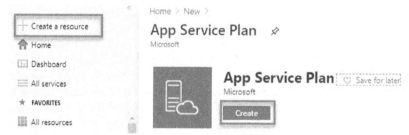

Figure 11.1: App service plan

Before we create the app services plan, let us see how many plans we have in app services and its usage:

- **Shared compute:** In this plan, you will get the free apps services plan and shared services plan which can be used for the *dev/test* purpose as shown in the following table:

Selected features	Free	Shared
Web, mobile, or API apps	10	100
Disk space	1 GB	1 GB
Auto scale	NA	NA
Deployment slots	NA	NA
Max instances	NA	NA

Table 11.1: Web services shared plan

- **Dedicated compute:** It is used for production purpose. In this plan, you will get a basic, standard, premium, and premium V2 tier. This can be seen in the following table:

Selected features	Basic	Standard	Premium
Web, mobile, or API apps	Unlimited	Unlimited	Unlimited
Disk space	10 GB	50 GB	250 GB
Auto scale	NA	Supported	Supported
Deployment slots	NA	5	20
Max instances	Up to 3	Up to 10	Up to 30

Table 11.2: Web services dedicated plan

- **Isolated:** It will provide the dedicated VM instance which is integrated with the dedicated VNet. It provides complete isolation as well. Take a look at the following table:

Selected features	Isolated
Web, mobile, or API apps	Unlimited
Disk space	1 TB
Auto scale	Supported
Deployment slots	20
Max instances	Up to 100

Table 11.3: Web services isolated plans

Please take a look at the following screenshot:

Figure 11.2: App services plan size

Once you click on **Create app service**, follow the given steps:

1. Select the resource group.

2. Please provide the name of the app service.

3. Please select the OS: **Windows/Linux** as per your requirements.

4. Please click on `Review + create` as shown in the following screenshot:

Create App Service Plan

App Service plans give you the flexibility to allocate specific apps to a given set of resources and further optimize your Azure resource utilization. This way, if you want to save money on your testing environment you can share a plan across multiple apps. Learn more ☒

Project Details

Select a subscription to manage deployed resources and costs. Use resource groups like folders to organize and manage all your resources.

Subscription * ⓘ		⌄
Resource Group * ⓘ	BPB	⌄
	Create new	

App Service Plan details		
Name *	Bpbappseviceplan	⌄
Operating System *	◯ Linux ⦿ Windows	
Region *	East US	⌄

Pricing Tier

App Service plan pricing tier determines the location, features, cost and compute resources associated with your app. Learn more ☒

Sku and size *	Standard S1
	100 total ACU, 1.75 GB memory
	Change size

Review + create	< Previous	Next : Tags >

Figure 11.3: App service plan creation

Once you click on `Review + create`, your app service plan will be created in 5 to 10 minutes.

Create and configure the app service

Let us now create the app services as we have already created and understood the app services plan. To do this, follow the given steps:

1. Click on **+ Create a resource**.

2. Search for Azure app services.

3. Click on **Web App** as shown in the following screenshot:

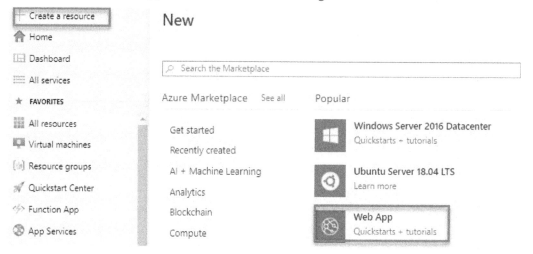

Figure 11.4: Web app

4. Once you click on **Web App**, provide the following details to create the new app services:

   • Subscription

   • Resource group

   • Provide the name of the instance

   • Publish can be **Code** or **Docker Container** as per your customer/ project requirements

5. Select the runtime stack as. **.NET CORE 3.1 (LTS)**.

6. Select the OS; either **Windows** or **Linux**.

7. Select the region.

8. Click on windows size or **App Service Plan** in app services. Take a look at the following screenshot:

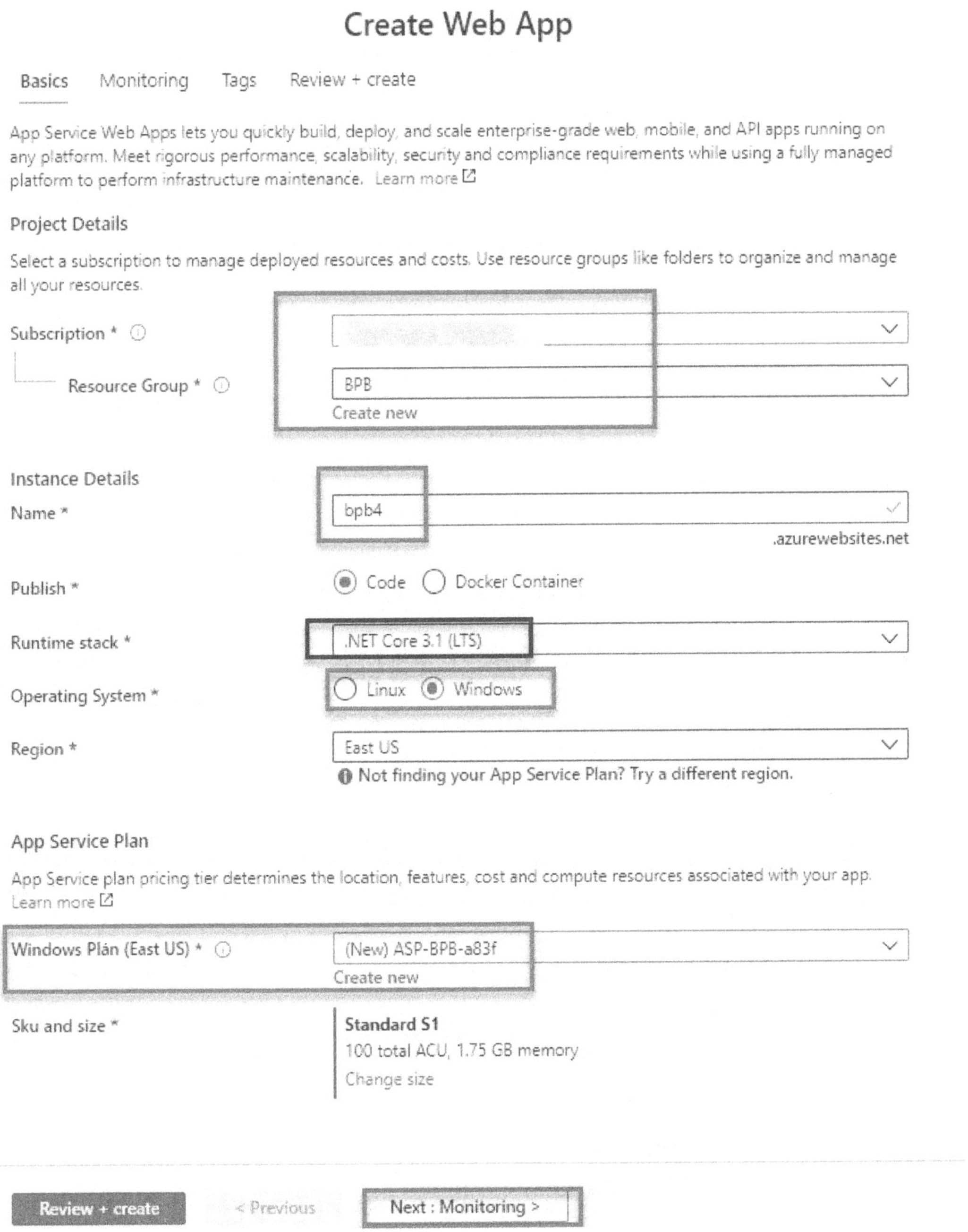

Create Web App

Basics   Monitoring   Tags   Review + create

App Service Web Apps lets you quickly build, deploy, and scale enterprise-grade web, mobile, and API apps running on any platform. Meet rigorous performance, scalability, security and compliance requirements while using a fully managed platform to perform infrastructure maintenance. Learn more 🗗

Project Details

Select a subscription to manage deployed resources and costs. Use resource groups like folders to organize and manage all your resources.

Subscription * ⓘ	⌄
Resource Group * ⓘ	BPB ⌄
	Create new

Instance Details

Name *	bpb4 ✓
	.azurewebsites.net
Publish *	⦿ Code ◯ Docker Container
Runtime stack *	.NET Core 3.1 (LTS) ⌄
Operating System *	◯ Linux ⦿ Windows
Region *	East US ⌄
	❶ Not finding your App Service Plan? Try a different region.

App Service Plan

App Service plan pricing tier determines the location, features, cost and compute resources associated with your app. Learn more 🗗

Windows Plán (East US) * ⓘ	(New) ASP-BPB-a83f ⌄
	Create new
Sku and size *	**Standard S1**
	100 total ACU, 1.75 GB memory
	Change size

[Review + create]   < Previous   [Next : Monitoring >]

Figure 11.5: *Web app details*

9. Click on **Next: Monitoring >** and select the **Monitoring** tab and create a new application insight for monitoring of app services.

10. Once this is done, click on **Review + create**, and after 10 minutes, your app services will be created. Take a look at the following screenshot:

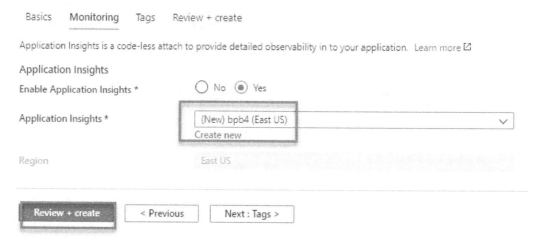

Figure 11.6: Web app creation

Custom domain configuration

A custom domain is used to configure your own custom domain for your web apps. For example, if you want to configure the xyz.com to bpb.com, then you need to configure the custom domain.

Now, we will configure the custom domain for app services. Please follow the given steps:

1. Go to **App Service**.

2. Click on **Custom domains**.

3. Click on **+ Add custom domain**.

4. Provide the custom domain name.

5. Click on the **Validate** button.

Once you click on **Validate**, add the *A record* and *TXT record* in your public domain registration to validate, and then try to validate.

I will successfully validate after that, and now you can configure the Azure web apps services. Take a look at the following screenshot:

Figure 11.7: Custom domain

App services security

The app services security will help you to reduce the attack and enable the authentication to your web apps for your users. For example, you can integrate it with Azure AD, Facebook, Microsoft account, Google, and Twitter account. For more details, please take a look at the following screenshot:

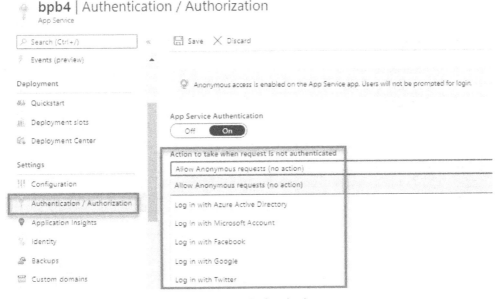

Figure 11.8: Authentication

We can even enable the Transport Layer Security (TLS) to services and add the TLS/SSL certificate binding for the HTTPS configuration under the TLS/SSL settings configuration.

- **TLS:** It stands for **transport layer security** which is designed to provide the privacy and data security of communication over the internet.

- **SSL:** It is a **secure socket layer** that helps to protect the connection between the server and client while encrypting the link. The examples include websites, main servers, browsers, and so on. Take a look at the following screenshot:

Figure 11.9: TLS/SSL settings

App services backup

If you need to enable the backup of Azure app services, it is not simple to enable it directly from the **backup vault**, but the app services can use the backup vault with their configuration. Please follow the given steps to configure the app services backup:

1. Go to **App Service**.

2. Click on the **Backups** option.

3. Click on **Backup** to configure as highlighted in the following screenshot:

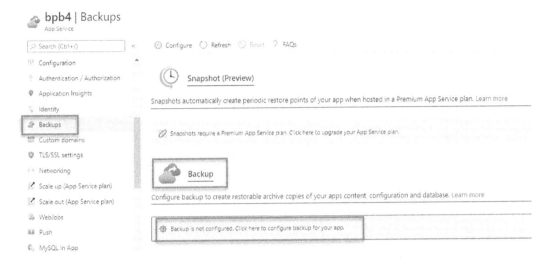

Figure 11.10: App backup

4. Click on the **Storage** tab and select the storage account for backup.

5. Select the **On** button for enabling the backup.

6. Set up the backup frequency.

7. Please mention the backup schedule start.

8. Select the retention period.

9. Click on the **Save** button, and your app services backup will be enabled. Take a look at the following screenshot for more details:

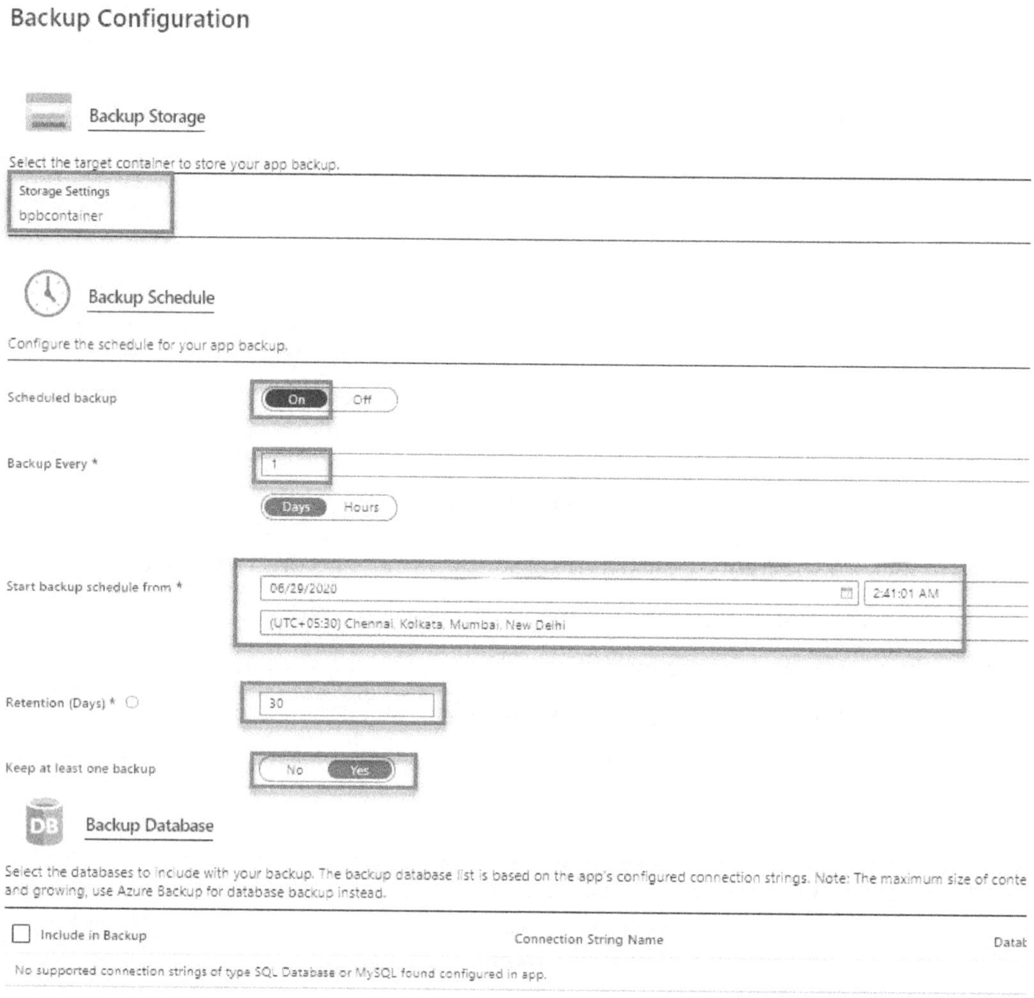

Backup Configuration

Backup Storage

Select the target container to store your app backup.

Storage Settings
bpbcontainer

Backup Schedule

Configure the schedule for your app backup.

Scheduled backup   [On   Off]

Backup Every *   [1]

                     [Days   Hours]

Start backup schedule from *   [06/29/2020   📅 [2:41:01 AM]

                     [(UTC+05:30) Chennai, Kolkata, Mumbai, New Delhi]

Retention (Days) * ◯   [30]

Keep at least one backup   [No   Yes]

Backup Database

Select the databases to include with your backup. The backup database list is based on the app's configured connection strings. Note: The maximum size of conte and growing, use Azure Backup for database backup instead.

☐ Include in Backup   Connection String Name   Datab

No supported connection strings of type SQL Database or MySQL found configured in app.

Figure 11.11: App backup configure

Conclusion

In this chapter, we discussed the Azure app services and app services plan. We also discussed how to configure the Azure app services backup and custom domain. We covered the app services security as well in this chapter.

In the next chapter, we will discuss how to integrate the on-premises network to Azure using the site-to-site connection and express route. We will also discuss the VNet-to-VNet peering and more.

References

- App service overview: **https://docs.microsoft.com/en-us/azure/app-service/overview**

- Web apps: **https://docs.microsoft.com/en-us/rest/api/appservice/webapps**

- Create an ASP.NET core web app in Azure: **https://docs.microsoft.com/en-us/azure/app-service/app-service-web-get-started-dotnet**

- Create a web app in an app service environment v1: **https://docs.microsoft.com/en-us/azure/app-service/environment/app-service-web-how-to-create-a-web-app-in-an-ase**

CHAPTER 12
Configuring Virtual Networking and Integrating On-Premises to Azure Network

In this chapter, we will discuss the networking services and use their components such as the Azure virtual network and see how to create and use these services. We will also cover the VNet peering that can be used to connect to VNet, how to configure the VNet-to-VNet connectivity and the Azure virtual network gateway. Let us start with all of these topics and learn how to use networking services.

Structure

The following topics will be covered in this chapter:

- Azure virtual network
- ExpressRoute connection
- ExpressRoute configuration

Objectives

In this chapter, you will learn how to define the network in your Azure subscription using Azure VNet and subnet. We will discuss how to configure a site-to-site connection and on-premises to Azure connectivity using ExpressRoute.

Azure virtual network

An Azure virtual network is defined as the Azure network within your subscription. VNet integration enables you to access Azure resources like Azure virtual machine, SQLDB, and so on securely to the Azure network or on-premises network. It is just like your on-premises network that you have configured and have access to in your data center. Please take a look at the following components that are required to create the virtual network:

- **Address space:** An address space is nothing but a range of your virtual network IP address.

- **Subnet:** A subnet is a collection of the IP address which can be used to assign an Azure virtual machine. Please take a look at the following diagram:

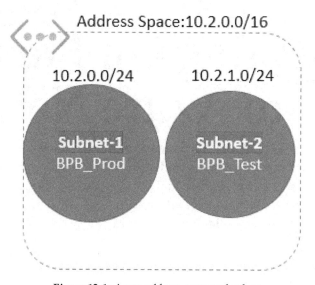

Figure 12.1: Azure address space and subnet

Azure virtual network creation

If you need to create the Azure virtual network, then follow the given steps:

1. Log in to the portal.
2. Go to **All services** and click on **Networking**.
3. Select **Virtual networks** as shown in the following screenshot:

Figure 12.2: Azure virtual network

4. Provide the virtual network name.
5. Mention the address space as per your requirements.
6. Select the subscription, location, and resources group.
7. Provide the name of the subnet.
8. Then, provide the range of the subnet within the address space range.

9. Click on **Create**, and after that, it will take some time to create the virtual network. Please take a look at the following screenshot:

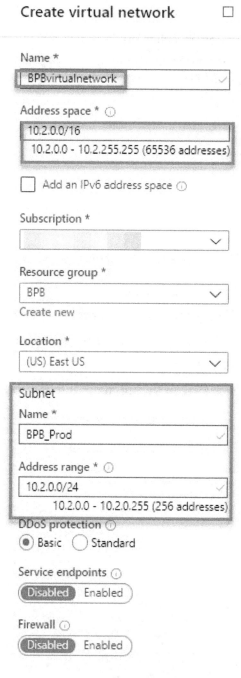

Figure 12.3: Azure virtual network details

Once the virtual network is created, you can see the following details as shown in the following screenshot

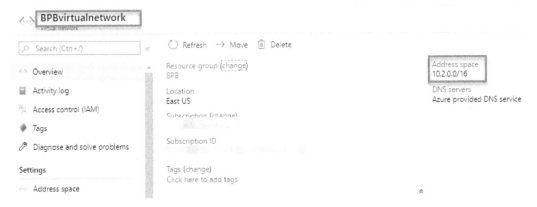

Figure 12.4: VNet configuration

Azure VNet peering

The Azure virtual network can be used to connect two different virtual networks. It provides a seamless connectivity from the Microsoft backbone infrastructure. VNet peering can connect two different VNets, and it provides low-latency and high-bandwidth.

Azure VNet peering are of two types:

- **VNet peering:** It is used to connect two virtual networks within the same region.

- **Global VNet peering:** It is used to connect two virtual networks across regions.

Please take a look at the following diagram:

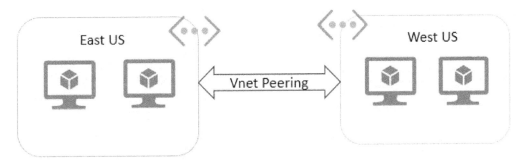

Figure 12.5: VNet peering

Now, we have understood the use of Azure VNet peering, so let us now understand how to create the Azure VNet peering.

Suppose if you have multiple VNets from various environments and you want to communicate with all the VNets, then you can have VNet peering. For VNet peering, we require a minimum of two VNets either in the same region or different region. Let us see how to create the VNet peering:

1. Log in to the portal and choose the two VNets in which you want to configure the VNet peering.

2. Select the VNet you want to peer.

3. Please select the VNet.

4. Under the **Settings** tab, select the **Peerings** option.

5. Click on **+ Add**. Take a look to configure the VNet peering as shown in the following screenshot:

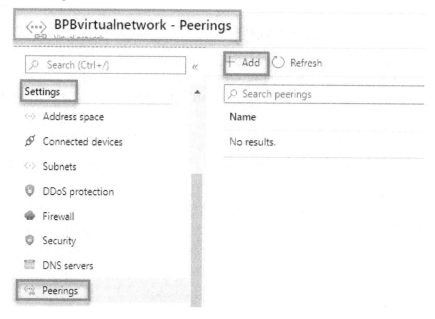

Figure 12.6: VNet peering configuration

6. Provide the VNet peering name.

7. Select the deployment **Resources manager** as default. The classic model can be used if you have resources in the classic mode (it is an old model and MS has stopped supporting this model).

8. Then, select the second virtual network name from the drop-down menu for which you want to enable the VNet peering.

9.　Provide the name of VNet peering again for the second VNet configuration. Take a look at the following screenshot:

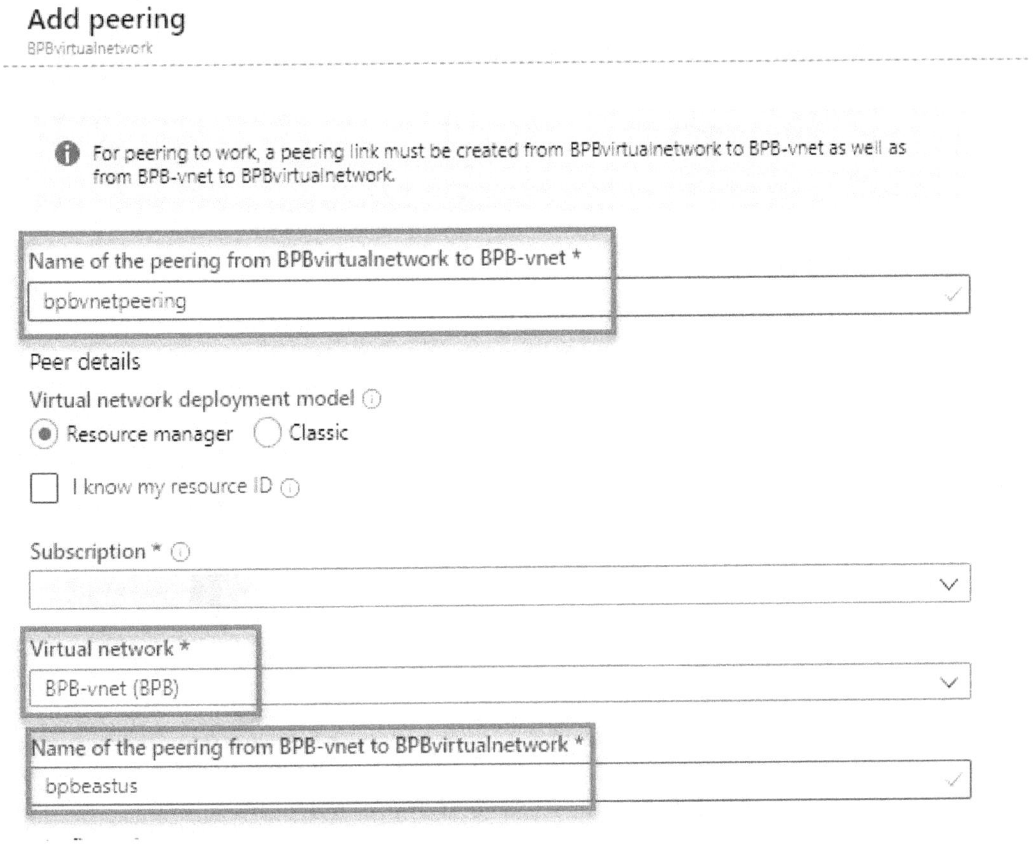

Add peering
BPBvirtualnetwork

   ℹ For peering to work, a peering link must be created from BPBvirtualnetwork to BPB-vnet as well as from BPB-vnet to BPBvirtualnetwork.

Name of the peering from BPBvirtualnetwork to BPB-vnet *

bpbvnetpeering

Peer details

Virtual network deployment model ⓘ
◉ Resource manager   ○ Classic

☐ I know my resource ID ⓘ

Subscription * ⓘ

Virtual network *

BPB-vnet (BPB)

Name of the peering from BPB-vnet to BPBvirtualnetwork *

bpbeastus

Figure 12.7: VNet peering configuration details

10.　Please select the configuration setting to enable to allow the VNet traffic from VNet 1 to VNet 2. You can even enable traffic from VNet 2 to 1 if required by your organization. The gateway transit is only required if VNet is configured with a virtual network gateway.

11.　Click on the **OK** button to configure it.

12. Once you click on Ok, it will take some time to configure, and it will allow traffic in both the VNets. Refer to the following screenshot:

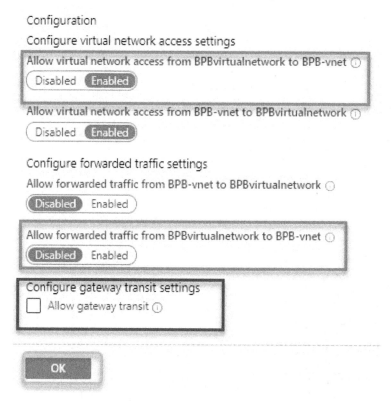

Figure 12.8: VNet peering configuration settings

13. Once the VNet peering is done, verify the connectivity under the **Peerings** section as shown in the following screenshot:

Figure 12.9: VNet connectivity verification

Virtual network gateway

The Azure virtual network gateway is used to send the encrypted traffic from the Azure network to the on-premises network. In other words, it is used to create connectivity between the Azure and on-premise network. A virtual network gateway is used to send the encrypted traffic over the Microsoft network. In a single VNet, you can configure only one VPN gateway, and if you want to connect from multiple connections, then you can use the same VPN gateway.

For the configuration, the following are pre-requisites:

- Azure VNet
- You might need a gateway subnet under the same VNet if you want to configure the virtual network gateway.
- You might need a gateway in which you can choose either a VPN or express route based on your requirements.
- It requires a public IP as well.

Before we create the virtual network, please make sure to understand the connectivity you want to use. If you need VNet-to-VNet and site-to-site connection, you can use the VPN, but if you want to configure with the express route, then select the gateway type as **EXPRESS ROUTE**.

Let us see how to configure the Azure virtual network gateway:

1. Please go to the marketplace and search for the Azure virtual network gateway.

2. Select **Virtual network gateway** and click on **Create**. The following screenshot shows the VNet network gateway creation:

Figure 12.10: VNet network gateway creation

3. Provide the subscription and resource group name of your virtual network resources.

4. Then, provide the virtual network gateway name and region for which you want to create the VNet gateway, and it will provide the same location as your VNet.

5. Choose the VNet gateway type as follows:

    *   **VPN:** It is used to connect the VNet-to-VNet and site-to-site connectivity.

    *   **Express route:** If you are planning for the express route connectivity, then please select the express route gateway type. I will explain this later in this chapter.

    *   The VPN type is explained as follows:

        *   **Policy-based:** It is a combination of both the networks and based on the firewall policy. It will filter the encrypted/decrypted traffic. It is a built-in firewall device which performs traffic filtering. In another way, it is a static VPN device configuration and it has some limitations.

            Please take a look at the following diagram:

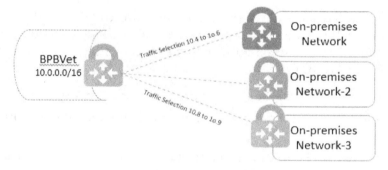

Figure 12.11: VPN type policy-based

        *   **Route-based:** In this scenario, VPN devices are used to send the traffic or route/filter the traffic from any device to any device or internet by an IPsec tunnel. Please take a look at the following diagram:

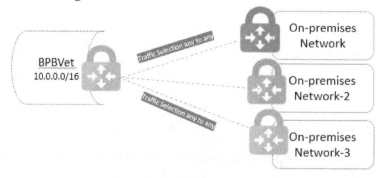

Figure 12.12: VPN type route-based

6. Please select the VPN SKU; it is nothing but a VNet device capability configuration. For more details, please take a look at the following screenshot:

VPN Gateway Generation	SKU	S2S/VNet-to-VNet Tunnels	P2S SSTP Connections	P2S IKEv2/Op	Aggregate Throughput Benchmark	BGP	Zone-redundant
Generation	Basic	Max. 10	Max. 128	Not Supp	100 Mbps	Not Supported	No
Generation	VpnGw1	Max. 30*	Max. 128	Max. 250	650 Mbps	Supported	No
Generation	VpnGw2	Max. 30*	Max. 128	Max. 500	1 Gbps	Supported	No
Generation	VpnGw3	Max. 30*	Max. 128	Max. 1000	1.25 Gbps	Supported	No
Generation	VpnGw1AZ	Max. 30*	Max. 128	Max. 250	650 Mbps		

Figure 12.13: VPN SKU

7. Once you provide all the details and select the option, it will look like the following screenshot:

Create virtual network gateway

Basics   Tags   Review + create

Azure has provided a planning and design guide to help you configure the various VPN gateway options. Learn more.

Project details

Select the subscription to manage deployed resources and costs. Use resource groups like folders to organize and manage all your resources.

Subscription *

Resource group ⓘ   Select a virtual network to get resource group

Instance details

Name *

Region *   (US) West US

Gateway type * ⓘ   ◉ VPN   ◯ ExpressRoute

VPN type * ⓘ   ◉ Route-based   ◯ Policy-based

SKU * ⓘ   VpnGw1

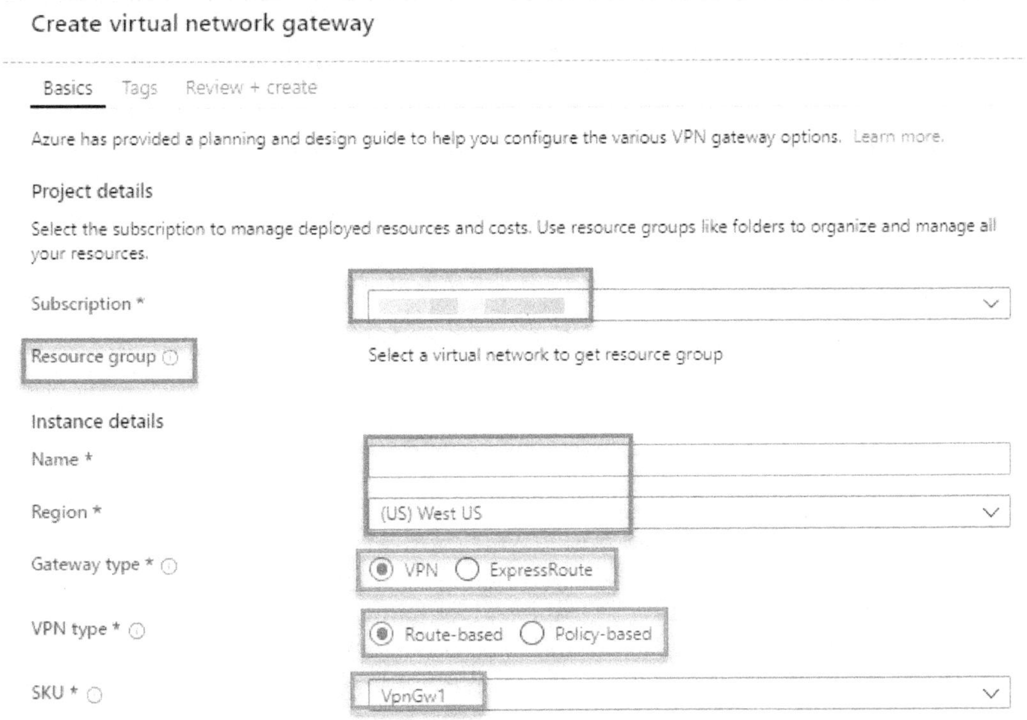

Figure 12.14: VPN gateway configuration

8. Select the generation which is **Generation 1**, and let it be the default.

9. Select the virtual network from the drop-down menu.

10. Provide the public IP name or use an existing one.

11. Select **Enable active-active mode** which will be the default value, but if you want to configure it, then you need to add another public IP in the configuration.

12. Select the default option in **Configure BGP ASN** as **Disabled**.

13. Click on **Review + create**. Please take a look at the following screenshot:

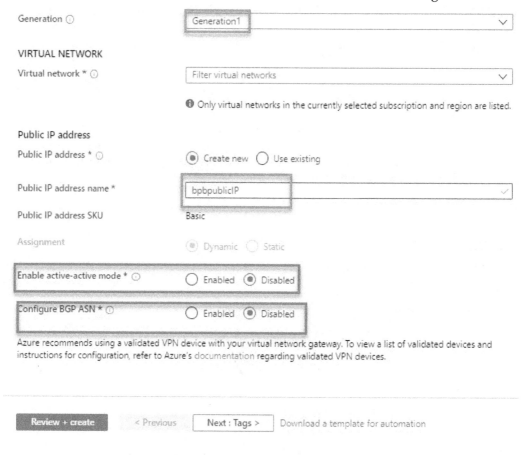

Figure 12.15: VPN gateway creation

It will take up 30 to 45 minutes to create a VNet gateway. Once it gets created, you can configure the site-to-site VPN and VNet-to-VNet connectivity, and we will explain this in the next section.

Now, let us see how to configure the VNet-to-VNet gateway. The VNet gateway is required to be created for both the VNets, and it is used to connect the two subscriptions and two different regions.

Site-to-site VPN

The Azure site-to-site VPN is used to connect the Azure network to on-premises data centers over the IPsec IPsec/IKE (**IKEv1** or **IKEv2**) tunnel. It requires an on-premises VPN device to configure an S2S connection. Take a look at the following diagram:

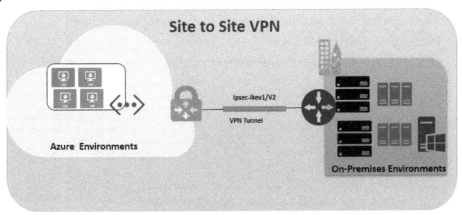

Figure 12.16: Azure site-to-site VPN

To create a site-to-site VPN, it requires the following requirement list:

- Azure VNet
- VNet gateway
- Local network gateway
- Connection
- On-premises VNet connection

Local Area network Gateway: It represents the hardware or software VPN device in your local network. We can use this with a connection to set up a site-to-site VPN connection between an Azure virtual network and your local network.

As I have mentioned all the steps to create the VNet and Vet gateway, let us now see how to create a local area network:

1. Please go to marketplace and search for `Local network gateway.` Take a look at the following screenshot:

Figure 12.17: Azure local area network gateway

2. Please provide the local gateway name.
3. Please provide the public IP address of your on-premises VPN devices.
4. Please provide the address range of the on-premises network.
5. Please provide the resources group, name, and location.
6. Please click on **Create**. Take a look at the following screenshot:

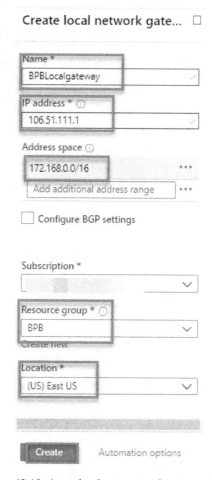

Figure 12.18: Azure local area network gateway details

Once the local area network gateway is created, please create the connection and configure the site-to-site VPN.

Site-to-site VPN connection creation

Once you configure the site-to-site VPN, perform all the given steps:

1. Please go to the marketplace and search for **Connection**.

2. Click on **Connection**.

3. Click on **Create**. Please take a look at the following screenshot:

Figure 12.19: Azure S2S connection creation

4. Once you click on **Create**, follow the given steps:

   a. Please select the connection type as **Site-to-site (IPsec)**, **VNet-to-VNet**, or **ExpressRoute** from the drop-down menu.

   b. Select the subscription.

   c. Please select the resource group.

   d. Select the location. Please take a look at the following screenshot:

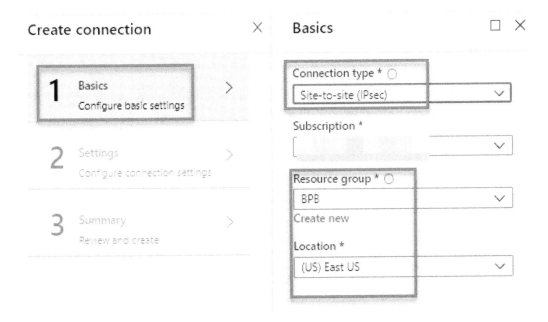

Figure 12.20: Azure S2S connection basic details

5. Go to the **Settings** tab and perform the following steps:
    a. Please select the VNet gateway in your specific region.
    b. Select the local area network gateway as we created earlier.
    c. Provide the name of the connection.
    d. Provide the passkey. It can be created in your on-premises VPN device or Azure connections.
    e. Select the protocol **IKEv2** and let it be the default value.
    f. Click on **OK**. Please take a look at the following screenshot:

Figure 12.21: Azure S2S connection basic details

6. In **Summary**, please verify the details and click on **OK** to create the connection. Please take a look at the following screenshot:

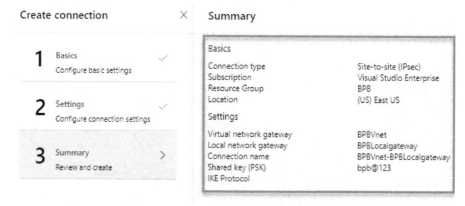

Figure 12.22: Azure S2S connection summary

7. Once the connection is created, you will see the status connecting and data in and out. It will take some time to connect, and after that, you need to ask your network team to create the S2S tunnel in your on-premises VPN device as well. Please take a look at the following screenshot:

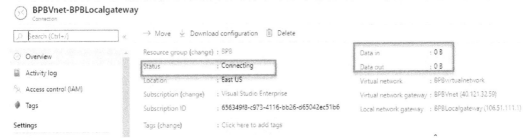

Figure 12.23: Azure S2S connection summary

Now, you can create an S2S connection. Let us see how to create the VNet-to-VNet connectivity.

VNet-to-VNet connectivity creation

Let us see how to create the VNet-to-VNet connectivity. You would require the following configuration before you set up the VNet-to-VNet connections:

- Azure VNet
- You would need two VNet gateways for both the VNets
- Connection

Once you set up the preceding components, follow the given steps to create the connections:

1. Please go to the marketplace and search for a connection.

2. Then, click on the connection to create the VNet-to-VNet connection. Please take a look at the following screenshot:

Figure 12.24: Azure VNet-to-VNet connection summary

3. Select the connection type **VNet-to-VNent**.

4. Select the subscription and resources group.

5. Select the location as **(US) East US**. Please take a look at the following screenshot:

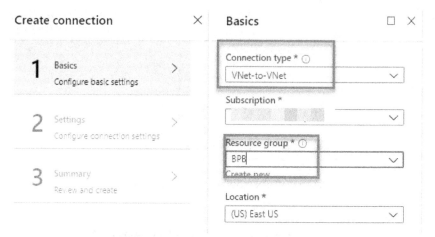

Figure 12.25: Azure VNet to VNet connection basic settings

6. Please select the source and destination VNet gateway.

7. Please provide the name of the connections.

8. Please provide the shared access key.

9. Click on **OK**. Please take a look at the following screenshot:

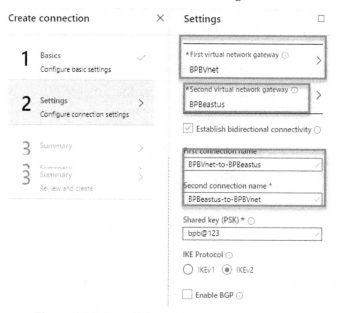

Figure 12.26: Azure VNet-to-VNet connection settings

10. Please verify the **Summary** section and click on **OK** to create the VNet-to-VNet connections. Refer to the following screenshot:

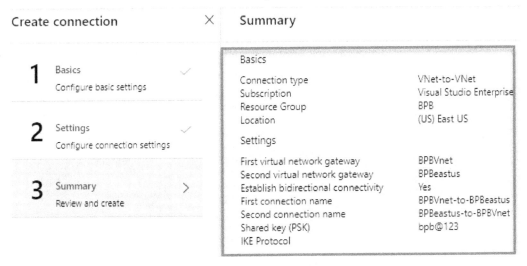

Figure 12.27: Azure VNet-to-VNet connection summary

11. Once the VNet connection is created, you can see that the status is **Connected**. Please take a look at the following screenshot:

Figure 12.28: Azure Vnet-to-VNet connection status

Now, we learned how to configure the site-to-site connection and VNet-to-VNet connectivity. In the next section, I will discuss the express route and set up the express route connection which is almost the same we did in the site-to-site connectivity.

ExpressRoute connection

ExpressRoute is a direct, dedicated connection from your WAN (not over the public internet) to Microsoft services and Azure. We can configure the site-to-site VPN and ExpressRoute connections for the same virtual network for load balancing or high availability.

We can configure a site-to-site VPN as a secure failover path for ExpressRoute or use site-to-site VPNs to connect to sites that are not part of your network, but that are connected through ExpressRoute. Please take a look at the following diagram that shows ExpressRoute:

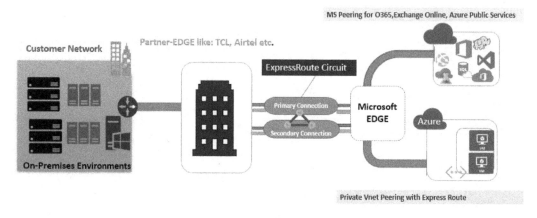

Figure 12.29: ExpressRoute

ExpressRoute configuration

Now, we will discuss how to configure the express route. For this, we require the following:

- Azure VNet
- ExpressRoute circuit
- VNet gateway with ExpressRoute
- Connection

I have explained how to create an Azure VNet and VNet gateway. Let us now see how to configure the ExpressRoute circuit in Azure:

1. Please search for express route from the marketplace.
2. Click on **+Add**.
3. Please provide the express route circuit name.
4. Please provide the name that will be your ISP provider name like **Airtel, AT&T**, and so on.
5. Please select the peering location from the drop-down menu.
6. Please select the bandwidth **50Mbps** to **10Gbps.**
7. Then, click on create.

Please take a look at the following screenshot:

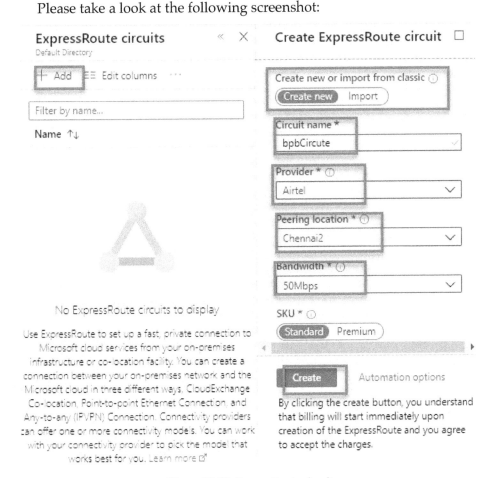

Figure 12.30: ExpressRoute circuit

8. Once the ExpressRoute circuit is created, follow the site-to-site connection steps and select the ExpressRoute circuit name. Then, create the connections.

Note: ISP providers can configure the on-premises express route setup and the circuit creation will be done by your ISP and with your network team.

Conclusion

In this chapter, we discussed VNet and how to set up the VNet gateway and configure the site-to-site connection, express route, and VNet-to-VNet connections. In the next chapter, we will discuss the Azure network security group and IP address types. We will also discuss how to create and configure the Azure security group rules and how to associate a subnet NSG with VMs and subnets.

References

- Configure a VNet-to-VNet VPN gateway connection using PowerShell: **https://docs.microsoft.com/en-us/azure/vpn-gateway/vpn-gateway-vnet-vnet-rm-ps**

- What is an Azure virtual network: **https://docs.microsoft.com/en-us/azure/virtual-network/virtual-networks-overview**

- Connect Azure VPN gateways to multiple on-premises policy-based VPN devices using PowerShell: **https://docs.microsoft.com/en-us/azure/vpn-gateway/vpn-gateway-connect-multiple-policybased-rm-ps**

- VPN gateway: **https://docs.microsoft.com/en-us/azure/vpn-gateway/vpn-gateway-about-vpngateways**

- Virtual network peering: **https://docs.microsoft.com/en-us/azure/virtual-network/virtual-network-peering-overview**

- Modify local network gateway settings using the Azure portal: **https://docs.microsoft.com/en-us/azure/virtual-network/virtual-network-peering-overview**

- ExpressRoute connectivity models: **https://docs.microsoft.com/en-us/azure/expressroute/expressroute-connectivity-models**

- ExpressRoute circuits and peering: **https://docs.microsoft.com/en-us/azure/expressroute/expressroute-connectivity-models**

- For more details, visit Azure4you blog post: **https://azure4you.com/**

Chapter 13
Configuring Load Balancing

In this chapter, we will discuss Azure DNS and learn how to create public and private DNS zones. We will also discuss the Azure load balancer and see how to create and configure the Azure load balancer and DNS. We will also cover the Azure application gateway and traffic manager.

Structure

The following topics will be covered in this chapter:

- Azure DNS
- Configure the custom DNS settings
- Configure private and public DNS zones
- Configure the internal load balancer
- Configure load balancing rules
- Configure the public load balancer
- Troubleshoot load balancing
- Application gateway
- Traffic manager

Objectives

In this chapter, you will learn how to configure and set up the load balancer for Azure VMs/applications using the Azure load balancer, Traffic manager, and application gateway. We will also cover Azure DNS and see how to create your custom Azure DNS and configure it.

Azure DNS

Azure DNS is a hosting service that provides the DNS domain and the name resolutions using the Azure infrastructure. You can host the domains in Azure and manage the records. Using Azure DNS, you cannot buy the custom domain. To buy the domain name, you need to use third-party domain register name sites like godaddy.com, and so on.

Azure DNS manages the Azure records, and we can use it for external resources as well. Azure DNS is an integrated part of the Azure portal and it is used for Azure services like billing, support contract, and so on.

The following are the details of the Azure DNS delegation, zones, and DNS registrar usage:

- **Zone delegation**
    - o Azure DNS allows us to host a DNS zone and manage the DNS records for a domain in Azure.
    - o Azure DNS is not the domain registrar.

- **Domains and zones**
    - o The domain name system is a hierarchy of domains. The hierarchy starts with the root domain.
    - o Top-level domains such as `.com, .net, .org, .uk, or .jp.`
    - o Second-level domains such as `org.uk` or `co.jp`, and so on.
    - o The domains in the DNS hierarchy are hosted using separate DNS zones.
    - o Zones are globally distributed and hosted by DNS name servers around the world.

- **DNS zone**
    - o The domain is a unique name in the domain name system, for example, `Bpbcloud.com`.
    - o A DNS zone is used to host the DNS records for a domain.

o For example, the domain `rcloudweb.com` may contain several DNS records such as mail. `rcloudweb.com` (for a mail server) and `www.rcloudweb.com` (for a website).

- **Domain registrar**

  o The domain registrar is a company who can provide internet domain names.

  o They will verify if the internet domain you want to use is available and allows you to purchase it.

  o Once the domain name is registered, you will be the legal owner of the domain name.

If you already have an internet domain, you will be able to use the current domain registrar to delegate to Azure DNS.

Azure DNS creation

Now, let us try and create the Azure DNS services from the Azure portal:

1. Please go to the marketplace.

2. Please search for **DNS** and click on **DNS zone**.

3. Click on **Create** as shown in the following screenshot:

Figure 13.1: Azure DNS creation

4. Please select the subscription and resource group name.

5. Please provide the DNS name in this format **XYZ.com**.

6. Please click on **Review + create** as shown in the following screenshot:

Create DNS zone

Basics   Tags   Review + create

A DNS zone is used to host the DNS records for a particular domain. For example, the domain 'contoso.com' may contain a number of DNS records such as 'mail.contoso.com' (for a mail server) and 'www.contoso.com' (for a web site). Azure DNS allows you to host your DNS zone and manage your DNS records, and provides name servers that will respond to DNS queries from end users with the DNS records that you create. Learn more.

Project details

Subscription *

        Resource group *   BPB

Create new

Instance details

Name *   bpbdns.com

Resource group location ⓘ   (US) East US

Review + create   < Previous   Next : Tags >   Download a template for automation

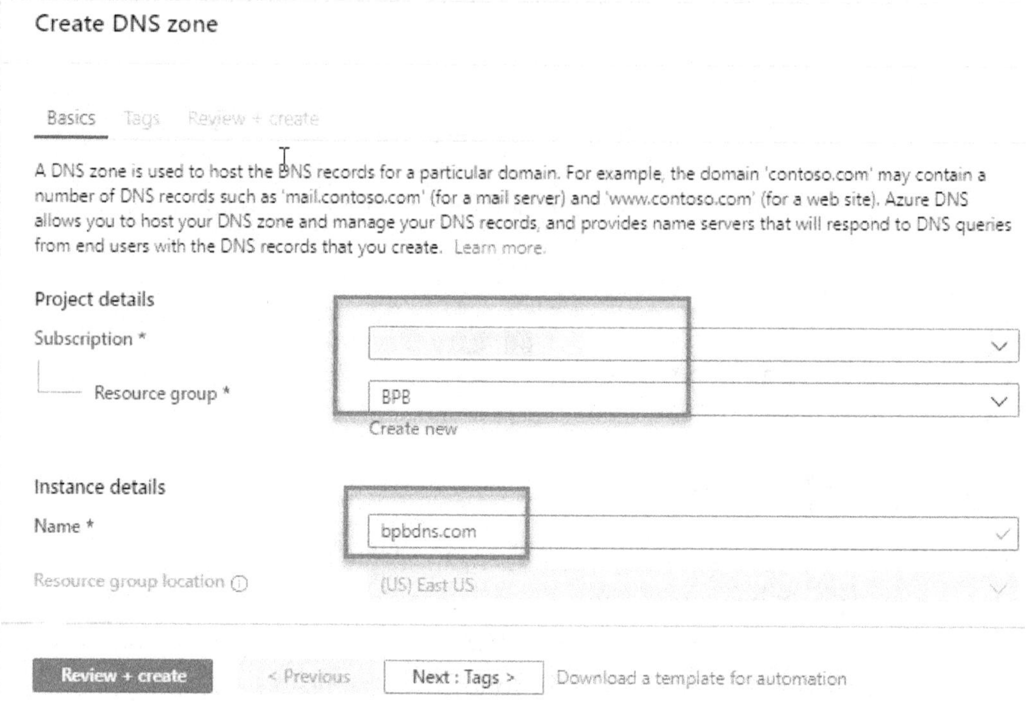

Figure 13.2: Azure DNS

Once the DNS zones are created, it will look like the following screenshot:

Figure 13.3: Azure DNS configuration

Azure DNS record creation

Azure DNS records various types of data and helps to identify the services based on the records. Generally, records map a domain to its IP address. The following records in the table will help you to understand the usage of each record:

Record name	Full name	Usage
A(IPv4) AAAA(IPv6)	Address	It maps a host name like, mail.bpb.com to an IP address 153.120.10.20.
CNAME	Chronicle name	It is used to point one host record to another like test.Bpb.com to **email.Azure4you.com**.
MX	Mail exchange	It points to the host that will receive an email from that domain. The MX record must be a point to A record not to the CNAME record.
NS	Name server	It delegates a DNS zone to the specified authoritative name server.
SOA	Start of authority	It defines the authoritative record of zones.
SRV	Services	It is a location host that provides specific services like Skype-**Session Initiation Protocol (SIP)**, which is used in Skype, Teams, and so on.
TXT	Text	It records a human-readable text field in DNS.

Table 13.1: Record names and their usage

Let us try and create the Azure DNS records:

1. Please go to **DNS zone**.

2. Please click on **+Record set**.

3. Please provide the name of the A record.

4. Please select the type of record from the drop-down menu.

5. Provide the **Time-to-Live (TTL)** value.

6. The IP address of the A record or any other record name/IP is based on the description asked. Please take a look at the following screenshot:

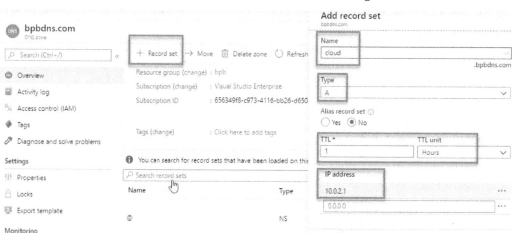

Figure 13.4: Azure DNS configuration

Now, we have shown how to create the DNS server in Azure and explained its usage.

Azure load balancer

The Azure load balancer can be used to distribute the traffic across the backend server and resources which will help to scale your services and create a high availability of your services. It provides low latency and high throughput. Load balancers support **Transmission Control Protocol (TCP)** and **User Datagram Protocol (UDP).**

Azure load balancers are of the following two types:

- **Internal load balancer:** It is used to load balance the internal traffic between Azure virtual machines. You can use hybrid connectivity if you want to load balance the on-premises VMs. In this load balancer, there are private IP addresses that are assigned to the front-end IP configuration.

- **External load balancer:** It is used for your external application which communicates with the internet traffic. In this load balancer, there are public IP addresses that are assigned to the front-end IP configuration.

Azure load balancers provide the following two types of Stock-keeping-Unit(SKU):

- **Basic:** The basic SKU supports up to 100 instances and the virtual machine should be in an availability set, single, or in the scale set. The protocol has been supported on TCP and UDP. It does not support TCP reset on idle, SLA, multiple front-end and availability zone, and so on.

- **Standard:** The standard SKU supports up to 1000 instances and the virtual machine should be in an availability set, single or in a scale set. The protocol has been supported on TCP, HTTP, and HTTPS. It supports TCP reset on idle, SLA, multiple front-end and availability zone, and so on.

Azure internal load balancer

Let us try to create an Azure private load balancer and understand its components.

Before you create an Azure internal load, you need an Azure virtual network to be created and Azure virtual machine in an availability set or single VMs which can be used to associate with the Azure internal load balancer backend pool:

1. Please go to the marketplace and search for an Azure load balancer.
2. Click on **Create** as shown in the following screenshot:

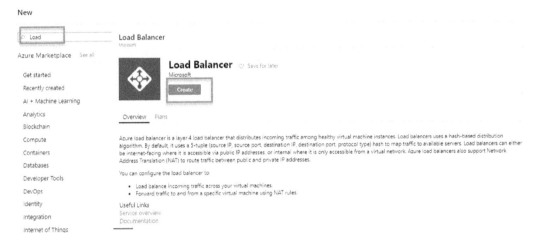

Figure 13.5: Azure load balancer

3. Please select the subscription for which you want to create an internal load balancer.
4. Please select the appropriate resource group.
5. Please provide the name of the load balancer.
6. Select the region for which you want to deploy the load balancer.
7. Please select the load balancer type: *internal* or *external* based on your project.
8. Please select the SKU type as **Basic**.
9. Please select the virtual network and subnet.
10. Please select the IP address assignment. Let it be the default, but if you are deploying for production, please select **Static** instead of **Dynamic**.

11. Please click on **Review + create** as shown in the following screenshot:

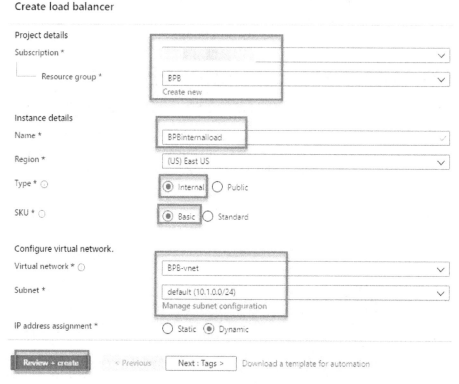

Figure 13.6: Azure load balancer creation details

12. Once you click on create, the Azure load balancer will be created after 10 to 15 minutes. Once it is created, it will look like the following screenshot. Let us see how to configure the backend pool, health probe, load balancing rule, NAT rule, and so on:

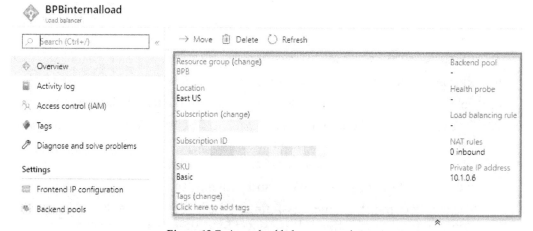

Figure 13.7: Azure load balancer overview

Front-end IP configuration

All the traffic will come first to the front-end IP addressed and it will distribute the traffic based on the backend pool connectivity and the load balancers rule.

Perform the following steps:

1. Go to the load balancer and select **Front-end IP configuration** under the **Settings** tab.
2. Click on **+ Add**.
3. Provide the name of the front-end load balancer.
4. Select the subnet from the drop-down menu.
5. Click on **Add** to add the frontend IP.

By default, when you create the load balancer, an automatic front-end IP configuration will be configured, but if you want to add the front-end IP, you need to follow the preceding process to add the new front-end configuration. Take a look at the following screenshot:

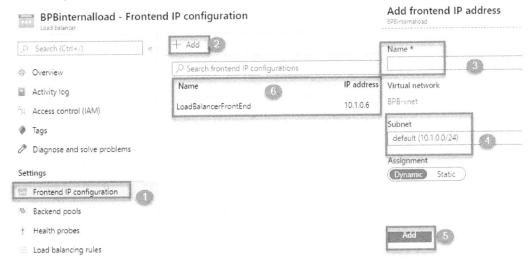

Figure 13.8: Azure load balancer frontend IP configuration

Once your front-end IP configuration is done, please configure the backend pool.

Azure backend pool

The Azure backend pool has your server or services configuration which needs to be load-balanced and it routes the traffic from the front-end IP. It should be a single virtual machine or scale set to configure it.

1. Provide the backend pool name.
2. Select the virtual machine or scale set you want to associate.
3. Select the virtual machine and the IP address from the drop-down menu.
4. Click on **+ Add** as shown in the following screenshot:

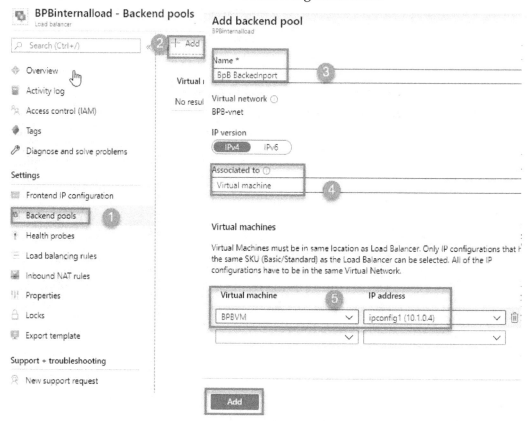

Figure 13.9: Azure load balancer backend pool configuration

Health probes

It helps us to find the failure of the application on the backend endpoint. The health probe helps to find out when to send the new traffic flow to the backend endpoint just like a busy/free status. If the backend endpoint status fails, it stops and does not send any new traffic flow to that instance.

Let us create the health probe for the load balancer configuration:

1. Please go to **Health probes** under the **Settings** tab.
2. Please click on **+ Add**.
3. Please provide the name of the health probe.

4. Please select the TCP/UDP protocol from the drop-down menu.

5. Let the Interval be set to the default value, which means the health probe will check the backend endpoint status in a specific time as configured in the interval.

6. Please configure the unhealthy threshold as per your project requirements. It means that if it continuously fails for two times or more, then it will consider the backed endpoint status as failed and stop sending the traffic.

7. Click on **OK** to add the health probe.

   Please take a look at the following screenshot:

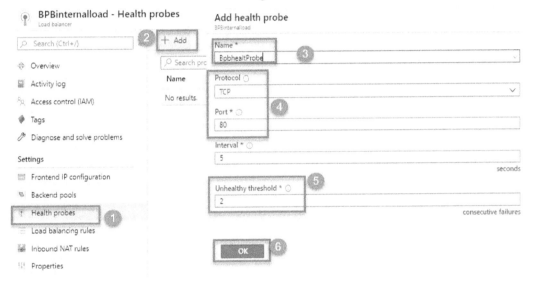

Figure 13.10: Azure load balancer health probe configuration

8. Please click on **Load balancing rules** under the **Settings** tab.

9. Please provide the rule name.

10. Please provide the protocol type **TCP/UDP**.

11. Please provide the port number and backend port of services.

12. Please select the backend pool and health probe.

13. Please select the session persistence and idle timeout.

14. Please click on the **OK** button to create a load balancing rule.

Take a look at the following screeснhot:

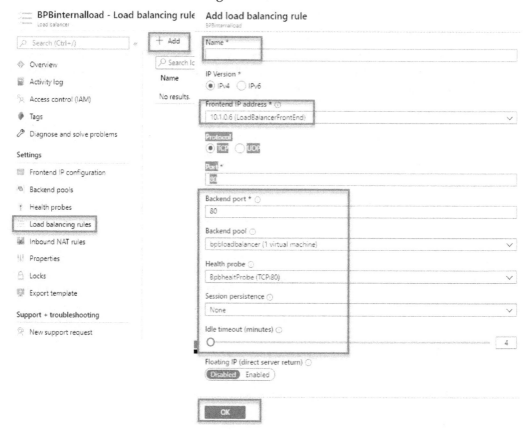

Figure 13.11: *Azure load balancer rule configuration*

Now, your load balance configuration has been completed and your services will use the Azure load balancer capability.

Application gateway

An application gateway is an application layer (OSI layer 7) load balancing, which helps the web traffic load balancer to enable the management traffic to your web applications. The application gateway can make the routing decision as per the HTTP/HTTPS request to route the traffic to the URI path or the host VM.

The Azure application gateway can do the URL-based routing. It provides the following features:

- **Secure sockets layer (SSL/TLS) termination:** In this feature, the application gateway provides an SSL/TLS termination at the gateway and after that, traffic will flow (encrypted) to the backend servers/applications.

- **Autoscaling:** The application gateway `standard_v2` supports and provides an autoscaling feature that helps to scale up and down the application gateway if there are any changes in the traffic load.

- **Zone redundancy:** The application gateway `standard_v2` supports multiple zones availability.

- **Static VIP:** The application gateway `standard_v2` supports a static VIP which means it will make sure your VIP associated with this application gateway does not change.

- **Web application firewall:** It provides centralized protection to your web application for common vulnerabilities. It is based on the OWASP 3.1, 3.0, and 2.9. It helps you protect from SQL injection, scripting attack, and so on.

- **URL-based routing:** This URL-based routing allows you to route traffic to the backend server pool based on your URL path. Let us say **https://bpb. com/video or https://bpb.com/images**, and so on.

- **Multiple-site hosting:** We can host up 100 web applications in one application gateway, and each application can be directed to its backend pool.

- **Redirection:** It provides the HTTP/HTTPs based redirection to make sure all the communication between users and its application has been encrypted.

- **Session affinity:** The cookie-based session provides the feature – if you want the user session on the same server for processing the request.

  Please take a look at the following diagram:

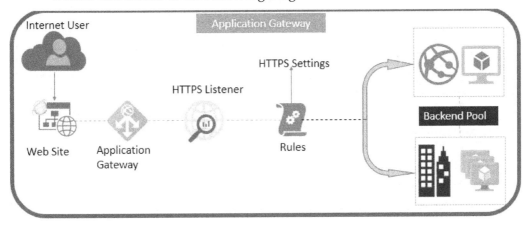

Figure 13.12: Application gateway

Let us see how to create the application gateway and configure it:

1. Please click on **Create a resource**.
2. Search for **Application gateway**.

3. Click on the **Create** button to create an application gateway as shown in the following screenshot:

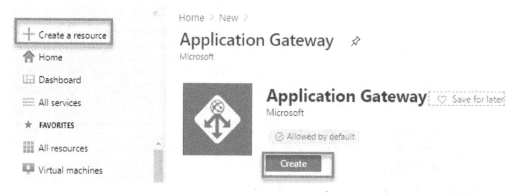

Figure 13.13: Application gateway creation

Once you click on the application gateway creation, follow the given steps:

1. Select the subscription for which you want to create an application gateway.

2. Create or select an existing resources group.

3. Provide the application gateway name as per your organization's standard.

4. Select the region.

5. Select the tier:

   - **Standard:** This standard tier does not support autoscaling and zone redundancy.
   - **Standard V2:** This standard tier supports autoscaling and zone redundancy.
   - **WAF:** It supports WAF 2.9 and 3.0.
   - **WAF V2:** It supports WAF 3.1.

6. Provide the autoscaling as **Yes** or **No**. If yes, then provide the minimum and maximum scale unit.

7. Provide the virtual network and subnet which does not have a routing table.

8. Once you provide all the details as shown in the following screenshot, please click on **Next** to configure the front-end configuration:

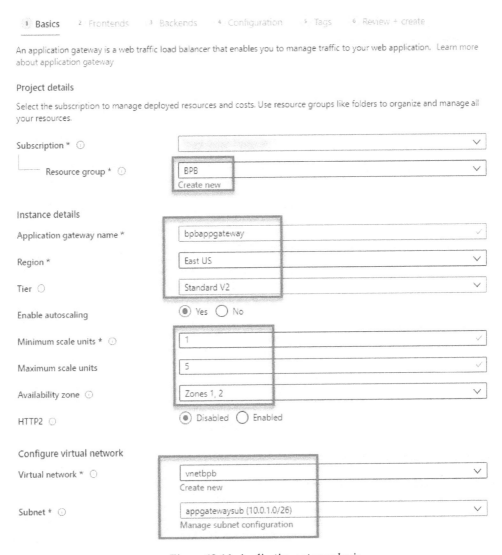

Figure 13.14: Application gateway basic

The application gateway front-end is where all the reapplication traffic will arrive and then get routed to your apps.

Let us configure the front-end IP configuration and follow the given configuration:

- **Public:** If you have a public-facing application, then select **Public** and configure the public IP.

- **Private:** If you have your internal application, then configure the **Private** option.

- **Both:** If you want you to configure your public and internal application, then select **Both**.

Please take a look at the following screenshot:

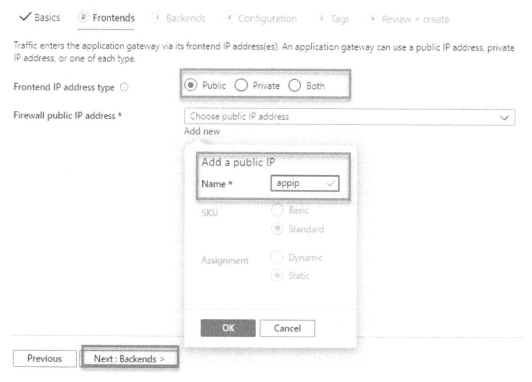

Figure 13.15: Application gateway front-end configuration

Once you are done with this configuration, please select the backend configuration. The application backend pool is where your application/host has been configured to route the traffic based on your user request.

1. Please click on **Add a backend pool**.

2. Provide the name of the backend pool.

3. Please select **Yes** or **No** in **Add backend pool without targets**. If yes, please provide the backend pool configuration as follows:

   - IP address or FQDN name

- Virtual machine
- VMMS
- App services

4. Once you select this, please click on **Next** for the configuration as shown in the following screenshot:

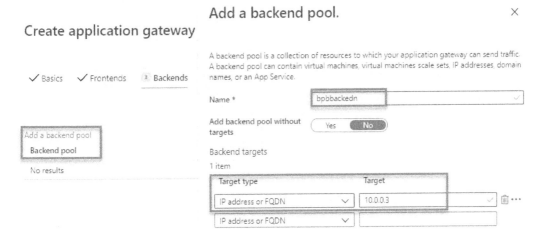

Figure 13.16: Application gateway backend configuration

5. Once you are done with the backend configuration, let us look at the configuration part where you need to set up the routing rule for your application.

We will now configure the HTTP/HTTPS listener and backend routing rule to redirect the traffic.

Let us just configure the listener:

1. Provide the name of the listener.

2. Select the front-end.

3. Select the protocol **HTTP** or **HTTPS** and port **80** or **443**.

4. Select the listener type as **Multi site** if you are planning to add multiple sites or select **Basic**.

5. Select the error page URL as shown in the following screenshot:

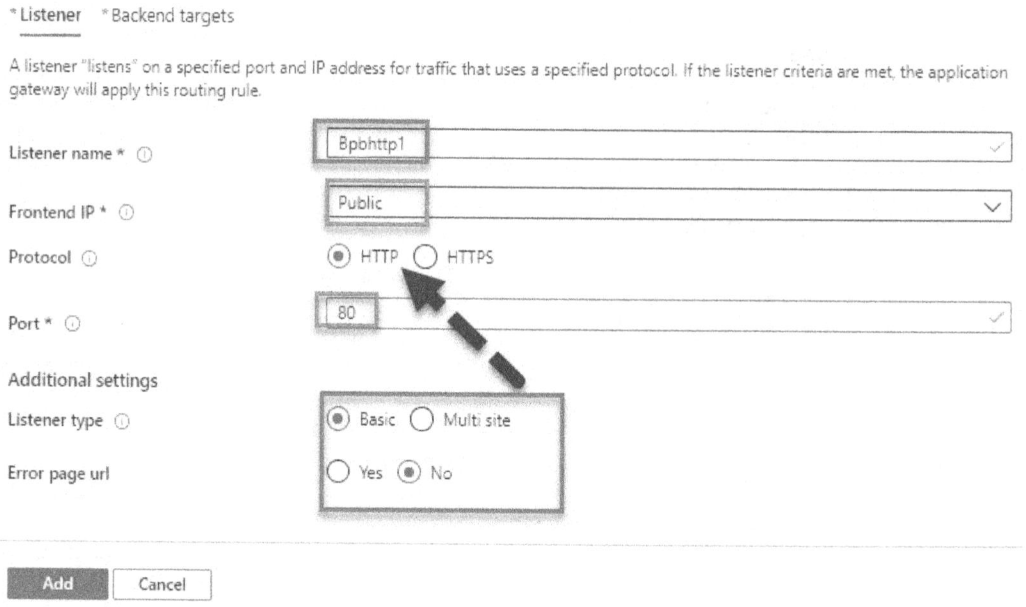

* Listener   * Backend targets

A listener "listens" on a specified port and IP address for traffic that uses a specified protocol. If the listener criteria are met, the application gateway will apply this routing rule.

Listener name * ⓘ	Bpbhttp1
Frontend IP * ⓘ	Public
Protocol ⓘ	⦿ HTTP ◯ HTTPS
Port * ⓘ	80
Additional settings	
Listener type ⓘ	⦿ Basic ◯ Multi site
Error page url	◯ Yes ⦿ No

Add   Cancel

Figure 13.17: Application gateway listener

As we have configured the listener, we will now configure the backend target:

1. Provide the rule name.

2. Select the target type either as **Backend pool** or **Redirection** based on your requirements.

3. Select the backend pool from the drop-down menu as shown in the following screenshot:

Add a routing rule   ✕

Configure a routing rule to send traffic from a given frontend IP address to one or more backend targets. A routing rule must contain a listener and at least one backend target.

Rule name * | bpbaps   ✓ |

* Listener   * Backend targets

Choose a backend pool to which this routing rule will send traffic. You will also need to specify a set of HTTP settings that define the behavior of the routing rule.

Target type   ⦿ Backend pool   ◯ Redirection

                       | bpbbackedn   ⌄ |
Backend target * ⓘ   Add new

                       | bpbuser   ⌄ |
HTTP settings * ⓘ   Add new

Path-based routing

You can route traffic from this rule's listener to different backend targets based on the URL path of the request. You can also apply a different set of HTTP settings based on the URL path.

Path based rules

Path   Target name   HTTP setting name   Backend pool

No additional targets to display

Add multiple targets to create a path-based rule

| Add | | Cancel |

Figure 13.18: Application gateway backend target

4. Please click on **HTTP settings** and click on **Add new**.

5. Provide the HTTP setting name.

6. Select the backend pool and port number.

7. Select the cookies-based session and connection draining as per your requirements.

8. Please select the request timeout.

9. If you need to configure a new hostname or the custom hostname, you can also configure it as shown in the following screenshot:

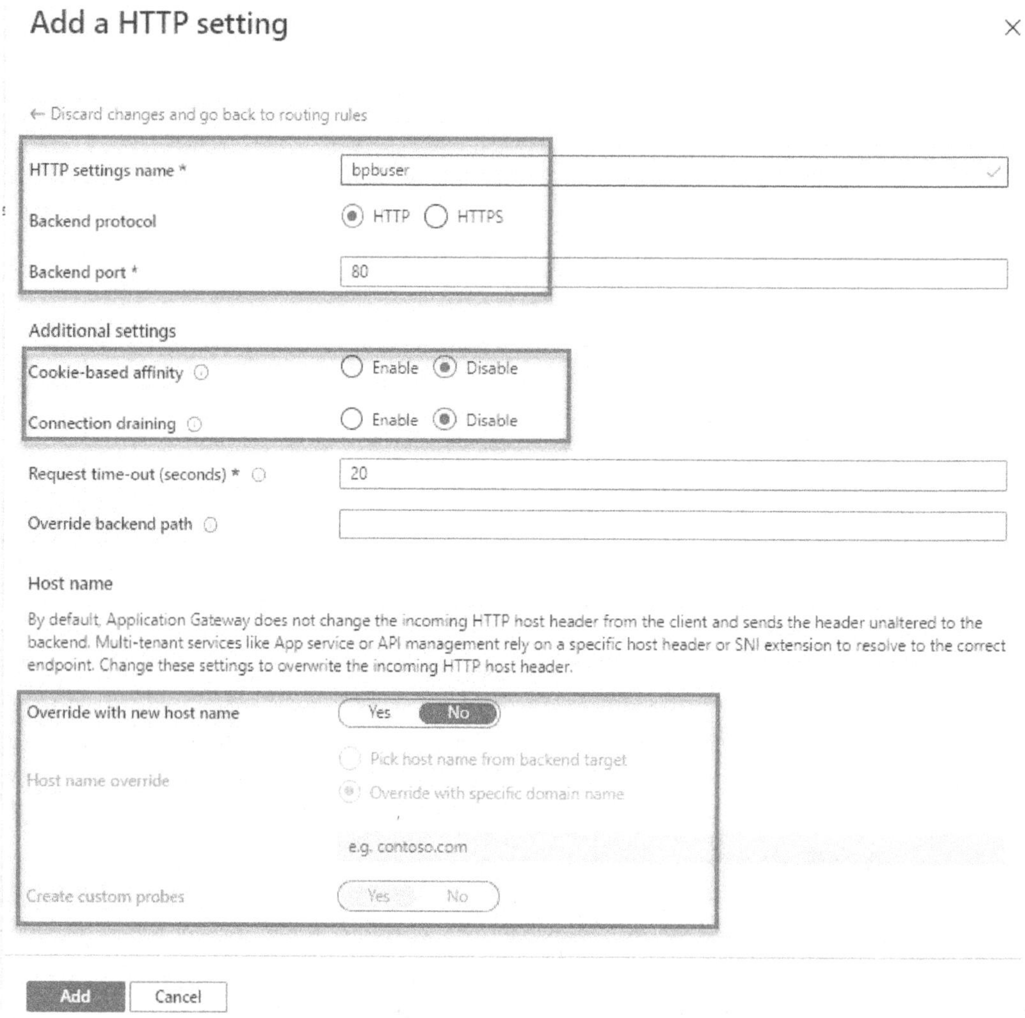

Add a HTTP setting   ✕

← Discard changes and go back to routing rules

HTTP settings name *	bpbuser	✓
Backend protocol	◉ HTTP ◯ HTTPS	
Backend port *	80	

Additional settings

Cookie-based affinity ⓘ	◯ Enable ◉ Disable
Connection draining ⓘ	◯ Enable ◉ Disable

Request time-out (seconds) * ⓘ   20

Override backend path ⓘ

Host name

By default, Application Gateway does not change the incoming HTTP host header from the client and sends the header unaltered to the backend. Multi-tenant services like App service or API management rely on a specific host header or SNI extension to resolve to the correct endpoint. Change these settings to overwrite the incoming HTTP host header.

Override with new host name	Yes **No**
Host name override	◯ Pick host name from backend target ◉ Override with specific domain name e.g. contoso.com
Create custom probes	Yes No

Add   Cancel

Figure 13.19: Application gateway HTTP setting

Once we are done with this configuration, click on the **Tags** tab. If you want to add the tags, please click on **Review + create** as shown in the following screenshot:

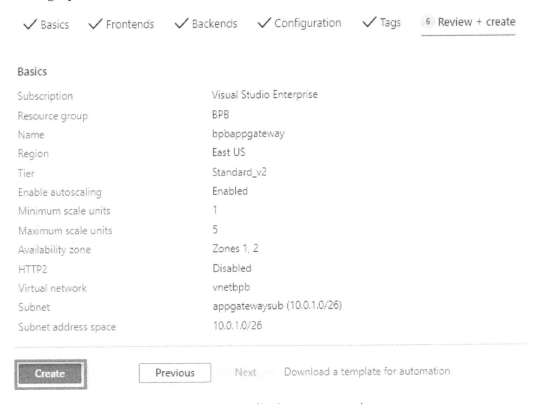

Figure 13.20: Application gateway creation

When you click on the application gateway creation, the application gateway will get created in 10 to 15 minutes.

Azure traffic manager

The Azure traffic manager is a DNS-based traffic load balancer that enables the distribution of traffic and provides high availability to web applications. The traffic manager uses a DNS to direct the traffic to the most appropriate service endpoint based on the traffic routing method.

It provides the following features:

- Application availability
- Application performance
- Hybrid application
- Distributes the traffic to complex environments

Let us create an Azure traffic manager and configure it. Please follow the given steps:

1. Please click on **Create a resource**.

2. Please search for the traffic manager.

3. Please click on the **Create** button to create the traffic manager as shown in the following screenshot:

Figure 13.21: Traffic manager profile creation

4. Please provide the name of the traffic manager.

5. Please provide the routing method from the following to configure it:

    *   **Priority:** It is used when you want to configure the primary site's endpoint for all the traffic and secondary sites for backup.

    *   **Weighted:** Weighted can be configured when you want to distribute the traffic to set off endpoints, according to the weight.

    *   **Performance:** It is used when you want to route the traffic to geographic locations and you want the closest endpoint for low network latency.

    *   **Geographic:** It is used to redirect the traffic to a specific endpoint such as Azure, external, and so on based on the geographic location.

    *   **MultiValue:** This can be configured only when the endpoint has an IPv4/IPv6 address.

    *   **Subnet:** Subnet traffic-routing is used to map sets of end-users IP address (subnet) ranges to a specific endpoint in the traffic manager profile.

6. Select the subscription.

7. Select the resource group.

8. Please click on the **Create** button as shown in the following screenshot

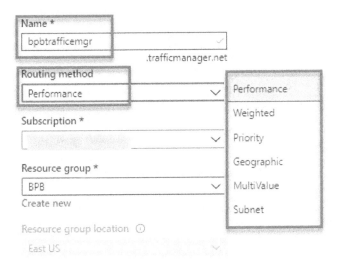

Figure 13.22: Traffic manager creation

Now, we can create the traffic manager and route the traffic using various routing methods in the traffic manager profile.

Conclusion

In this chapter, we discussed the configuration of Azure DNS and how to set up the Azure DNS private and public zones. We also discussed the Azure DNS components and records. We covered the usage of the Azure load balancer and explained how to configure and set up the Azure load balancer. We covered the application gateway and traffic manager profile. We also covered how to configure the application and how to load balance and secure your application.

References

- Azure DNS: **https://docs.microsoft.com/en-in/azure/dns/dns-overview**

- Azure private DNS: **https://docs.microsoft.com/en-in/azure/dns/private-dns-overview**

- Create an Azure DNS zone and record using the Azure portal: **https://docs.microsoft.com/en-in/azure/dns/dns-getstarted-portal**

- Virtual network service endpoints: **https://docs.microsoft.com/en-us/azure/virtual-network/virtual-network-service-endpoints-overview**

- Azure load balancer: **https://docs.microsoft.com/en-us/azure/load-balancer/load-balancer-overview**

- Create a standard load balancer to load balance VMs using the Azure portal: **https://docs.microsoft.com/en-us/azure/load-balancer/quickstart-load-balancer-standard-public-portal**

- Azure application gateway: **https://docs.microsoft.com/en-us/azure/application-gateway/overview#:~:text=Azure%20Application%20Gateway%20is%20a,destination%20IP%20address%20and%20port.**

- Traffic manager: **https://docs.microsoft.com/en-us/azure/traffic-manager/traffic-manager-overview#:~:text=Traffic%20Manager%20uses%20DNS%20to,the%20health%20of%20the%20endpoints.andtext=Traffic%20Manager%20provides%20a%20range,needs%20and%20automatic%20failover%20models.**

- For more details, visit Azure4you blog post: **https://azure4you.com/**

CHAPTER 14
Securing Access to Virtual Networks

In this chapter, we will explain the network security group and its uses. The network security group contains the security rules which allow or deny the inbound/outbound traffic within the subscription and to the outer world. We will discuss network routes and learn how the routes will help to distribute the traffic as per route rules. We will explain the types of IP addresses and learn how they can be assigned to Azure VMs. We will cover the Azure firewall, route table and how to access the VM using Azure Bastion services.

Structure

The following topics will be covered in this chapter:

- Configuration of private and public IP addresses
- Network security group
- Route table
- Configure and deploy the Azure firewall
- Configure and deploy Azure Bastion services
- Evaluate effective security rules

Objectives

One of the objectives is to discuss the Azure firewall and its features. We will discuss how you can protect your Azure network using the Azure firewall. Suppose your customer wants to connect VMs securely so this can be made possible using the Azure Bastion services.

Configuration of private and public IP addresses

The public IP address can be used if you want to connect your application publicly or outside the Azure network. Refer to the following public IP table:

Public IP addresses	IP address association	Dynamic	Static
Virtual machine	NIC	Yes	Yes
Load balancer	Front-end configuration	Yes	Yes
VPN gateway	Gateway IP configuration	Yes	No
Application gateway	Front-end configuration	Yes	No

Table 14.1: Public IP VS private IP

The private IP address can be used for internal communication within the Azure network. Refer to the following private IP table:

IP addresses	IP address association	Dynamic	Static
Virtual machine	NIC	Yes	Yes
Internal load balancer	Front-end configuration	Yes	Yes
Application gateway	Front-end configuration	Yes	Yes

Table 14.2: IP Address association

IP addresses can be assigned dynamically by default from the Azure portal, and you have make them static IP addresses. Let us understand what is a static IP and dynamic IP address.

Static IP is a fixed IP address, and it can't be changed even if you restart your services and deallocate the VM. Dynamic IP is the dynamic IP address that can be changed if you restart your services or deallocate the VM.

Let us understand how to make changes in IP addresses, and we will try to change dynamic IP to static IP:

1. Please select the Azure VMs for which you want to change the IP address from dynamic IP to static IP.

2. Under the **Settings** tab, click on **Networking**.

3. Click on the NIC card name.

4. Go to the **IP configurations** tab.

5. Click on the IP address on the right-hand side of the screen. Take a look at the following screenshot:

Figure 14.1: Azure private IP configuration

6. Please change dynamic to static and click on the **Save** button.

7. After a few minutes, your dynamic IP address will change to static IP as shown in the following screenshot:

Figure 14.2: Azure private IP dynamic IP to static IP

If you want to change the public IP address from dynamic IP to static IP, please follow the given steps:

1. Please go to the **Networking** tab.

2. Select the public IP address name and click on **Configuration**.

3. Please change the selection from **Dynamic** to **Static**.

4. Now, your public IP address will change to static IP address. Take a look at the following screenshot:

Figure 14.3: Azure public IP dynamic IP to static IP

Network security group

Azure network security rules contain the setup of security rules and are used to allow or deny traffic in your Azure network. NSG is followed by two types of rules which are inbound and outbound rules where you can define the port number, IP address, and source and destination for which you want to allow or deny the network traffic.

- **Inbound rule:** The network traffic that allows traffic from the internet to your VM is called an **inbound rule** or allows calls/traffic to your VM from the outer world.

- **Outbound rule:** The network traffic that allows traffic from your VM to the internet is called an **inbound rule** or denies calls/traffic to your VM from the outer world.

Let us see how to create a network security group and how to add an inbound and outbound rule:

1. Go to the marketplace and search for the **network security group**.

2. Click on **Create** as shown in the following screenshot:

Figure 14.4: Network security group

3. Provide the network security group subscription and resource group.

4. Provide the security group name.

5. Select the region you want to create the NSG.

6. Click on **Review + create** the NSG. Take a look at the following screenshot:

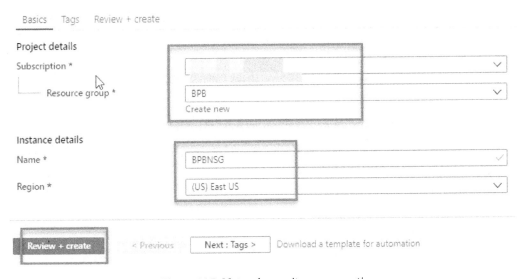

Figure 14.5: Network security group creation

After a few minutes, your network security group will be created and it will be look as follows:

- After the creation of NSG, the default rule will be created with the priority of **65000**, **65001**, and **65500**.

- You can maximum rules that will be created up to **65500** not more than that. Please take a look at the following screenshot:

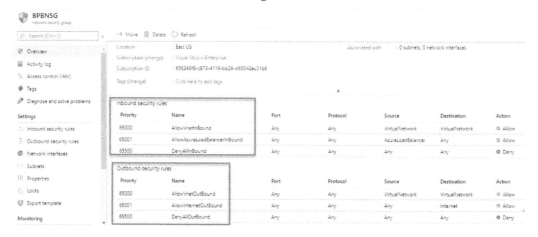

Figure 14.6: Network security group default rule

Let us create the inbound rules in NSG:

1. Select the source **IP Addresses**, virtual network, or services tag.

2. Provide the source IP address.

3. Provide the port number you want to allow.

4. Provide the destination as **IP Addresses**, virtual network, or services tag as shown in the following screenshot:

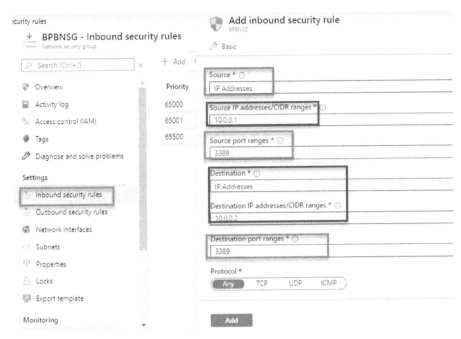

Figure 14.7: Network security group inbound rule

5. Select the action either as **Allow** or **Deny**.

6. Provide the priority **100** or above as the NSG priority will start from **100** to **65500**. Lower the priority, higher the importance; which means the rule has lower priority as **100** will be applied first.

7. Provide the name of NSG and description and click on **Add** as shown in the following screenshot:

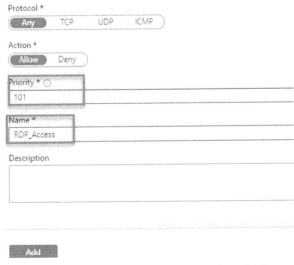

Figure 14.8: Network security group inbound rule

Similarly, if you need to create the outbound rule, you can follow the same steps as given in the inbound rule creation.

Network security group association

The network security group can be associated with Azure VMs, NICs and subnet levels.

NSG when applied on the VM NIC card will have high priority. Let us understand this. If you apply the NSG rule 3389 in the subnet which is allowed, but when traffic reaches the NIC card, NSG which has the denied rule 3389 will deny the traffic at NIC NSG level. You can allow the common ports to the subnet and block the specific port in VMs NIC NSG.

Let us see how to associate the NSG in the subnet:

1. Select the NSG you want to associate with the subnet.
2. Click on **Subnets** under the **Settings** tab.
3. Click on **+ Associate**.
4. Select the virtual network.
5. Select the subnet under the virtual network which you want to associate the NSG with.
6. Click on **OK** to process further as shown in the following screenshot:

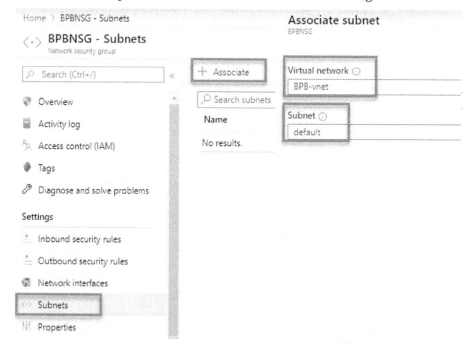

Figure 14.9: Network security associate with subnet

Let us see how to associate the NSG in the NIC card of the VM:

1. Select the **Networking** under the **Settings** tab.

2. Click on the NIC card.

3. Select the **Network security group** option under the **Settings** tab.

4. Click on **Edit** as shown in the following screenshot:

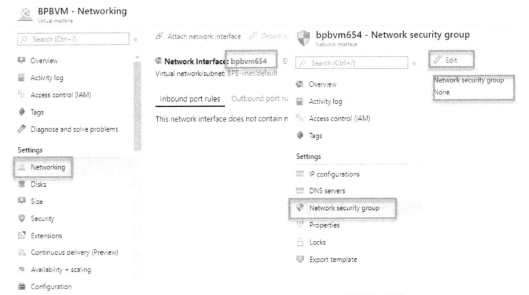

Figure 14.10: Network security associate with VM's NIC

5. Select the NSG and click on **Save**. After some time, NSG will be associated with the VMs NIC and you will be able to see all the rules as shown in the following screenshot:

Figure 14.11: Network security in VM's NIC

Route table

The Azure route table can be used to route the traffic in Azure and on-premises network. Routes will be created automatically when you create the subnet and associated it with automatically. You can create the custom routes to define how the traffic route uses the route table. Let us say you have configured the firewall in between the Azure and on-premises. You can configure the route table and set the rule that all the traffic first will go to the firewall and then to the internet. Hence, you can control the network traffic in Azure and route it as per your organization standards.

Now, let us see how to create the route table and configure it:

1. Search for **Route tables** in the marketplace.
2. Click on **+ Add**.
3. Provide the route table name.
4. Select the resource group name and location.
5. Click on **Create**. After some time, your route table will be created as shown in the following screenshot:

Figure 14.12: Route table creation

Once the route table is created, it will look like the following screenshot:

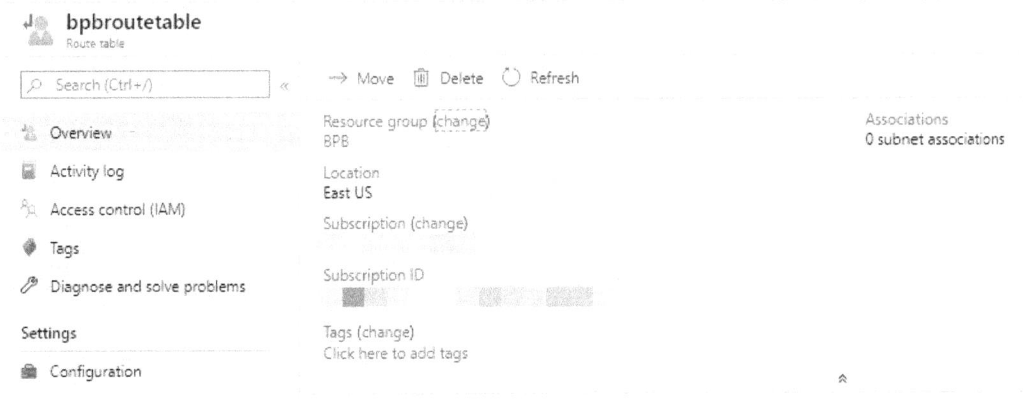

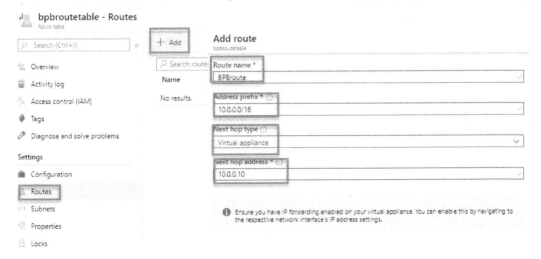

Figure 14.13: Route table

Now, we will configure the route table:

1. Click on **Routes** under the Settings section.

2. Click on **+ Add**.

3. Provide the name of the route table.

4. Provide the address prefix range.

5. Select the virtual appliance (firewall), VNet, VNet gateway, and internet.

6. Click on *Add* to add routes.

    Take a look at the following screenshot:

Figure 14.14: Route table configuration

7. Once the route is configured, please associate it with the subnet.

8. Select **Subnets** under the **Settings** tab.

9. Click on **+ Associate**.

10. Select the VNet.

11. Select the subnet from the drop-down menu.

12. Click on **OK** and associate the VNet. It will take some time to save the settings as shown in the following screenshot:

Figure 14.15: Route table subnet association

Configure and deploy the Azure firewall

Azure firewalls manage the Azure network security and its services which is managed by a virtual network. It is a fully stateful firewall as a service which provides built-in high availability and cloud scalability.

The Azure firewall can be created centrally and managed to enforce the rules and log application and network connectivity policies across subscriptions and virtual networks. The Azure firewall is fully integrated with the Azure Monitor for logging and analytics purpose.

Let us see how to create the Azure firewall and configure it for our subscription:

1. Go to the marketplace or search for **Firewall**.

2. Click on the **Create** button as shown in the following screenshot:

Figure 14.16: Azure firewall

When you click on **Create**, follow the given steps and provide the details as follows:

- Subscription and resource group.
- Name of the firewall.
- Region and availability zone.
- If you want to use an existing or new VNet, select one as per your requirements.
- Provide the virtual network name and address space.
- Provide the subnet.
- Provide the firewall IP address and click on Review + Create.

3. Once you provide all the details, click on Review + create:

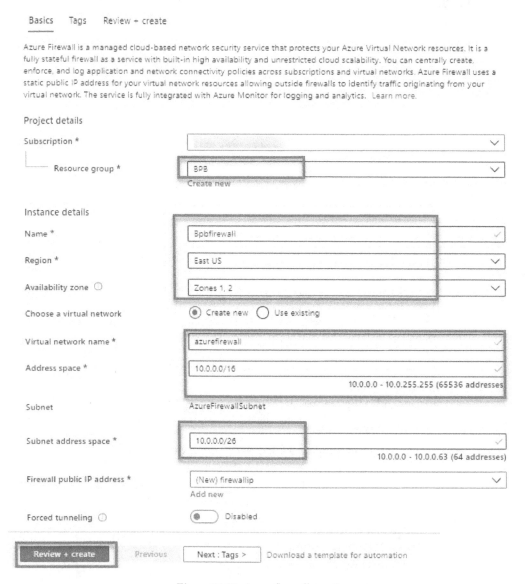

Figure 14.17: Azure firewall creation

It will take a few minutes to create the Azure firewall. Let us see how we can configure the Azure firewall rule.

Go to the Azure firewall and follow the given steps:

1. Provide the name of the rule.

2. Provide the priority of the rule.

3. Provide the following details as shown in the following screenshot:

   - **Protocol: TCP/UDP.**

   - **Source type: IP address/IP group.**

   - Provide the source and destination IP.

   - Provide the translated address and its port.

   Once done, you will be able to create the NAT rule.

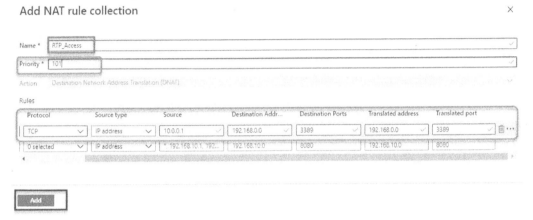

Figure 14.18: Azure firewall NAT rule creation

Once we configure the NAT rule, it will allow the Remote Desktop Protocol (RDP) access to the services.

Let us try to configure an application rule which helps to allow the URL or specific domain URL services such as **http://www.microsoft.com**,.*windows.net, and so on.

1. Provide the name of the rule.

2. Provide the priority of the rule and action as either **Allow/Deny**.

3. Provide the following details as shown in the following screenshot.

4. **FQDN Tags** as follows:

   - Name of the rule

   - Source type as either IP address/IP group

   - Source IP address

   - Add the tags in the drop-down menu

5. **Target FQDNs** as follows:

   - Name of the rule

   - Source type as either IP address/IP group

- Source IP address
- Protocol will be in `msql:1433, TCP:80`, and so on
- Provide the target FQDN or URL you are trying to connect and then click on **Add** as shown in the following screenshot:

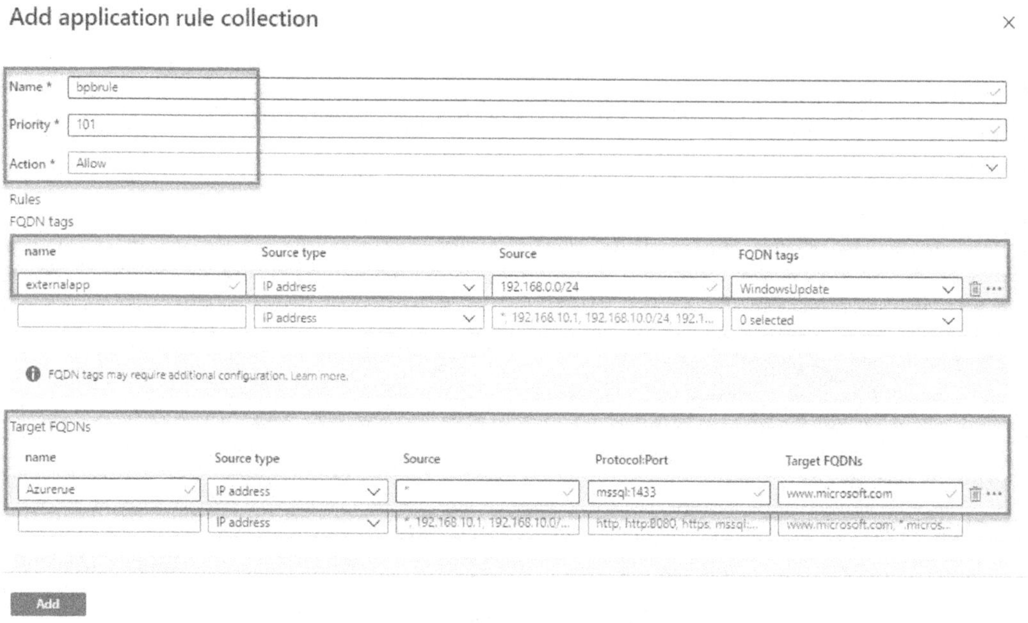

Figure 14.19: Azure firewall application rule

When you click on *Add*, your application rule will be added to the firewall and your Azure services will be able to access the specific target.

Configure and deploy Azure Bastion services

Azure Bastion provides a secure and seamless RDP/SSH access to your virtual machine in your Azure portal. It is PaaS services that have to be provisioned inside your virtual network. If you try and connect the VMs through Bastion services, then your VM does not require a public IP to be associated with it.

It provides the following features of the services:

- **RDP and SSH directly in Azure portal:** We can directly connect the RDP and SSH session from the Azure portal using a single click.
- **Remote session:** It uses an HTML5-based web client that is automatically streamed to your local device, so we can connect to the RDP/SSH session over TLS on port 443.

- **Don't need a public IP to VM:** Azure Bastion opens the RDP/SSH connection to your Azure virtual machine using private IP on your VM. You don't need a public IP on your virtual machine.

- **No hassle of managing NSGs:** You don't require to manage the NSG rules and so on, as it is internally hardened to provide the RDP/SSH connection securely.

Let us just see how we can create the Azure Bastion services in Azure:

1. Go to the Azure portal.

2. Click on **Create a resource**.

3. Search for **Bastion** and click on **Create** as shown in the following screenshot:

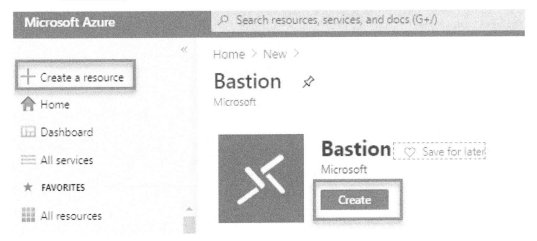

Figure 14.20: *Azure Bastion*

When you click on **Create**, please fill-up the following parameters:

- Subscription
- Resources group
- Name
- Region
- Virtual network
- Subnet with the name of the Azure Bastion subnet with a prefix of at least with /27.

- Provide public IP address details. Refer to the following screenshot:

Create a Bastion

Basics   Tags   Review + create

Bastion allows web based RDP access to your vnet VM. Learn more.

Project details

Subscription *   Visual Studio Enterprise   ⌄

└─── Resource group *   BPB   ⌄
Create new

Instance details

Name *   azurebastionbpb   ✓

Region *   East US   ⌄

Configure virtual networks

Virtual network * ○   azurefirewall   ⌄
Create new

Subnet *   AzureBastionsubnet (10.0.1.0/27)   ⌄
Manage subnet configuration

Public IP address

Public IP address * ①   ⦿ Create new   ○ Use existing

Public IP address name *   azurefirewall-ip   ✓

Public IP address SKU   Standard

Assignment   ○ Dynamic ⦿ Static

Review + create   Previous   Next : Tags >   Download a template for automation

Figure 14.21: Azure Bastion creation

4. Once you are done with the Azure Bastion services creation, verify the services connecting to RDP over the browser. Click on the Azure VM, and then follow the given steps:

    1. Go to the Azure VM settings.

2. Then, click on **Connect**.

3. Select **BASTION**.

4. Provide the user ID/password as shown in the following screenshot:

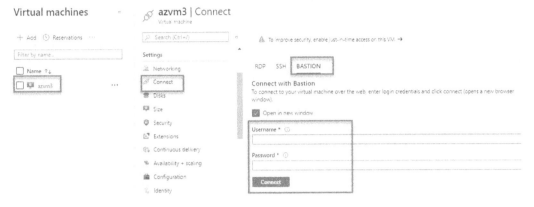

Figure 14.22: Azure Bastion verification

When you click on **Connect**, you will be able to connect to the VM as shown in the following screenshot:

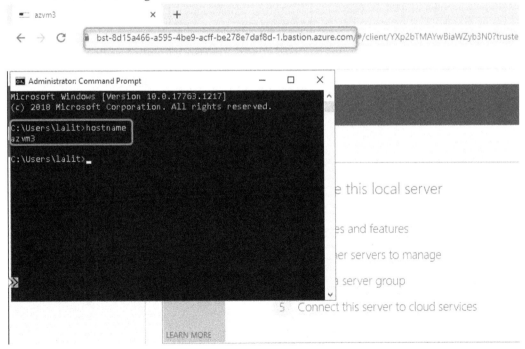

Figure 14.23: Azure Bastion RDP access

Now, we can access the VM using the Bastion services.

Evaluate effective security rules

Network security group effective rules will help you to understand the rules that have been enabled in inbound/outbound on the same page. You can review all those NSG rules at a one-shot.

Let us see how we can see those rules:

Please go to the network security group and select the **Network security group** option and follow the given steps:

- Please go to **Support + troubleshooting**.

- Then, click on the effective security rules.

It will show which VM NSG has been attached and the rules. You can download those rules as shown in the following screenshot:

After downloading the rules, you can review all the rules. You will be able to understand the rules that result in a mismatch as per your requirements:

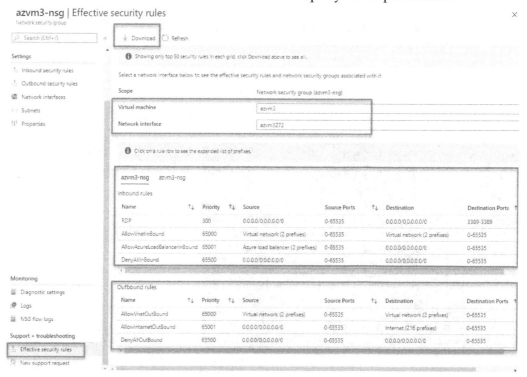

Figure 14.24: Effective security rules

Now, we are able to see how we can evaluate effective security rules.

Conclusion

In this chapter, we discussed the configuration of private and public IP addresses and learned how to change the IP address from dynamic to static. We discussed the Azure network security group and how to associate with the subnet/VM NIC card. We covered the route table and learned how it can be used to route the traffic.

We will discuss the Azure network monitoring in the next chapter. We will explain the network watcher and on-premises to Azure network connectivity monitoring, and so on. For more details, please go through the next chapter.

References

- Virtual network traffic routing: **https://docs.microsoft.com/en-us/Azure/virtual-network/virtual-networks-udr-overview**

- Security groups: **https://docs.microsoft.com/en-us/Azure/virtual-network/security-overview**

- Virtual network service tags: **https://docs.microsoft.com/en-us/Azure/virtual-network/service-tags-overview**

- Virtual network service endpoints: **https://docs.microsoft.com/en-us/Azure/virtual-network/virtual-network-service-endpoints-overview**

- IP address types and allocation methods in Azure: **https://docs.microsoft.com/en-us/Azure/virtual-network/virtual-network-ip-addresses-overview-arm**

- For more details, visit Azure4you blog post: **https://Azure4you.com/**

CHAPTER 15

Monitoring and Troubleshooting of Virtual Networking

In this chapter, we will discuss Azure Network Watcher and its usage. We will also discuss how to troubleshoot the on-premises connectivity using the network watcher.

We will cover network performance monitoring, how to use the IP flow verify, VPN troubleshooting, packet capture, and so on.

Structure

The following topics will be covered in this chapter:

- Network watcher
- Monitor on-premises connectivity
- Network performance monitor

Objectives

In this chapter, you will learn about Azure Network Watcher. If your customer is troubleshooting a network issue from the Azure network to on-premises, then Azure Network Watcher will help your customer to trace the traffic at various levels and help you. We will describe the network watcher capabilities in detail.

Network watcher

Azure Network Watcher provides the tools to monitor, diagnose, and view the metrics. We can enable or disable the logs in the network watcher.

It is designed to monitor and repair the Azure infrastructure services, which include the Azure virtual machine, virtual network, application gateway, and so on.

Let us see how we can implement the Azure Network Watcher services:

1. Go to **All services** and search for **network watcher**. Please select the **Network Watcher** option as shown in the following screenshot:

Figure 15.1: Network watcher

2. Once you click on **Network Watcher**, please enable it for the regions you want to select it for. Let us follow the given steps to enable it:

   1. Click on **Overview**.

   2. Select the region and click on the **Overview** tab to enable the network watcher.

   3. It will take some time to enable it. Please take a look at the following screenshot for more details:

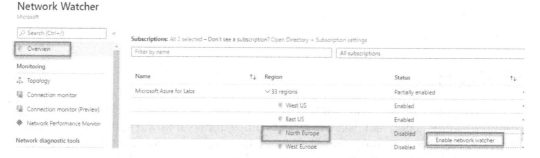

Figure 15.2: Network watcher enable

Network watcher topology

Under the **Monitoring** tab, if you click on **Topology**, it will show you the complete architect connectivity of your VNet which connects to all the resources like the VM, application gateway, and so on as shown in the following screenshot:

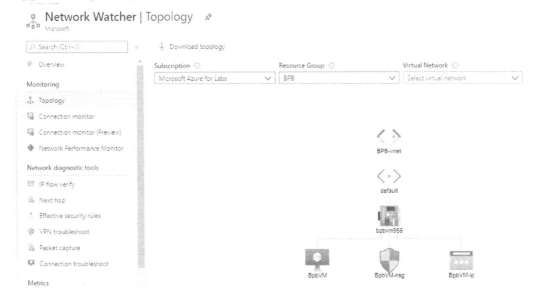

Figure 15.3: *Network watcher enable*

Monitor on-premises connectivity

Using **Connection monitor**, we will monitor the traffic between two virtual machines or between the Azure VM and the on-premise server. We can monitor the Fully Qualified Domain Name (FQDN) name or individual IP address as well. Once you select the connection monitoring, follow the given instructions to add the monitoring:

1. Provide the name of the monitor.

2. Select the subscription.

3. Select the virtual machine.

4. Select the destination as **Select a virtual machine or Specify manually** (URI, FQDN, or IPv4).

5. Select the port number for which you want to monitor the services.

6. Click on **Add** as shown in the following screenshot:

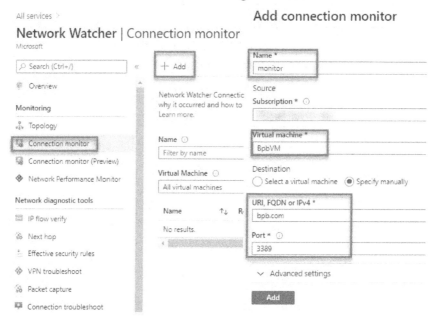

Figure 15.4: Network watcher connection monitor

After you click on **Add**, you will be able to see the connectivity of each service when you click on a specific monitor. Please take a look at the following screenshot for more details:

Figure 15.5: Network watcher connection monitor status

IP flow verify

IP flow verify helps you to track the packets and checks whether the packets have been allowed or denied. Click on **IP flow verify** under the **Network diagnostic tools** section and provide the following details:

- **Subscription**
- **Resource group**
- **Virtual machine**
- **Direction: Inbound** or **Outbound**
- Provide the local IP address and remote IP address with the port number to verify.
- Please click on the **Check** button.

  For more details, take a look at the following screenshot:

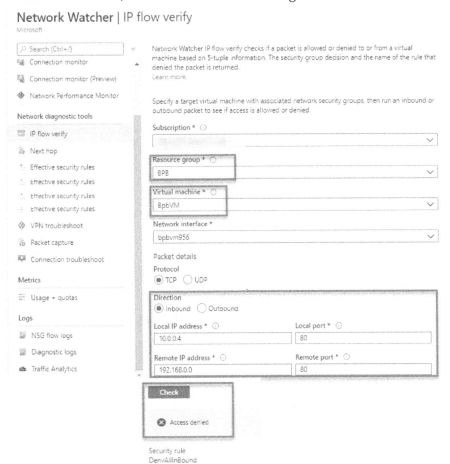

Figure 15.6: Network watcher IP flow

Next hop

Next hop will help you identify the next hope and IP address of the packet from a specific VM and NIC card. It will help you to determine whether the traffic has been directed to a specific destination or not.

Next hop helps you to identify where your traffic has been routed to such as to the virtual network, virtual appliance or system route, and so on. Take a look at the following screenshot:

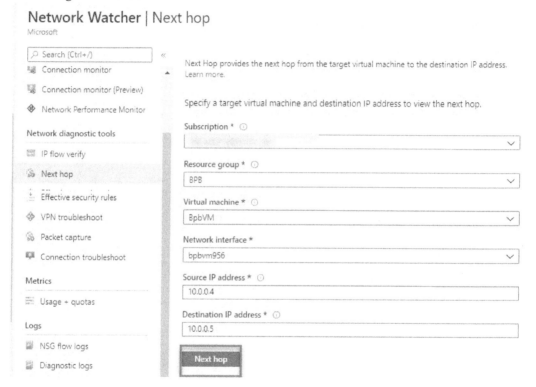

Figure 15.7: Network watcher next hop

Network performance monitor

The network performance monitor helps us to monitor the Azure express route traffic. It is a cloud-based hybrid monitoring solution which helps to monitor the various points of the network infrastructure.

Let us take a look at how to configure the Azure network and performance monitor by following the given steps.

1. Click on the **+** sign.

2. Search for **Network Performance Monitor**.

3. Click on **Create**.

   Look at the following screenshot for more details:

Figure 15.8: Network performance monitor

4. Select **Log Analytics Workspace**.

5. Once you select the workspace, click on **Create** as shown in the following screenshot.

6. It will take up to 5 minutes to create the network performance monitor:

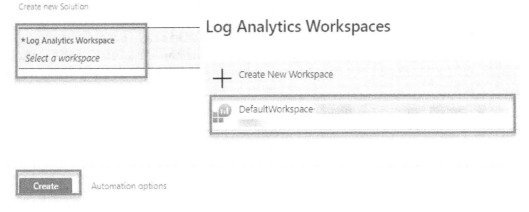

Figure 15.9: Network performance monitor creation

7. Once the network performance monitor is created, you can check it in log analytics.

8. In log analytics, you will see that one solution has been deployed in the **Overview** tab, which is the network performance monitor. Let us try and configure it. Click on **Solution requires additional configuration** under the **Network Performance Monitor** tab on the right-hand side of the **Overview** section. Take a look at the following screenshot:

Figure 15.10: Network performance monitor overview

9. When you click on **Solution requires additional configuration**, one window will open up with the network performance monitor configuration where you need to configure the following services, including the express route:

   • You can download the agent and install it on the stand-alone VMs/ devices to configure the monitor.

   • You can set up the performance monitor.

   • You can configure the services connectivity monitor for network devices.

   • You can set up the express route monitor to get the traffic of the express route and fix the issue when it arrives.

Once all the preceding configurations are done, you will start getting the data within 24 hrs in log analytics. We have now successfully configured the network performance monitoring in the Azure environment.

Take a look at the following screenshot:

Figure 15.11: Network performance monitor configuration

Conclusion

In this chapter, we discussed Azure Network Watcher and its usage, how to troubleshoot the network using various tools, how to troubleshoot the on-premises network and Azure connectivity, how the IP flow verify and next hope will help your on-network troubleshooting. We also discussed the Azure network performance monitor and how to configure it.

In the next chapter, we will discuss the Azure monitor and its subsets to analyze the utilization and consumption of the Azure services. We will also discuss how to set up alerts in Azure environments.

References

- IP flow: **https://docs.microsoft.com/en-us/azure/network-watcher/ network-watcher-ip-flow-verify-overview**
- Network watcher monitoring: **https://docs.microsoft.com/en-us/azure/ network-watcher/network-watcher-monitoring-overview**
- Connection troubleshoot in Azure Network Watcher: **https://docs.microsoft. com/en-us/azure/network-watcher/network-watcher-connectivity-overview**
- Resource troubleshooting in Azure Network Watcher: **https://docs.microsoft. com/en-us/azure/network-watcher/network-watcher-troubleshoot-overview**
- Effective security rules view in Azure Network Watcher: **https://docs. microsoft.com/en-us/azure/network-watcher/network-watcher-security-group-view-overview**
- For more details, visit Azure4you blog post: **https://azure4you.com/**

CHAPTER 16

Analyzing Resource Utilization and Consumption

In the previous chapter, we covered how to create and manage the different types of Azure subscriptions and resources. In this chapter, we will learn about Azure monitor and its utilization of the resources and how to monitor the different services using Azure Log Analytics. We will see how to use the log search query functions in the log analytics space.

Structure

The following topics will be covered in this chapter:

- Azure Monitor
- Setup and configuration of alerts
- Utilize log search query functions

Objectives

We will cover Azure Monitor in detail which will help you to set up the monitoring alerts for your Azure subscription resources. We will discuss how to set up and configure the alerts, which will help you to send the notifications.

Azure Monitor

Azure Monitor is a comprehensive solution for all the Azure services that reside in the Azure subscription, and it uses various tools to monitor the IaaS, PaaS, and SaaS components. It collects the logs data, application performance data, and so on to provide the best result for services, and based on them, the customer can get notified.

For more details, take a look at the following screenshot:

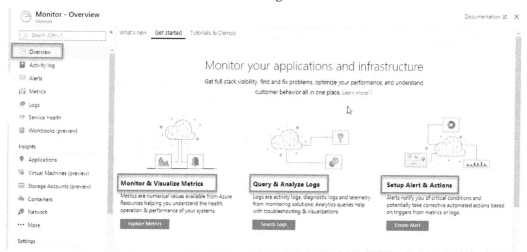

Figure 16.1: *Azure Monitor*

Azure Monitor supports a variety of Azure resource collection data which provides the metrics/alerts on the Azure portal.

The types of data provided by Azure monitors are as follows:

- **Application monitoring data:** It collects consistent data of application functionality, performance, and maintenance with respect to application code-related issues.

- **Guest OS monitoring data:** It collects data of Azure VMs running on the subscription and it has an application running on it.

- **Resource monitoring data:** It collects the application resource operation data.

- **Subscription monitoring data:** It collects the complete subscription data, including Azure resources health of the Azure services in terms of the region, and so on.

- **Tenant monitoring data:** It collects the tenant level data such as any operations or any issues that may have occurred on your Azure AD services.

- **Activity logs:** Activity logs are nothing, but the activities that have been performed by the user or owner in terms of all the services. They will be collected and recorded. Refer to the following screenshot:

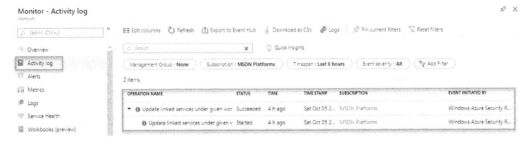

Figure 16.2: Activity logs

Setup and configuration of Azure alerts

If you would like to configure an alert of your services, then please follow the given steps:

1. Click on **Alerts**, and then click on **+ New alert rule** under Azure Monitor or resources as shown in the following screenshot:

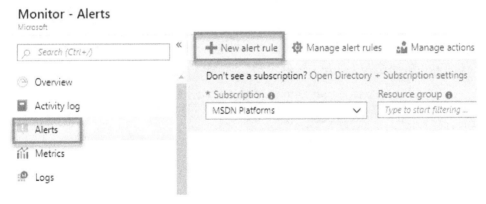

Figure 16.3: New alert

2. Select resources like subscription, VMs, and so on for alert creation, as shown in the following screenshot:

Figure 16.4: Alert creation

3. Select the condition under all administrative logs, specific resources logs, and so on to add the condition as shown in the following screenshot:

Figure 16.5: Alerts rules

4. Click on the action group:

- Provide the action group name
- Short name of maximum 116 characters
- Subscription name
- Resource group name
- Action name like where or how to get an alert:
    o **Automation Runbook**
    o **Azure Function**
    o **Email/SMS/Push/Voice**
    o **ITSM** like services ticketing tool
    o **Webhook** and other services

Add action group details as shown in the following screenshot:

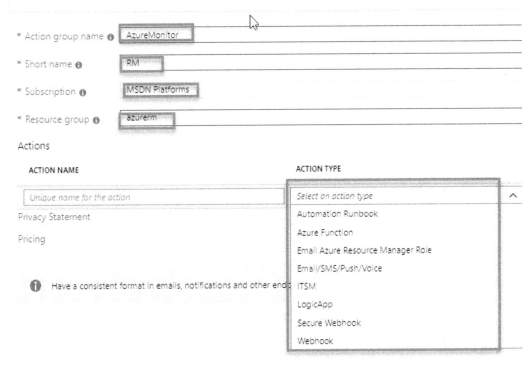

Figure 16.6: Add action details

5.   Click on **OK**.

6.   Provide the details of the alert:
   - Alert name
   - Description
   - Save alert to the resource group name
   - Enable or disable rule on creation
   - Click on **Create alerts**

For more details on alerts, take a look at the following screenshot:

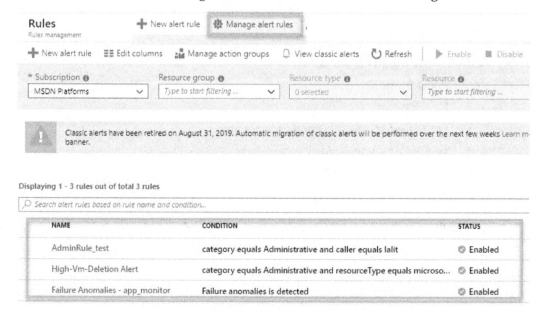

ALERT DETAILS

* Alert rule name ⓘ

Subscription Administror Alerts ✓

Description

It's inclide all the operation Alerts ✓

* Save alert to resource group ⓘ

azurerm ⌄

Enable rule upon creation

[Yes   No]

ⓘ It can take up to 5 minutes for an Activity log alert rule to become active.

Create alert rule

Figure 16.7: Alert details

Once the alerts are created, you can view all the alerts in the **Manage alert rules** window. For more alert manager details, take a look at the following screenshot:

Rules
Rules management
╋ New alert rule   ⚙ Manage alert rules

╋ New alert rule   ☰☰ Edit columns   Manage action groups   ♫ View classic alerts   ⟳ Refresh   ▶ Enable   ■ Disable

* Subscription ⓘ	Resource group ⓘ	Resource type ⓘ	Resource ⓘ
MSDN Platforms ⌄	Type to start filtering... ⌄	0 selected ⌄	Type to start filtering...

⚠ Classic alerts have been retired on August 31, 2019. Automatic migration of classic alerts will be performed over the next few weeks Learn m- banner.

Displaying 1 - 3 rules out of total 3 rules

🔍 Search alert rules based on rule name and condition...

NAME	CONDITION	STATUS
AdminRule_test	category equals Administrative and caller equals lalit	⊘ Enabled
High-Vm-Deletion Alert	category equals Administrative and resourceType equals microso...	⊘ Enabled
Failure Anomalies - app_monitor	Failure anomalies is detected	⊘ Enabled

Figure 16.8: Manager of the alert rule

This is how you can create and manage the alerts. You can also modify the Azure resource alerts.

Azure Metrics

Azure Metrics are numerical values of the resources utilization which are collected in real-time. Based on the numerical values, it shows the metrics performance of the resources, as shown in the following screenshot:

1. You can select the resources.

2. Click on **Metrics** as shown in the following screenshot:

Figure 16.9: Metrics

Azure Services Health

Azure Service Health will help you analyze the resources under the subscription and various region service availability options. Let us understand them:

- **Planned maintenance:** You can see the planned maintenance of the Azure datacenter if there is any global impact and then you can take the primitive action on that.

- **Resource health:** Resources health will help you to understand the health of the resources.

- **Health alerts:** We can set up the resource health alerts as well based on the customers' requirements. For more details, take a look at the following screenshot:

Figure 16.10: Azure Services Health

Diagnostic logs

It provides auditing and diagnostic information about the Azure resources.

It helps to collect the logs and sends the logs to log analytics for further analysis. It can be sent to the event hub to get the notification. It can also store the logs to storage accounts for any further update or archival.

Enabling the diagnostic settings

Perform the following steps:

1. Click on `Azure Monitor`.
2. Click on `Diagnostic settings` under `Settings` and click on the resource. Please take a look at the following screenshot for diagnostic settings:

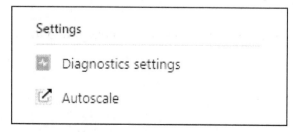

Figure 16.11: Diagnostic settings

3. Click on the resource menu on the Azure portal. Then, click on **Diagnostic settings** under **Monitoring** as shown in the following screenshot:

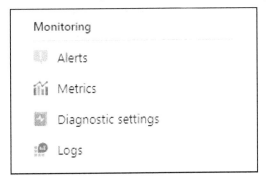

Figure 16.12: Diagnostic settings details

4. If there are no settings that exist on the resource, then click on turn on diagnostic settings and enable it as shown in the following screenshot:

Monitor - Diagnostics settings
Microsoft

🔍 Search (Ctrl+/)	☼ Refresh

☼ Service Health

🖼 Workbooks (preview)

Insights

🔮 Applications

🖥 Virtual Machines (preview)

🖼 Storage Accounts (preview)

👬 Containers

🔗 Network

••• More

Settings

💠 Diagnostics settings

📝 Autoscale

Support + Troubleshooting

* Subscription 🛈   Resource group 🛈

MSDN Platforms   azurerm

MSDN Platforms > azurerm > Recoverypiyush

Diagnostics settings

NAME	STORAGE ACCOUNT	EVENT HUB

No diagnostic settings defined

+ Add diagnostic setting

Click 'Add Diagnostic setting' above to configure the collection of the following data:

- AzureBackupReport
- AzureSiteRecoveryJobs
- AzureSiteRecoveryEvents
- AzureSiteRecoveryReplicatedItems
- AzureSiteRecoveryReplicationStats
- AzureSiteRecoveryRecoveryPoints
- AzureSiteRecoveryReplicationDataUploadRate
- AzureSiteRecoveryProtectedDiskDataChurn

Figure 16.13: Monitor diagnostic settings

5. Once you click on **Diagnostic settings**, follow the given steps:

    1. Please provide the storage account details.

2. Provide the solution where to store the logs: **Send to Log Analytics** or **Stream to an event hub**.

3. Select the storage account and retention period of the logs.

4. Click on **OK** and save the settings as shown in the following screenshot:

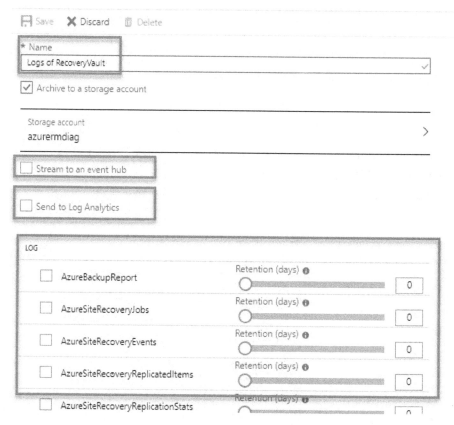

Figure 16.14: Diagnostic settings configuration

Now, your diagnostic settings have been enabled to recovery services and it can be done with other services in your Azure subscription resources.

Azure Log Analytics

Azure Log Analytics is a service that collects the data from various Azure resources and on-premises devices and sends it to your log analytics.

The collected data is stored in the log analytics workspace which can be used for a query language, alerting, and so on. Log analytics analyses the metric data and provides the result based on that.

Create the Azure workspace

You can follow the given steps to create the Azure workspace:

1. Click on **+ Create a resource**.
2. Search for **Log Analytics**.
3. Click on **Log Analytics**.
4. Click on the **Create** button to create the log analytics workspace as shown in the following screenshot:

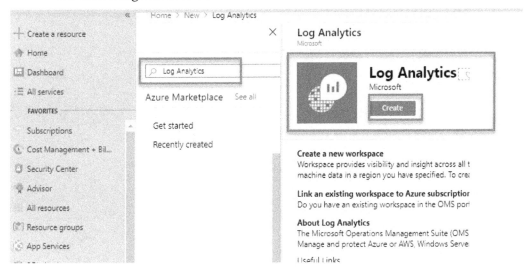

Figure 16.15: Log analytics workspace

5. Once the preceding steps are complete, perform the following steps:

   a. Provide the log analytics name.

   b. Provide the subscription name.

   c. Provide the resource group name.

   d. Provide the location based on your customer or project.

   e. Provide the pricing tier.

6. Click on **Create** as shown in the following screenshot:

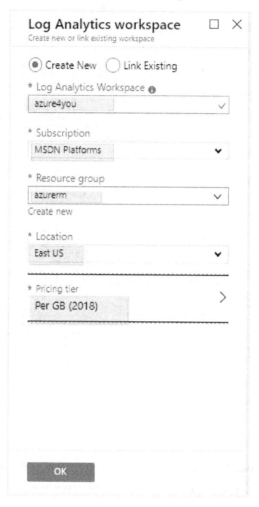

Figure 16.16: Log analytics details

Now, your log analytics workspace has been created. You can start connecting your devices or using them.

If you would like to install or connect the VMs to the workspace manually, then click on the **Advanced settings** option under **Log Analytics** and click on the Windows or Linux agent to download it. Take a look at the following screenshot for more details:

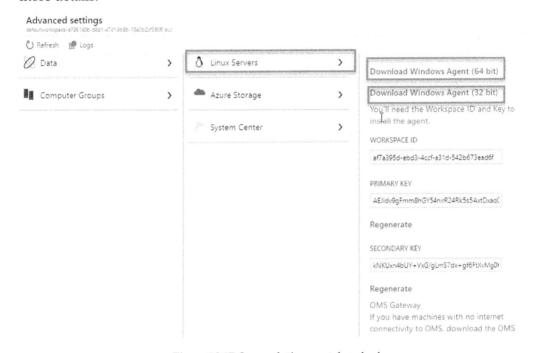

Figure 16.17: Log analytics agent download

Utilize log search query functions

The log query function will provide you with the values from the data collected from log analytics or Azure monitor. The query is a powerful language that allows you to combine the data from the multiple tables, aggregate the larger data, and provide a complex operation with minimal code.

You can query the data using the following steps:

1. Click on the log analytics which you have created.

2. Go to **Workspace summary**.

3. Click on **Logs**.

4. Once you click on **Logs**, you will be able to see the dashboard of the log analytics. Take a look at the following screenshot:

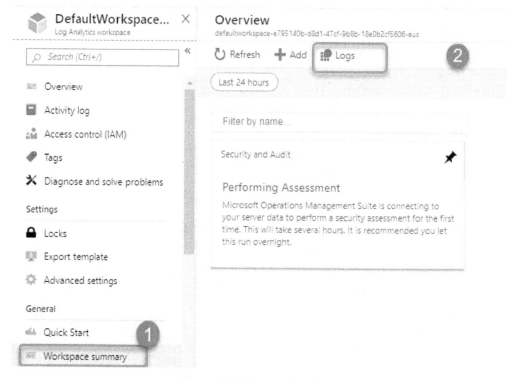

Figure 16.18: Log analytics logs

Here, you can run the query search for your port, dashboard or alert, and so on.

A query can be used to create the custom dashboard of Azure monitoring based on your customers' requirements:

1. Click on **Sample queries**.
2. Type the query.
3. Click on **Run**.
4. You will get a result.

5. You can use the same query and create an alert as well as shown in the following screenshot:

***Figure 16.19:** Log analytics search query*

This is how we can use the query search to get the result of Azure resources and use it to monitor and query the result of the services. We can enable the alert based on the query.

Conclusion

In this chapter, we covered analyzing the resources and explaining the Azure monitor. We discussed how to create the alerts and how to use those alerts. We covered how to create the Azure log analytics workspace and query search of Azure data based on the query. Using the query, we can create the alerts.

We will discuss Azure backup and Disaster recovery in the next chapter. We will also cover how to enable the backup of your Azure virtual machine and migrate the VM or set up disaster recovery in Azure.

References

- Metrics in Azure Monitor: **https://docs.microsoft.com/en-us/azure/azure-monitor/platform/data-platform-metrics**
- Log query search: **https://docs.microsoft.com/en-us/azure/azure-monitor/log-query/log-query-overview**
- Log Analytics: **https://docs.microsoft.com/en-us/azure/azure-monitor/log-query/log-query-overview**
- Alert configuration: **https://docs.microsoft.com/en-us/azure/azure-monitor/platform/alerts-metric**

- Azure Monitor: **https://docs.microsoft.com/en-us/azure/azure-monitor/overview**
- Azure4you: **https://azure4you.com/**

CHAPTER 17

Implementation of Azure Backup and Disaster Recovery

In this chapter, we will discuss the Azure backup services, Azure backup recovery vault, and usage of the Azure backup policy. We will also discuss how to create the backup reports and see how the restoration process works in Azure. We will cover the various types of backup operations and so on.

Structure

The following topics will be covered in this chapter:

- Azure backup
- Azure backup vault creation
- Azure VM backup configuration
- Azure backup report
- Azure restoration of VMs
- Azure backup operation details
- Use soft delete to recover Azure VMs
- Site-to-site recovery by using Azure site recovery

Objectives

In this chapter, you will learn about Azure backup and disaster recovery services. You will also learn how to configure the backup to protect the VMs from accidental deletion and ensure faster restoration process in detail.

Azure backup

Azure backup services come under the Azure site recovery vault. Azure backup services are used to take the backup of your virtual machines, Azure storage file share, and SQL servers which are hosted in Azure VMs. It provides the files and folder-level backup as well.

We can take the on-premise servers backup to Azure using Azure backup. The Azure backup vault supports Windows as well as Linux VMs to take the backup. It enhances the backup capability and provides a secure way to backup your infrastructure. It provides centralized monitoring and protects all the Azure VMs. We can control the access using the RBAC roles to meet the compliance level.

Azure backup vault creation

Let us see how to create the Azure backup vault and how to backup the services. Please follow the given steps:

1. Log in to the portal.

2. Go to **All services**, or you can go to the marketplace and search for the **Backup and Site Recovery** service.

3. Click on the **Backup and Site Recovery** service. For more details, take a look at the following screenshot:

Backup and Site Recovery
Microsoft

Backup and Site Recovery ♡ Save for later
Microsoft

Create

Overview   Plans

A disaster recovery and data protection strategy keeps your business running when unexpected events occur.

The Backup service is Microsoft's born in the cloud backup solution to backup data that's located on-premises and in Azure. It replaces your existing on-premises or offsite backup solution with a reliable, secure and cost competitive cloud backup solution. It also provides the flexibility of protecting your assets running in the cloud. You can backup Windows Servers, Windows Clients, Hyper-V VMs, Microsoft workloads, Azure Virtual Machines (Windows and Linux) with its in-built resilience and high SLAs. Learn more.

The Site Recovery service ensures your servers, virtual machines, and apps are resilient by replicating them so that when disasters and outages occur you can easily fail over to your replicated environment and continue working. When services are resumed you simply failback to your primary location with uninterrupted access. Site Recovery helps protect a wide range of Microsoft and third-party workloads. Learn more.

Useful Links
Backup Pricing details
Site Recovery Pricing details

Figure 17.1: Azure backup vault marketplace

4. Provide the backup vault name.

5. Provide the resources group name and subscription details.

6. Click on **Create**. For more details, please take a look at the following screenshot:

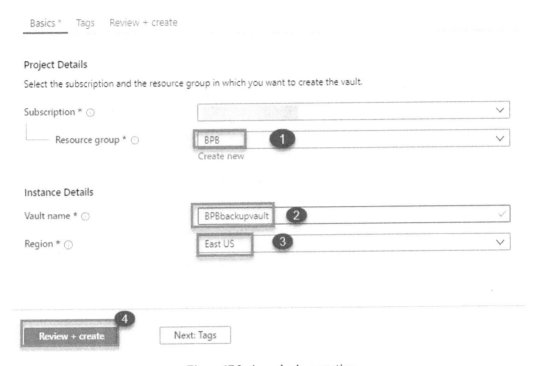

Figure 17.2: Azure backup creation

Now, you will be able to create the Azure backup vault. The backup vault has been created, and we will start the backup using the same recovery vault.

Azure VMs backup configuration

Now, I will show you how to configure the backup of your VMs:

1. Click on **Recovery Service vault**.

2. Click on the **+ Backup** button.

3. Set up the quota limit as per customers' requirements.

4. Click on **Create**. For more details, please take a look at the following screenshot:

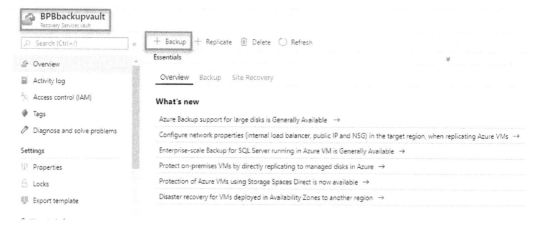

Figure 17.3: Azure backup configuration

5. You can select the Azure environment, and you can get two or more options to backup the Azure stack and on-premise servers.

6. Select **Azure** and select the Azure VMs, but you can also backup **Azure FileShare (Preview)** and **SQL Server in Azure VM**. For more details, take a look at the following screenshot:

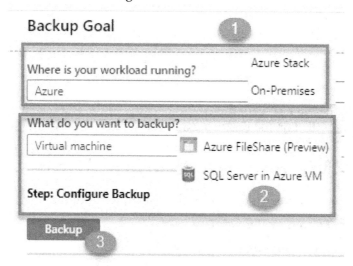

Figure 17.4: Azure backup configuration setup

7. Once you click on the backup, it will ask you for the Azure policy so let me explain how the Azure backup policy will help you schedule the backup for daily purpose.

Azure backup policy

The Azure backup policy helps you set the rules for your backup infrastructure like VMs. You can have the retention policy which will help you to retain the data in the Azure backup vault up to 99 years. A retention policy can be set based on a daily, weekly, monthly, and yearly basis. For more details, refer to the following screenshot:

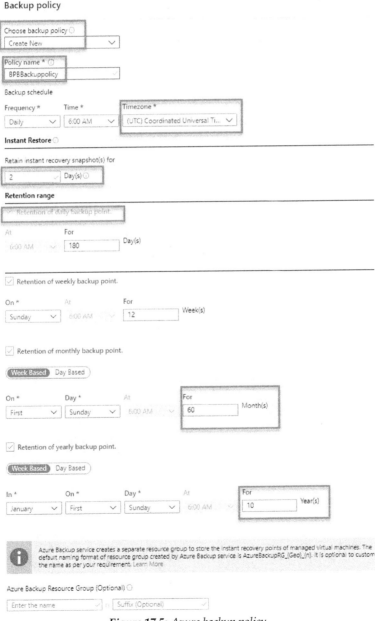

Figure 17.5: Azure backup policy

Perform the following steps to create the backup policy:

1. Click on **OK** to create the backup policy. Once your backup policy is created, the backup vault will allow you to choose the VMs.

2. Click on **Items to backup** and select the virtual machine.

3. Click on Enable backup.

4. Once you click on **Enable backup**, it will trigger a job that installs the recovery agent. It will start taking the backup of your services. For more details, please take a look at the following screenshot:

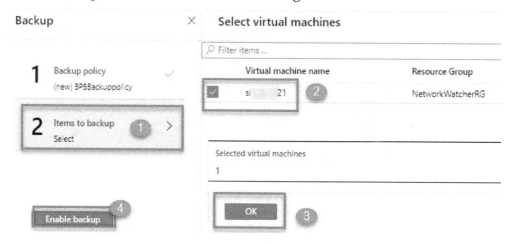

Figure 17.6: Azure backup enable

5. Once done, it will start the deployments. It will take some time to enable the backup as shown in the following screenshot:

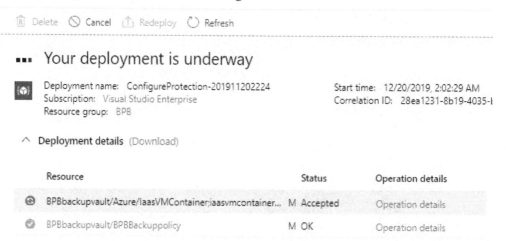

Figure 17.7: Azure backup deployment

6. Once the backup is enabled, you can see that the VMs will be added to your backup services vault. You can see the numbers of the VMs in your VM backup vault as shown in the following screenshot:

Figure 17.8: Azure backup verification

7. Click on **Backup item** and select the Azure VMs tab and then select the Azure VM.

8. Click on the **Backup now** button to enable the backup.

9. When you click on **Backup now**, the backup will get triggered, or it will start based on the Azure backup policy as per your schedule. Take a look at the following screenshot:

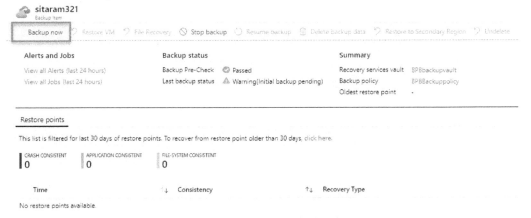

Figure 17.9: Enabling Azure backup for VM

Azure backup report

Azure backup reports will help you to identify the backup of your VMs and its storage provides the transaction and backup failure. It also provides restoration and size of the backup size of your backup vault.

Before we create the backup report, we need the following:

- Azure storage account.
- Log restoration time 30 days to 1 year max.
- An important part is to have the Power BI licensed version to configure the Azure backup report.

Let us see how to set up the Azure backup report from the Azure backup vault:

1. Go to the Azure backup vault for which you want to configure the backup report.

2. In that backup vault, go to **Manage** and select **Backup Reports**. For more details, please take a look at the following screenshot:

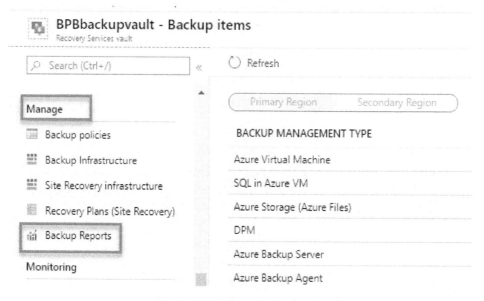

Figure 17.10: Azure backup report

Now, you need to follow the step-by-step instructions to enable the backup report as shown in the following screenshot:

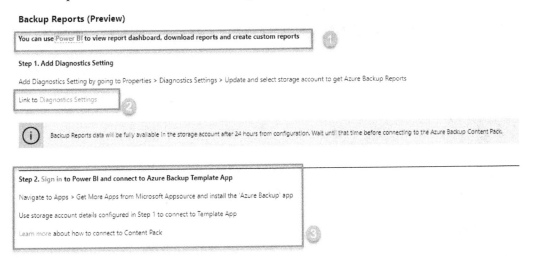

Figure 17.11: Backup report configuration

3. When you click on the Azure backup diagnostic settings, it will ask you to store the log, and you can select the Azure storage account, stream logs to an event hub, or send the logs to log analytics. I have selected the Azure storage to configure the backup report. Please take a look at the following screenshot:

Figure 17.12: Backup report diagnostic configuration

4. Once this process is complete, please log in to the Power BI report tool and add backup apps from the storage to configure the backup report. Take a look at the following screenshot:

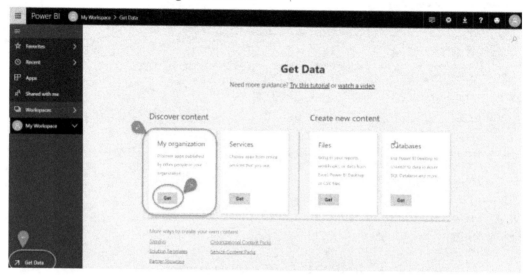

Figure 17.13: Backup report Power BI configuration

5. Now, you can create the Azure file sync. We will create the Azure file sync group. Take a look at the following screenshot:

Figure 17.14: Azure backup from Power BI

6. Provide the storage account name you need to configure the diagnostic setting from the Azure backup vault.

7. Provide the Azure storage account and Azure storage account key.

8. Once you are done with the setup, it will take some time to add the report.

9. It might take 24 to 48 hrs to generate the report as to store the logs and generate the reports.

10.   Once the report is published, take a look at the Power BI backup report as shown in the following screenshot:

Figure 17.15: Azure backup storage configuration Power BI

11.   After the storage configuration backup report is published, you can customize the Azure backup dashboard.

Azure restoration of VMs

The Azure backup restoration is processed to restore the VMs, files, and so on in case of corruption of images or any services interruption to services, or just for restoring to the previous version. Now, I will show you the option of how to restore the VM using the recovery vault.

Please follow the given steps:

1.   Please select the recovery vault where you have taken the backup.

2.   Then, click on the **Backup** tab from **Protected items**.

3.   Select the virtual machine for which you want to restore the VM.

4. When you click on **Restore VM** or **File Recovery**, you will see the restore option. Take a look at the following screenshot:

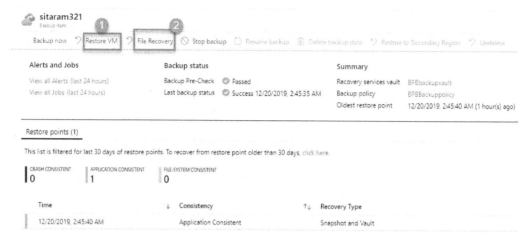

Figure 17.16: VM backup restoration

5. Please click on the **Restore point** option.

6. When you click on it, it will show you the restoration time.

7. You can restore the backup in terms of application, crash, and file consistency as well. Take a look at the following screenshot:

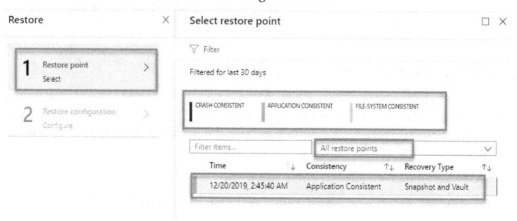

Figure 17.17: VM backup restoration point

8. Once you select the restore configuration, you can select whether you want to create a new VM or replace the existing setup which will replace the disk.

9. Let us select the new VM creation.

10. Now, you need to provide the name of the VMs, and VNet will select the default or you can change it within the same region.

11. Please select the storage account and click on the **Restore** button.

12. After 10 to 15 minutes, your VM will be created or based on the data; it might take a longer time. Please take a look at the following screenshot:

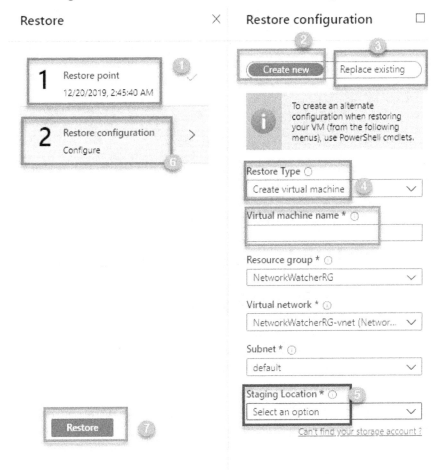

Figure 17.18: New VM creation using restoration

Azure backup operation details

Azure backup operations help you to understand whether your backup job has been successful or unsuccessful. It provides the end-to-end Azure operation errors to understand and troubleshoot the issue. Activity logs will also help in the Azure backup operation. Please take a look at the following screenshot:

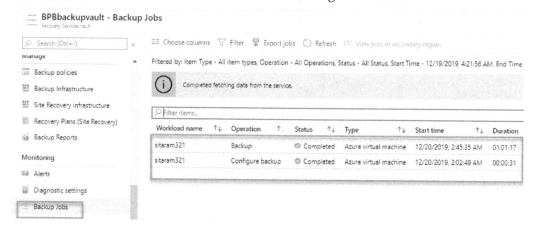

Figure 17.19: Azure backup operations

Use soft delete to recover Azure VMs

The Azure soft delete backup will help you to recover the VM even after you delete it from the backup vault. You will be able to recover the VM from the backup vault within 14 days.

It helps you if you have deleted the backup by mistake or due to some malicious activity, it got deleted, then you will be able to recover the VM. Whenever you create the backup vault, soft delete will be enabled by default.

Let us see how we can enable or disable the soft delete Azure VM using the site recovery:

1. Select the Azure backup vault.
2. Go to **Properties**.
3. Select **Security Settings** and click on **Update**.
4. Click on enable the soft delete.

5.   Click on **Save** to enable it. Take a look at the following screenshot:

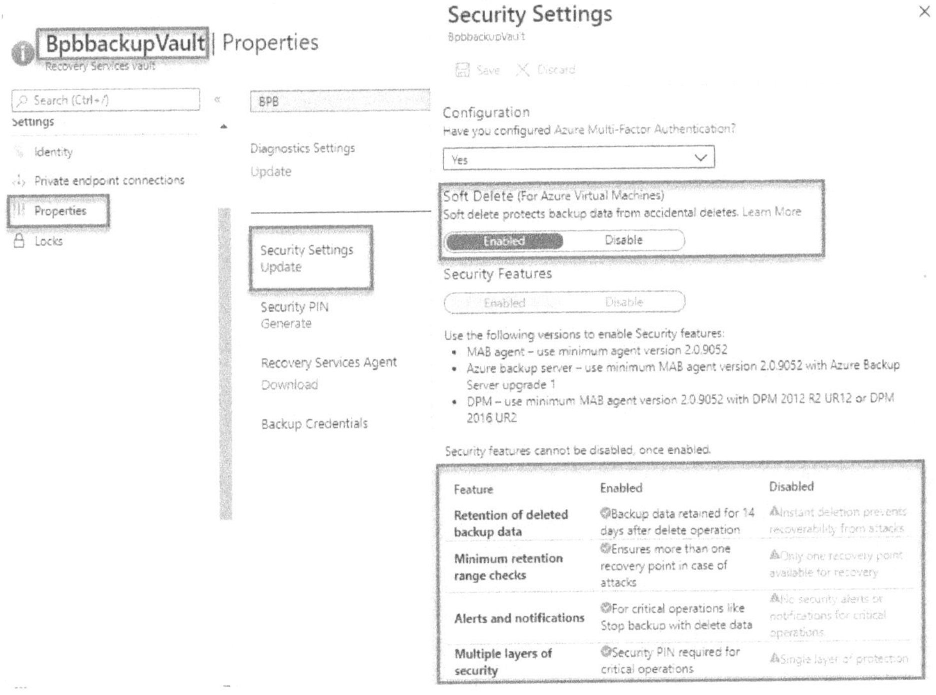

Figure 17.20: Azure backup soft delete

6.   When you delete the backup, you will get the following message that if you have enabled the soft backup to delete, then you will able to recover the data within 14 days. Take a look at the following screenshot:

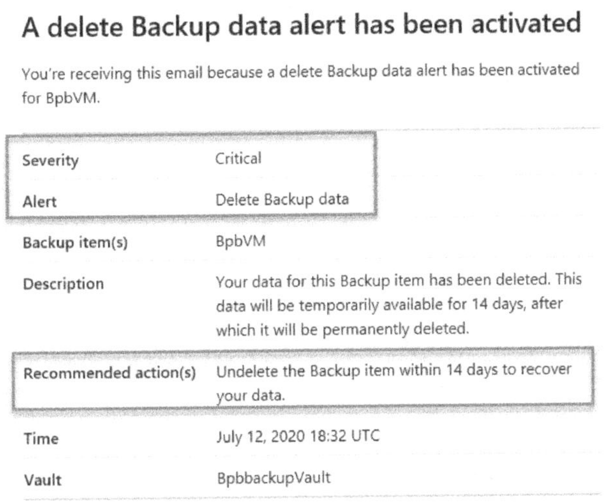

A delete Backup data alert has been activated

You're receiving this email because a delete Backup data alert has been activated for BpbVM.

Severity	Critical
Alert	Delete Backup data
Backup item(s)	BpbVM
Description	Your data for this Backup item has been deleted. This data will be temporarily available for 14 days, after which it will be permanently deleted.
Recommended action(s)	Undelete the Backup item within 14 days to recover your data.
Time	July 12, 2020 18:32 UTC
Vault	BpbbackupVault

Figure 17.21: Azure backup soft delete

7.　If you want to recover the data, then go the backup vault and select the deleted VMs backup and click on **Undelete** as shown in the following screenshot:

Figure 17.22: Azure backup soft undelete

Site-to-site recovery by using Azure site recovery

Azure site recovery helps you to ensure your business continuity by running due to unplanned or planned outage. Azure site recovery services will help you to replicate the on-premise and Azure workload from the primary site to the secondary site whenever there is an outage on primary sites. Once the primary sites are up and running, you can failback to primary sites.

The site recovery manages the following replications:

- Azure VMs can replicate between Azure regions.
- On-premises VMs, Azure stack VM, physical server, Hyper-V, and VMware servers.

Let us see how to enable the Azure site recovery:

1.　Go to site recovery and click on **+ Replicate** as shown in the following screenshot:

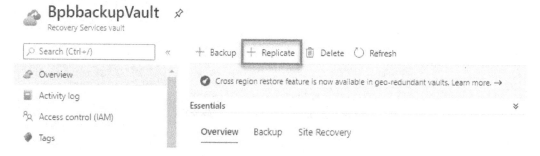

Figure 17.23: Azure site recovery replicate

2. Once you click on **+ Replicate**, select the source and provide the details as follows:

- Provide Source as Azure.

- Source location is your Azure VM location.

- Please provide the source resource group.

- Please provide the subscription.

- Please select the availability zone and click on **OK**. Please take a look at the following screenshot:

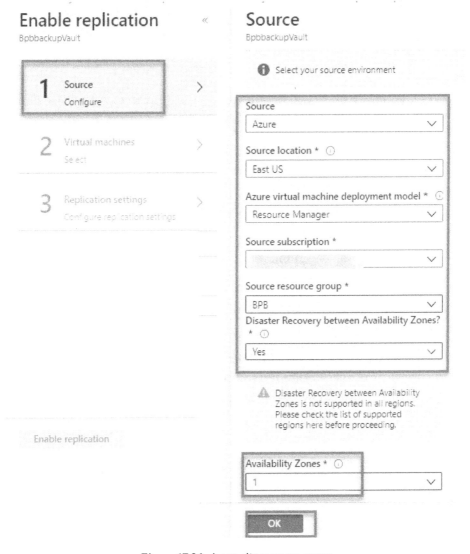

Figure 17.24: Azure site recovery source

3. Click on **OK** and select the Azure virtual machine. Refer to the following screenshot:

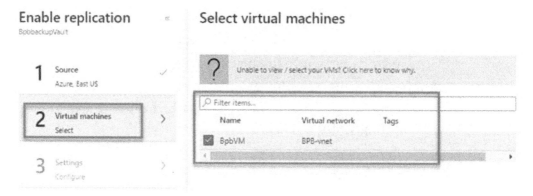

Figure 17.25: Azure site recovery virtual machine

4. When you click **OK**, it will be directed to the **Settings** tab. Please define the settings as follows:

    - Select the target location.

    - Select the **Disaster Recovery (DR)** subscription you want to configure in Azure.

    - Select the target resource group.

    - Target virtual network.

    - Cache storage account.

    - Replica the managed disk.

    - Target the AV set if you want to configure.

    - Replication policy:
        o 24-hour retention policy
        o Recovery point retention
        o Application consistent settings
        o Replication group

5. Click on **Create target resources** as shown in the following screenshot:

Enable replication
BpbbackupVault

1 Source
Azure, East US ✓

2 Virtual machines
1 Selected ✓

3 Settings
Configure →

Enable replication

Configure settings

Target location * ⓘ

West US ▾

Target subscription   ✎ Customize

Microsoft Azure for Labs

> ⚠ If you are choosing General Purpose v2 storage accounts, ensure that operations and data transfer prices are understood clearly before you proceed. Learn more

Resource group, Network, Storage and Availability   ✎ Customize
By default Site Recovery will mirror the source site configuration to target site by creating/using the required resource groups, storage accounts, virtual network and availability sets as below. Click 'Customize' above to change the configuration. The resources created are appended with "asr" suffix.

Target resource group ⓘ	**Target virtual network** ⓘ
(new) BPB-asr	(new) BPB-vnet-asr
Cache storage accounts ⓘ	**Replica managed disks** ⓘ
(new) rp0vpwbpbbackupvaercache	(new) 1 premium disks(s), 0 standard disk(s)
Target availability sets ⓘ	
Not Applicable	

Replication Policy   ✎ Customize

Name: 24-hour-retention-policy
Recovery point retention: 24 hour(s)
App consistent snapshot frequency: 4 hour(s)
Replication group: None

Extension settings   [+] Show details

Site Recovery manages site recovery extension updates for all your replicated items. 1 new automation account will be created.

[**Create target resources**]

Figure 17.26: Azure site recovery target resource

6. Once the target resource is created, enable the replication as shown in the following screenshot:

Figure 17.27: Azure site recovery replication enables

7. Once the replication is enabled, you will be able to successfully set up the DR using the site recovery. It will start the replication, and once the replication is complete, you can do the failover.

Now, we can successfully create the DR site.

Conclusion

In this chapter, we discussed the Azure backup and its usage. We learned how to create a backup report and its usage. We discussed how to set up the Azure site recovery for Azure VMs and explained the Azure backup reports.

In the next chapter, we will discuss the exam guidelines and assessments. We will provide the details on how to register for the exam and provide 75 questions to prepare for the exam.

References

- Create a recovery services vault: **https://docs.microsoft.com/en-us/azure/backup/backup-create-rs-vault#modifying-default-settings**

- Recovery services vaults overview: **https://docs.microsoft.com/en-us/azure/backup/backup-azure-recovery-services-vault-overview**

- Monitor and manage recovery services vaults: **https://docs.microsoft.com/en-us/azure/backup/backup-azure-manage-windows-server**

- Recover files from the Azure virtual machine backup: **https://docs.microsoft.com/en-us/azure/backup/backup-azure-restore-files-from-vm**

- Restore Azure VM data on the Azure portal: **https://docs.microsoft.com/en-us/azure/backup/backup-azure-arm-restore-vms**

- Configure Azure backup reports: **https://docs.microsoft.com/en-us/azure/backup/backup-azure-configure-reports**

- For more details, visit Azure4you blog post: **https://azure4you.com/**

CHAPTER 18
Exam Preparation Guidelines and Assessment Based on Live Questions

In this chapter, I will discuss the AZ-104 live scenario-based questions and answers, which will help you to understand the exam pattern. These are dummy questions which have been created by me and might help you in your exam practice. It's not related to your exam, but it will help you to understand the topics. It will give clarity on what types of questions will be asked in the exam so that you can prepare well for your exam. We will try to cover all the topic questions which have been written in this book and try to cover the question as much as we can.

> Note: Certified author swill create all the questions but if there is any match to your exam question, then it is just a coincidence and neither the author or publisher will be responsible for those questions.

The following topics will be covered in your exam as per the Microsoft exam center official site **https://docs.microsoft.com/en-us/learn/certifications/azure-administrator**.

Please follow the given topics to start preparing for the exam:

- Manage Azure subscriptions and resources (15-20%)
- Implement and manage storage (15-20%)
- Deploy and **manage virtual machines (VMs)** (15-20%)

- Configure and manage virtual networks (30-35%)
- Manage identities (15-20%)

Exam preparation guidelines

Azure-104 Microsoft Azure administrator certification validates your expertise in the Azure administrator role. In this exam, your administrator skills and knowledge will be tested.

If you want to be certified on the AZ-104 exam, you should be aware of the Azure compute, storage, networking, Azure AD, monitoring, subscription management, and so on, which we have covered in this course. In this exam, you will have to perform the labs as well; hence, you will have hands-on practice. You can create the free subscription (**https://azure.microsoft.com/en-in/free/**) which will provide the 12K credit for 1 month and 25 most used applications which you can use for 12 months.

Exam AZ-104 Basic Information	
Name of the exam	Exam AZ-104: Microsoft Azure Administrator
Technology	Microsoft Azure
Prerequisites	Hands-on practice for Azure Admin labs and Azure concept understanding
Number of questions	40-60
Exam fee	USD 165 and INR 4800
Exam language	English

Table 18.1: Basic information for AZ-104

AZ-104 exam tips

- The Azure exam duration will be 180 minutes, and in those 180 minutes, 30 minutes will be given for instructions, comments, score reporting, and others. In 150 minutes, you must answer all the questions and complete the labs.

- You will get two labs which have 14 tasks to be completed and there will 3-5 case study-based questions.

- In the case study-based questions, you need to read and understand the questions very carefully to provide the correct answers. It is a time taking section because in these study cases, you might have to answer about 10 to 15 questions. In each case study, there will be approximate 2 to 5 questions which you need to answer.

- You will get multiple-choice questions as well in the following format:
  - o **Single-correct answer:** You have to say Yes/No.
  - o **Fill in the blanks:** You have understood the scenarios and you need to choose the right answer and do the drag and drop job.
  - o **Order statements:** In the exam, you need to create a site-to-site VPN by putting the preceding steps in order. Hence, you should be aware of the correct order and able to perform the steps.

- Exams will be divided into sections, and you can go back and correct the answers but within the section. Once you have moved to the next section, you will not be able to change the section. Please make sure you will be able to verify or review the question before going to the next section.

- Please read the question properly and understand the format of the question. It can be a scenario-based question. If it is a scenario-based question, understand the question been asked and you need to fill in the requirements to give the correct answer. Once you do this, it will take a few minutes to provide the correct answer.

- Try to complete single answer questions as early as you can so that you can save some time for scenarios-based questions and labs.

- Try to attempt and answer all questions which come in the exam because there is no harm in guessing the answers.

- A few of the questions will come from PowerShell and ARM. To answer with the given PowerShell command, let's just prepare the new module AZ PowerShell which will help.

- A few of the questions will come from cost management and Cloudyn. Please prepare the topics and answer them.

- Please practice the labs as there will around 14 tasks so you can get the free subscription and prepare well which will help you to clear the exam.

- Azure exam labs will be slow and you may face some issues. If you are running out of time and stuck in labs or any other technical issues during the exam, you can talk to the center person to reschedule the exam or the concerned person will help you. Pearson VUE supports emails to reschedule your exam.

- You won't be allowed to go out during the exam time, and please make sure to finish other activities before going to the exam.

- You will not be allowed any of your other stuff. The exam center requires two ID proofs to start the exam and the exam center team will help you with that.

- You can mark questions to be reviewed during the exam if you are not sure about the answer. Once you are done with the section, review the answer and proceed further.

- You might get the performance-based question about the Azure services, and you have to answer on that as well.

- In the case study question, you will need to give the business requirements and technical requirements of the existing environments and other information to answer the question.

- Case study questions might require you to look at your question back and forth, which might require information to be integrated with multiple sources in the question. Please make sure to read the case study properly, understand the requirements, and then answer the question.

Exam registration

If you are planning to register for the exam, if you are a first time user, please make sure you have a valid email ID like Outlook, Hotmail, and so on. Once you are ready with your email ID, follow the given steps to register for the exam:

- Please click on the link-AZ-104 exam registration link to register for the exam.

- Please provide the name, job title, and address.

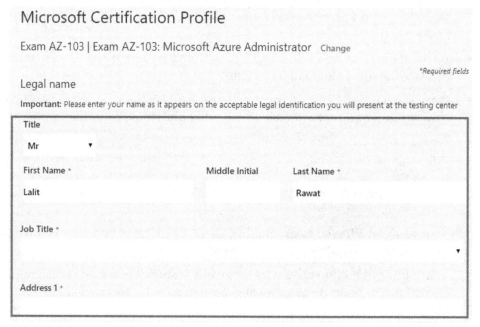

Figure 18.1: Exam schedule-1

- Please select the city and country for which you want to register for the exam.
- Provide the state postal code.
- Provide the country code and phone number.
- Provide the preferred email ID and language.

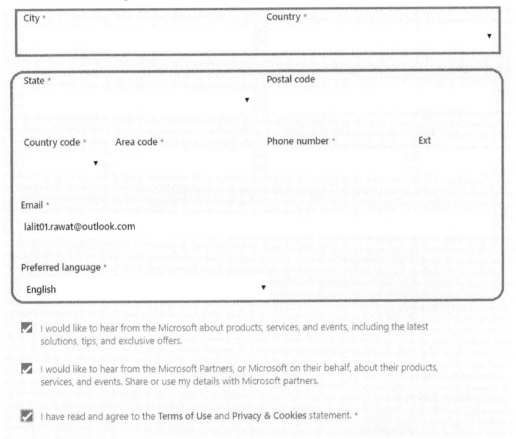

Figure 18.2: Exam schedule-2

Click on **Save & continue.**

- Once you click on **Save & continue**, it will ask you to go the Pearson VUE site to register for the exam.
- Select the local center, home, and so on options. Select the center option and click on the **Next** button.
- Select the language.
- Click on **Schedule the Exam**.
- Select the exam center or search for the center name.

- Select the date and time.

- Proceed to check out and proceed for payment.

Once you click on checkout, your exam will be scheduled. You will get an email from Pearson VUE.

Dummy objective exam questions

Q 1. **What kind of users can be invited using the guest user invite?**

1) B2C

2) B2B

3) Both

Ans: Both

Q 2. **How can we create multiple users in Azure AD?**

1) Using bulk user creation

2) Guest user invitation

3) Group management

Ans: Using bulk user creation

Q 3. **Which types of groups can we create in Azure AD?**

1) Security group

2) O365 group

3) Both

Ans: Both

Q 4. **What is the use of Azure AD connect?**

1) Hybrid connectivity

2) On-premises AD connect to Azure AD integration

3) MFA

Ans: On-premises AD connect to Azure AD integration

Q 5. **What is the permission requested to install the Azure AD Connect?**

1) Enterprise admin

2) Global administrator

3) Both

Ans: Both

Q 6.　What is the use of password writeback?

　　1)　It is used to sync the users.

　　2)　On-premises sync services

　　3)　To sync the password if it is changed through the Azure portal

Ans: To sync the password if it is changed through the Azure portal

Q 7.　Which is the PowerShell command to get the role definition?

　　1)　`Get-azRoledefinition "Contributor"`

　　2)　`Get-azRoledefinition "Contributor"|convertto-jason |out-file D:\ABPGroup`

　　3)　`Connect-azsubscription`

Ans: `Get-azRoledefinition "Contributor"`

Q 8.　How many types of role back Access are available in Azure?

　　1)　Read and write

　　2)　Viewer and editor

　　3)　Owner, contributor, and reader

Ans: Owner, contributor, and reader

Q 9.　How many custom roles can be created in one tenant?

　　1)　1000

　　2)　2000

　　3)　5000

Ans: 5000

Q 10.　If your company wants to buy a subscription directly from MS, which subscription would you chose?

　　1)　Free subscription

　　2)　Enterprise subscription

　　3)　CSP subscription

Ans: Enterprise subscription

Q 11.　What is a subscription in Microsoft Azure?

　　1)　It is a billing container which contains the Azure services.

　　2)　It just a container.

　　3)　It is Azure cloud services provider.

Ans: It is a billing container which contains the Azure services.

Q 12. A customer asks you to provide the IT admin access role that can manage the subscription and provide access. Which RBAC role access would you provide to the user?

1) Owner

2) Contributor

3) Reader

Ans: Owner

Q 13. What is the use of the Azure policy?

1) To meet the compliance.

2) To meet the cloud security.

3) To restrict the access.

Ans: To meet the compliance.

Q 14. A customer wants to allow only a few locations based on his presence in the Azure subscription. How would you do that?

1) Using the Azure policy

2) Using the Resources group

3) Using the RBAC access

Ans: Using the Azure policy

Q 15. Which types of storage accounts does Azure have?

1) Blob storage account

2) GPv1

3) GPv2

4) All of the above

Ans: All of the above

Q 16. What is storage account replication recommended by MS Azure?

1) RA-GRS

2) GRS

3) ZRS

4) LRS

Ans: RA-GRS

Q 17. **How many IOPS are provided by 1 TB premium storage account?**
1) 1000
2) 2000
3) 5000
4) 7500

Ans: 7500 IOPS

Q 18. **How to connect the Azure storage explorer? Please select two methods.**
1) SAS key
2) Storage account key
3) Through Azure portal

Ans: SAS key and Storage account key

Q 19. **What is the storage account contributor role?**
1) Provide access to read/write/delete access.
2) Provide read access.
3) Provide write access.

Ans: Provide access to read/write/delete access.

Q 20. **Why do we use the Azure import and export utility?**
1) To migrate the petabytes of data
2) To migrate 1 TB data
3) To migrate 50 GB data

Ans: To migrate the petabytes of data

Q 21. **Which OSes are supported by Azure fileshare?**
1) Windows and Linux
2) MAC
3) Linux

Ans: Windows and Linux, MAC

Q 22. **What is the limit of Azure fileshare?**
1) 2 TB
2) 5 TB
3) 4 GB

Ans: 5 TB

Q 23. **What is the use of Azure file sync?**
1) Centralized management for your files and folders
2) Used to sync docs Azure to Azure
3) Used for file sharing which is in cloud

Ans: Centralized management for your files and folders

Q 24. **What is Azure VMs size?**
1) Configuration of Azure VMs instance
2) VM image
3) None

Ans: Configuration of Azure VMs instance

Q 25. **Can we set the auto-scaling while creating the scale set?**
1) Yes
2) No
3) None of the above

Ans: Yes

Q 26. **Azure VMs size support GUP and SAP sizes as well?**
1) Yes
2) No
3) None

Ans: Yes

Q 27. **In which format does the ARM template save the documents?**
1) JSON
2) PowerShell
3) CLI

Ans: JSON

Q 28. **What are ways to deploy the ARM template?**
1) PowerShell
2) CLI
3) All of the above

Ans: All of the above

Q 29. How to deploy the ARM template from the portal?

1) Using a custom template

2) PowerShell

3) None

Ans: Using a custom template

Q 30. What is the way to connect to the on-premises network?

1) A site-to-site connection

2) Express route

3) Vnet-to-VNet connection

4) Options 1 and 2

Ans: Options 1 and 2

Q 31. How do you configure the Vnet-to-VNet connectivity?

1) VNet peering

2) Site-to-site connection

3) ExpressRoute configuration

Ans: VNet peering

Q 32. What is the use of a local area network?

1) It has on-premises VPN device configuration.

2) ExpressRoute configuration

3) None

Ans: It has on-premises VPN device configuration.

Q 33. Which are the types of Azure DNS zones?

1) Private zone

2) Public zone

3) Both

Ans: Both

Q 34. What are the different types of the Azure load balancer?

1) Internal

2) External

3) All of the above

Ans: All of the above

Q 35. **Which are the types of rules available in Azure NSG?**

1) Inbound
2) Outbound
3) Both

Ans: Both

Q 36. **What is the use of a route table?**

1) Route the traffic to the firewall
2) Route the traffic within Azure
3) All of the above

Ans: All of the above

Q 37. **Can we apply the NSG in web apps?**

1) Yes
2) No

Ans: No

Q 38. **What is the use of the Azure resource's health monitoring?**

1) Azure Resources Health Check
2) Subscription monitoring
3) PaaS service monitoring
4) None

Ans: Azure Resource Health Check

Q 39. **What is the use of log analytics?**

1) Resource monitoring
2) Analyzing the metrics and alerting
3) Data collection
4) All the above

Ans: All of the above

Q 40. **How to query the monitoring data?**

1) Using the log search query
2) Azure monitor
3) Log analytics
4) None

Ans: Using the log search query

Q 41. **What is use of the action group in an alert?**

1) Used to send the notification to tools/email ID.

2) Used to configure the Azure monitor.

3) Used to connect to log analytics.

4) None of the above.

Ans: Used to send the notification to tools/email ID.

Q 42. **What is the use of activity logs?**

1) It tracks all the operation activities within the subscription.

2) It collects the data from the Azure monitor.

3) It is used to connect to log analytics and analyze the logs.

Ans: It tracks all the operation activities within the subscription.

Dummy scenario-based exam questions

Q 1. **A BPB customer has more than 150 VMs, and now the customer wants to delete few of the VMs from his subscription. The customer wants to find out the unused disk which has been created during the VMs creation and deletion process. How can you identify the unused disk?**

1) You can use the Azure portal.

2) You can use Azure storage explorer.

3) You can use the cost management report.

4) You can use the Cloudyn optimization report.

Ans: 4. You can use the Cloudyn optimization report which will provide the report of an unused disk.

Q 2. **A BPB customer asked to create 10 Azure virtual machines with Linux OS that was required for the production workload. The customer needs to monitor the metrics. What are the options the customer can use to monitor the Linux metrics from the portal?**

1) Log analytics

2) Application insight

3) Azure performance diagnostic extension

4) Azure monitor

Ans: 3. Azure performance diagnostic extension will help the customer to collect the additional metric data and monitor the Linux metrics.

Q 3. A BPB customer has two different subscriptions: call subscriptions BPBDev and BPBProd and both the subscriptions need to communicate with each other. We have already configured the VNetDev for the subscriptions BPBDev and VNetProd with the BPBProd subscription. Now, you want to set up a communication between both the subscriptions. How can you configure it?

1) We will move the VNetDev to the BPBProd subscription.

2) Configure the VNet peering.

3) Configure Vnet-to-VNet connection between both the subscriptions.

4) Site-to-site connectivity between the subscriptions.

Ans: 3. Configure Vnet-to-VNet connection between both the subscriptions. Creating the vent-to-vent connectivity is a sillier process than site-to-site VP connectivity and the required local area connection needs to be created.

Q 4, Your customer wants to create an Azure storage account called bpbstorage, and under that, he wants to create an Azure fileshare. Once you create the Azure fileshare, you need to map it to an Azure fileshare supported port. Which port number will you choose to configure the Azure fileshare?

1) Port-443

2) Port-445

3) Port-80

4) Port-8080

Ans: 2. Port-445 because port 445 supports Azure fileshare. If the port 445 is blocked by your organization, then you will not be able to connect to fileshare.

Q 5. You are the administrator of your subscription which contains 30 virtual machines, and in your team, members want to create a couple more VMs with the NSG group. Now, your manager wants to block port 80 whenever any new NSG is created. What is your approach on this?

1) Use a custom Azure policy

2) Create lock on NSG

3) Block using the RBAC role

4) Provide limited access

Ans: 1. We will use a custom Azure policy which will help to define the policy. Whenever an engineer creates an NSG automatically, the deny rule will be created with port 80.

Q 6. **You are the administrator of your subscription and you have 50K users and you want to create 10 more users in the Azure AD and assign the user administrator role to those users. What options will you choose to provide access to those users?**

    1)   Only create the users.

    2)   Create the users and modify the directory role.

    3)   You can use the group policy to provide the access.

    4)   Use an active directory license to provide the access.

Ans: 2. We will create the user from Azure AD and use the directory role to modify and assign the user administrator role to those users.

Q 7. **You have 20K users, and now your organization IT head wants to buy 20 additional P2 licenses for higher management as they want to use the additional feature of premium AD. You have bought the 20 licenses. How will you configure them so that higher management can use the premium feature?**

    1)   You will assign the admin role to those users.

    2)   You will create a user group that allows you to use the premium feature.

    3)   You will assign the P2 licenses to each user using the license blade.

    4)   You will use the RBAC role.

Ans: 3. We will assign the P2 licenses to each user using the license blade because unless the license has been not configured, higher management cannot access the premium feature as those features will be available only if they have a valid license.

Q 8. **You have created a storage account in the resource group BPBRG32, and now you have applied a read-only lock to BPBRG32. Which operation will you perform?**

    1)   You will delete the resource group.

    2)   You can copy the storage key.

    3)   You can upload the data to the blob storage account.

    4)   You can change the replication settings.

Ans: 2. You can copy the storage key because the read-only lock allows you to copy the data, but it will not allow you to modify or delete anything from the resources group.

Q 9. **You have two Azure active directories bpb.com and azure4you.com. Now, you want to set up a default directory tenant to sign in to both the tenants. How can you configure it?**

1) Change the portal configuration settings.

2) Use the PowerShell command.

3) Change the directory from the portal.

4) You can change the subscription.

Ans: 3. We will change the directory from the portal to set up sign in.

Q 10. **Your customer wants to enable the backup solution on Azure web apps name called bpbapp1. How will you process this request?**

1) Set up the third-party backup solution.

2) Use the backup policy to implement.

3) Configure the backup using the recovery vault.

4) You can use the Azure backup server for app services.

Ans: 3. We will configure the backup using the recovery vault, which will help to take the backup of web apps.

Q 11. **A customer wants to transfer the data from the on-premises system to Azure. Which tool will you use to process it?**

1) Use the upload option directly to the blob storage.

2) Use the import and export option.

3) Create fileshare and map to on-premises.

4) Use the storage explorer to move the data.

Ans: 4. We will use the storage explorer to move the data as it is simple to use and tightly integrate with the Azure storage account and easy to move the data to the storage account.

Q 12. **You are the global administrator of your Azure AD, and now you want to enforce the multifactor authentication. How will you process it?**

1) Configure the playbook for MFA.

2) Use the custom policy.

3) Configure the Azure AD Connect.

4) Use the Azure AD conditional access policy.

Ans: 4. We will use the Azure AD conditional access policy which will help the MFA implementation organization. We can create a conditional access policy and apply it.

Q 13. **Your customer wants to configure the VNet name BPBVnetprod which supports the VNet gateway configuration to configure the site-to-site VPN?**

1) Create a Vnet.

2) Create subnet.

3) Create a VNet with the subnet gateway.

4) Create VNet with the subnet.

Ans: 3. We will create the VNet with the subnet gateway, which will help to configure the VNet gateway and the site-to-site VPN.

Q 14. **Your Azure tenant has enabled the privileged identity management, and you want to see how many users have been assigned the security admin role. You need to review the security admin access role. How can you process it?**

1) In identity protection manager, you will configure the risk policy.

2) You will configure the weekly ad report.

3) You will configure the access review from the privileged identify management.

4) You will enable the AD audit logs.

Ans: 3. We will configure the access review from the privileged identity management which help us to frequently understand access to that security admin and based on the report, we can decide it.

Q 15. **You have configured the multifactor authentication to all the users in your Azure tenant and few of the users are having an issue logging in to mobile devices and unable to reset the password. What is the solution you will apply?**

1) Self-service password reset.

2) Configure the mobile devices.

3) Create the password for those users.

4) Reinstall the app services.

Ans: 1. We will enable the self-services password reset which will help the users to reset their password whenever it is required. Then, they will be able to configure the apps in mobiles.

Q 16. **You have a couple of storage accounts and your customer wants to restrict the access to the internet in the production storage accounts. Which is the solution you will apply?**

1) In the storage account, enable encryption.

2) Create the SAS key.

3) Enable the VNet integration from the firewall settings.

4) Enable the replications.

Ans: 3. We will enable the VNet integration from the firewall settings from the Azure storage account, which will help to restrict the storage access to the internet.

Q 17. **Your clients have an on-premises network which contains multiple OS versions of servers. The client wants to migrate all the servers to Azure. You need to provide a solution to ensure that some of the servers which are available in single Azure data center and might go offline during planned and unplanned maintenance. What should be your recommendation to the client?**

1) Fault tolerance

2) Low latency

3) Scalability

4) Replication to Azure

Ans: 1. We will suggest having fault tolerance in the workload which will help during planned and unplanned maintenance.

Q 18. **You have 100 VMs in the Azure subscription, and now your customer wants to configure the backup. You have successfully created the backup. The client manager wants to enable the backup retention to 20 years? What is the solution you will propose to your customer?**

1) Backup reports

2) Azure backup policy

3) Manually take the backup

4) Enable the replication for 20 year

Ans: 2. We will enable the retention period in the Azure backup policy, which will help to retain the backup for upto 20 years.

Q 19. **You have 50 storage accounts in the Azure subscription, and now your customer wants to create a container in 20 storage accounts. What are the tools you will use to create the container in the storage account?**

1) From the portal.

2) You go to fileshare and create the container.

3) Manually create the container.

4) Azure storage explorer.

Ans: 4. We will be using the Azure storage explorer to configure the Azure storage containers.

Q 20. Your customer plans to map a network drive from several computers that run Windows 10 and Linux to Azure Storage. You need to create a storage solution in Azure for the planned mapped drive. What will be the solutions you will provide to the mapped drive?

1) Enable the port 80.

2) Using fileshare, connect and enable the port 445.

3) Use the blob storage account.

4) Use the Azure containers.

Ans: 2. We will use fileshare connect and enable the port 445, which provides the command to connect to Windows and Linux fileshare.

Q 21. Your company plans to deploy web servers and SQL database servers to the Azure subscription. Now, you need to recommend a solution to restrict the connection between Azure web servers and SQL BD servers. What is the solution you will provide?

1) You will restrict from the firewall.

2) You will use the route table.

3) Configure site-to-site connection.

4) Configure the **Network Security Group (NSG)**.

Ans: 4. We will configure the Network Security Group (NSG) which will help to allow or deny the traffic. It will help to restrict the outgoing traffic and it can only send the traffic to web servers to DB servers.

Q 22. Your customer plans to migrate to Azure and the company has several departments. All the Azure resources have been used by each department and managed by an IT administrator. Now, the customer wants to provide the solution which will minimize the administrative effect and will be easy to manage by each IT administrator. Please provide the solutions.

1) Multiple tenants with multiple subscriptions

2) Multiple region deployment

3) One tenant with multiple subscriptions

4) Multiple resource groups

Ans: 3. We will choose one tenant with multiple subscriptions which helps to separate the resources and its billing and also the administrative task to reduce the administrative workloads.

Q 23. Your organization has multiple offices, and every month, you plan to generate several billing reports from the Azure portal. Every report contains the resources of each subscription. What is the feature you will use before generating the report?

1) Azure policy
2) Tags
3) Cost management
4) Cloudyn

Ans: 2. We will use the tags before generating the reports, which will help us to provide the expected reports department wise.

Q 24. **You have multiple virtual machines, and now your customer wants to move the virtual machine from one subscription to another subscription. How can you process this request?**

1) Go to resources group, and click on Move.
2) From the virtual machine, we can go to move.
3) Using PowerShell, we can do that.
4) Will use third-party tools.

Ans: 1. We will go to resources group, and click on Move and select the subscription to move the resources to another subscription.

Q 25. **You have multiple virtual machines and the backup has been configured in all the virtual machines. Now, your customer wants to understand the backup process and wants to show the report to higher management. What is the solution you will propose?**

1) Go to backup report.
2) From the virtual machine, we can go to move.
3) Using PowerShell, we can do that.
4) Will use third-party tools.

Ans: 1. We will go to backup report and configure it, which will help us to provide the data and we can extract it in the PPT format for presentation.

Q 26. **You are the network administrator of your subscription and the customer has more than 50 VNet. Now, the customer wants to enable the VNet peering between VNetProd-to-VNetDev to enable the communication between both the VNet resources. What is the solution you will propose?**

1) Enable Vnet-to-VNet connection
2) Configure the VNet peering
3) Site-to-site VPN
4) Point to site VPN

Ans: 2. We will configure the Vnet-to-VNet peering between both the VNets, which allows the communication between both the VNets.

Q 27. You are the network administrator of your subscription and the customer wants to configure the Azure EXPRESSROUTE connectivity on-premises to Azure. The customer has decided the ISP, and the ISP has configured the on-premises connectivity. Now, you want to configure it. What is the service you can create to configure the EXPRESSROUTE?

1) VNet
2) VNet gateway
3) Site-to-site VPN
4) Expressroute circuit

Ans: 4. We will create the Expressroute circuit to configure the Expressroute connectivity. Then, we need to configure the VNet gateway for connectivity.

Q 28. You have 100 virtual machines in your subscription, and there are 20 virtual machines in production environments. Now, your manager wants to enable the alerts and whenever your VMs reboots, deallocates, you should get an alert. What is the solution you will propose?

1) We will create the rule.
2) We will configure with the Azure policy.
3) We will create two rules and one action group from monitoring.
4) We will set up alerts.

Ans: 3. We will create two rules and one action group from monitoring. One rule to stop deallocation and another rule to reboot the VM. We will be associated with one action group to configure the alerts.

Q 29. You have 20 virtual machines in your subscription and the customer has reported that few of the virtual machines are not connecting to the application, and the customer wants to fix the issue on priority. Which tool will you use to fix the issue?

1) Network performance monitor
2) Application insight
3) Weblog analytics
4) Network watcher

Ans: 4. We will use the network watcher tool, which will help to identify the issue of the servers and help to fix the issue quickly. It will also provide the input on traffic flow within Azure.

Best wishes for your exam!

Index

CPSIA information can be obtained
at www.ICGtesting.com
Printed in the USA
LVHW101530290321
682837LV00006B/455

9 789389 898767